Markus Mathes

Time-Constrained Web Services for Industrial Automation

Markus Mathes

Time-Constrained Web Services for Industrial Automation

Südwestdeutscher Verlag für Hochschulschriften

Impressum/Imprint (nur für Deutschland/ only for Germany)
Bibliografische Information der Deutschen Nationalbibliothek: Die Deutsche Nationalbibliothek verzeichnet diese Publikation in der Deutschen Nationalbibliografie; detaillierte bibliografische Daten sind im Internet über http://dnb.d-nb.de abrufbar.

Alle in diesem Buch genannten Marken und Produktnamen unterliegen warenzeichen-, marken- oder patentrechtlichem Schutz bzw. sind Warenzeichen oder eingetragene Warenzeichen der jeweiligen Inhaber. Die Wiedergabe von Marken, Produktnamen, Gebrauchsnamen, Handelsnamen, Warenbezeichnungen u.s.w. in diesem Werk berechtigt auch ohne besondere Kennzeichnung nicht zu der Annahme, dass solche Namen im Sinne der Warenzeichen- und Markenschutzgesetzgebung als frei zu betrachten wären und daher von jedermann benutzt werden dürften.

Verlag: Südwestdeutscher Verlag für Hochschulschriften Aktiengesellschaft & Co. KG
Dudweiler Landstr. 99, 66123 Saarbrücken, Deutschland
Telefon +49 681 37 20 271-1, Telefax +49 681 37 20 271-0
Email: info@svh-verlag.de
Zugl.: Marburg, Philipps-Universität Marburg, Dissertation, 2009

Herstellung in Deutschland:
Schaltungsdienst Lange o.H.G., Berlin
Books on Demand GmbH, Norderstedt
Reha GmbH, Saarbrücken
Amazon Distribution GmbH, Leipzig
ISBN: 978-3-8381-1469-9

Imprint (only for USA, GB)
Bibliographic information published by the Deutsche Nationalbibliothek: The Deutsche Nationalbibliothek lists this publication in the Deutsche Nationalbibliografie; detailed bibliographic data are available in the Internet at http://dnb.d-nb.de.

Any brand names and product names mentioned in this book are subject to trademark, brand or patent protection and are trademarks or registered trademarks of their respective holders. The use of brand names, product names, common names, trade names, product descriptions etc. even without a particular marking in this works is in no way to be construed to mean that such names may be regarded as unrestricted in respect of trademark and brand protection legislation and could thus be used by anyone.

Publisher: Südwestdeutscher Verlag für Hochschulschriften Aktiengesellschaft & Co. KG
Dudweiler Landstr. 99, 66123 Saarbrücken, Germany
Phone +49 681 37 20 271-1, Fax +49 681 37 20 271-0
Email: info@svh-verlag.de

Printed in the U.S.A.
Printed in the U.K. by (see last page)
ISBN: 978-3-8381-1469-9

Copyright © 2010 by the author and Südwestdeutscher Verlag für Hochschulschriften Aktiengesellschaft & Co. KG and licensors
All rights reserved. Saarbrücken 2010

Acknowledgments

I would like to acknowledge the help of several people during the course of this doctoral thesis.

First of all, I would like to thank my thesis supervisor Prof. Dr. Bernd Freisleben for his permanent support during the course of this thesis.

I would also like to thank Prof. Dr. Helmut Dohmann for numerous inspiring discussions about the subject of this thesis.

My thank also goes to the TiCS development team for helping to implement, test, and improve the framework: Christoph Stoidner, Roland Schwarzkopf, Steffen Heinzl, Tim Dörnemann, and Jochen Gärtner.

I dedicate this thesis to my parents: Ingrid and Hubert Mathes.
Both taught me that success comes along with hard work.

Abstract

Service-oriented architectures based on web services have become the de facto standard for the design and implementation of distributed applications. Due to their standardization, web services are widely adopted for inter-organizational communication, but their use for intra-organizational communication is challenging, especially within enterprises of the manufacturing domain. Business processes within an industrial enterprise have to satisfy predefined time constraints. More precisely, the manufacturing process has to guarantee real-time, i.e. predefined deadlines have to be kept. Today's industrial enterprises use specialized hard- and software at the manufacturing layer—industrial PCs (IPCs) and programmable logic controllers (PLCs)—that run under vendor-specific operating systems and are implemented using vendor-specific tools. This mixture of technologies of different vendors leads to numerous breaks in the communication paradigm. The interconnection of these technologies results in additional costs and is often quite error-prone.

This thesis investigates the seamless use of web services as a homogeneous communication backbone throughout the overall industrial enterprise with a focus on the manufacturing layer. The common layered organization of an industrial enterprise—consisting of the business layer, the intermediate layer, and the manufacturing layer—is avoided by using web services as the communication backbone. The need for real-time makes the use of web services in industrial automation challenging. Web service standards (e.g. SOAP for the invocation and WSDL for the description of web services) and technologies (e.g. available SOAP engines) have emerged from the Internet domain where processing is based on a best-effort basis (time constraints are of little or no interest).

The *Time-Constrained Services (TiCS)* framework presented in this thesis is a technical foundation for using web services in time-constrained environments with a specific focus on industrial automation. TiCS is a tool suite for the development, deployment, publication, composition, and execution of web services with time constraints, especially real-time constraints. TiCS consists of several components to ease the entire development process for automation engineers who are normally not familiar with web service technologies. The main components of the TiCS framework can be distinguished according to their functionality:

- permit access to the manufacturing layer using web services
- permit the composition of several web services to a value-added workflow that represents a production process
- offer a mechanism to describe the time constraints of web services and workflows
- permit the efficient transmission of binary web service parameters

To access the manufacturing layer using web services, the TiCS framework offers a real-time SOAP engine for IPCs called *SOAP4IPC* and for PLCs called *SOAP4PLC*. Both engines permit an evolutionary change to a web service based communication backbone, since existing hardware can be used further.

Most real-world production processes consist of several steps. Due to this reason, it is necessary to combine web services to a multi-step workflow. The *TiCS Modeler* supports an automation engineer to define such workflows with regard to the required time constraints.

The *WS-TemporalPolicy* language permits the description of time constraints for web services and entire workflows. Since time constraints may vary over time, e.g. compare processing during peak time and off-peak time, WS-TemporalPolicy permits the definition of a validity period for time constraints.

The protocol predominantly used for the invocation of web services is SOAP. Since SOAP is based on XML, it is necessary to encode binary parameters, resulting in a remarkable overhead. For an efficient parameter transmission—a fundamental prerequisite to process a web service within a given deadline—the TiCS framework contains a component called *Flex-SwA*.

Despite the fact that the technologies developed in this thesis focus on industrial automation, they can also be used in related research areas where web services are used as the communication technology.

Zusammenfassung

Service-orientierte Architekturen basierend auf Web Services sind der de facto Standard zum Design und der Implementierung verteilter Anwendungen geworden. Aufgrund ihrer Standardisierung sind Web Services auch für die Kommunikation zwischen Unternehmen weit verbreitet. Der Einsatz von Web Services für die innerbetriebliche Kommunikation innerhalb eines Industrieunternehmens ist derzeit aber noch schwierig. Geschäftsprozesse in Industrieunternehmen müssen vordefinierte Zeitbedingungen einhalten. Genauer gesagt, muss der Fertigungsprozess Echtzeit garantieren, d.h. vordefinierte Fristen müssen eingehalten werden. Heutige Industrieunternehmen verwenden spezielle Hard- und Software auf der Fertigungsebene – Industrie-PCs (IPCs) und speicherprogrammierbare Steuerungen (SPSen) – welche unter herstellerspezifischen Betriebssystemen laufen und mit herstellerspezifischen Tools programmiert werden. Diese Vermischung von Technologien verschiedener Hersteller führt zu einer Vielzahl an Brüchen im Kommunikationsparadigma. Die Kopplung dieser Technologien resultiert in zusätzlichen Kosten und ist oft sehr fehleranfällig.

Diese Doktorarbeit untersucht die durchgehende Verwendung von Web Services als homogenes Kommunikationssystem innerhalb des gesamten Industrieunternehmens. Der besondere Fokus liegt dabei auf der Fertigungsebene. Die klassische Organisation eines Industrieunternehmens in Geschäftsebene, Zwischenebene und Fertigungsebene wird durch den Einsatz von Web Services als durchgehendes Kommunikationssystem überflüssig. Der Einsatz von Web Services in der Industrieautomation ist jedoch aufgrund der Echtzeiterfordernisse schwierig. Web Service Standards (z.B. SOAP für den Aufruf und WSDL für die Beschreibung von Web Services) und Technologien (z.B. verfügbare SOAP Engines) wurden im Kontext des Internets entwickelt. Dort spielen Zeitanforderungen eine untergeordnete Rolle, da Anfragen nach dem best-effort Prinzip bearbeitet werden.

Das Time-Constrained Services (TiCS) Framework, welches in dieser Doktorarbeit präsentiert wird, ist die technische Grundlage zur Verwendung von Web Services in Umgebungen mit Anforderungen an das Zeitverhalten. Der besondere Fokus liegt dabei auf der Industrieautomation. TiCS ist eine Entwicklungsumgebung für die Implementierung, das Deployment, die Veröffentlichung, die Komposition und die Ausführung von Web Services mit Zeitanforderungen, insbesondere Echtzeitanforderungen. TiCS besteht aus mehreren Komponenten, um den gesamten Entwicklungsprozess für Automatisierungsingenieure zu vereinfachen, da diese normalerweise nicht mit Web Services vertraut sind. Die Hauptkomponenten des TiCS Frameworks können nach ihrer Funktionalität unterschieden werden:

- Zugriff auf die Fertigungsbene unter Verwendung von Web Services
- Komposition von mehreren Web Services zu einem Workflow, der einen Produktionsprozess repräsentiert
- Beschreibung der Zeitanforderungen von Web Services und Workflows
- effiziente Übertragung von binären Web Service Parametern

Zum Zugriff auf die Fertigungsebene unter Verwendung von Web Services bietet das TiCS Framework eine echtzeitfähige SOAP Engine für IPCs – *SOAP4IPC* – und für SPSen – *SOAP4PLC*. Beide Engines erlauben einen evolutionären Wechsel zu einem Web Service basierten Kommunikationssystem, da existierende Hardware weiterhin benutzt werden kann.

Viele realistische Produktionsprozesse bestehen aus mehreren Schritten. Aus diesem Grund ist es notwendig, mehrere Web Services zu einem Workflow zu kombinieren. Der *TiCS Modeler* unterstützt einen Automatisierungsingenieur bei der Definition solcher Workflows unter Beachtung der Zeitanforderungen.

WS-TemporalPolicy ermöglicht die Beschreibung der Zeitschranken von Web Services und kompletten Workflows. Da Zeitschranken variieren können, z.B. zwischen Stoß- und Nebenzeiten, ermöglicht WS-TemporalPolicy die Definition einer Gültigkeitsdauer für Zeitschranken.

Das überwiegend benutzte Protokoll zum Aufruf von Web Services ist SOAP. Da SOAP auf XML basiert, ist es notwendig, binäre Parameter zu kodieren. Dies führt zu einem beachtlichen Overhead. Für eine effiziente Übertragung von Parametern – eine grundlegende Voraussetzung um einen Web Service innerhalb einer gegebenen Frist zu verarbeiten – enthält das TiCS Framework die *Flex-SwA* Komponente.

Trotz der Tatsache, dass die Technologien, die in dieser Doktorarbeit entwickelt wurden, den Fokus auf Industrieautomation legen, können sie in angrenzenden Forschungsgebieten, die ebenfalls Web Services zur Kommunikation verwenden, genutzt werden.

x

Contents

1 Introduction   **1**
    1.1 Research Contributions 6
    1.2 Organization of this Thesis 14

2 Overview of the Time-Constrained Services Framework   **17**
    2.1 Introduction 17
    2.2 Requirements Analysis 18
    2.3 Architectural Blueprint 20
       2.3.1 Hardware Layer 20
       2.3.2 Real-time Infrastructural Layer 23
       2.3.3 Real-time Service Layer 26
       2.3.4 Tool Support Layer 28
    2.4 Design Considerations 30
    2.5 Summary 31

3 Web Services for PLCs   **33**
    3.1 Introduction 33
    3.2 Industrial Automation—Status Quo 34
    3.3 Benefits and Challenges of Web Services for PLCs 36
    3.4 Design Considerations 37
       3.4.1 WS-Infobase 40
       3.4.2 SOAP-Handler 41
       3.4.3 WSDL-Generator 42
       3.4.4 SOAP2PLC-Bridge 42
       3.4.5 Sequence-Controlled Web Services 43
    3.5 Summary 46

4 Web Services for IPCs   **49**
    4.1 Introduction 49
    4.2 Preliminary Design Considerations 50
       4.2.1 Mode of Operation 50

	4.2.2	Level of Concurrency	52
4.3	Architecture		52
4.4	Execution Time of Web Services		54
4.5	Summary		58

5 Composition of Time-Constrained Workflows — 61
- 5.1 Introduction 61
- 5.2 Characteristics of BPEL4WS 62
- 5.3 Time Behavior of BPEL4WS Activities 63
  - 5.3.1 The Receive and Reply Activities 64
  - 5.3.2 The Invoke Activity 65
  - 5.3.3 The Assign Activity 66
  - 5.3.4 The Wait Activity 66
  - 5.3.5 The Empty Activity 67
  - 5.3.6 The While Activity 67
  - 5.3.7 The Pick Activity 67
  - 5.3.8 The Flow Activity 68
  - 5.3.9 The Terminate Activity 68
  - 5.3.10 The Scope Activity 68
  - 5.3.11 The Sequence Activity 69
  - 5.3.12 The Switch Activity 69
- 5.4 Design Considerations 70
  - 5.4.1 DAVO's Data Model 72
  - 5.4.2 DAVO's Views and Controllers 74
- 5.5 Summary 74

6 Description of Time Constraints — 75
- 6.1 Introduction 75
- 6.2 Dynamic, Non-Functional Web Service Properties 76
- 6.3 Using WS-Policy and WS-TemporalPolicy 77
  - 6.3.1 WS-Policy 77
  - 6.3.2 WS-TemporalPolicy 78
- 6.4 Management of WS-TemporalPolicies 84
- 6.5 Use Cases 85
  - 6.5.1 Use Case I: Financial Services 85
  - 6.5.2 Use Case II: Real-time Processing 88
- 6.6 Summary 89

7 Efficient Data Transmission in Web Service Environments — 91
- 7.1 Introduction 91
- 7.2 Transmission of Web Service Parameters 92

7.3	Flex-SwA Protocol Stack	95
7.4	Communication Patterns	98
	7.4.1 Benefits using Flex-SwA	100
7.5	Summary	102

8 Implementation 103
8.1	Introduction	103
8.2	Java for Industrial Automation	104
	8.2.1 Real-time Specification for Java	106
	8.2.2 Java on Silicon	107
8.3	TiCS Source Code Organization	108
8.4	SOAP4PLC	108
	8.4.1 Experimental Soft- and Hardware Environment	109
	8.4.2 WS-Infobase	111
	8.4.3 WSDL-Generator	112
	8.4.4 SOAP-Handler	115
	8.4.5 SOAP2PLC-Bridge	115
8.5	SOAP4IPC	117
	8.5.1 JamaicaVM	117
	8.5.2 EntryPoint	118
	8.5.3 DependencyChecker	119
	8.5.4 Hot Deployment and Hot Undeployment	119
	8.5.5 Profiling Modes	120
	8.5.6 Monitoring of Job Execution Time	121
	8.5.7 Engine Configuration	123
	8.5.8 Parameterization of Engine Threads	123
8.6	TiCS Modeler	124
	8.6.1 Data Model	125
	8.6.2 Views and Controllers	127
	8.6.3 Shadow Model	129
	8.6.4 Adapting DAVO to Real-time Processing	130
8.7	WS-TemporalPolicy	135
	8.7.1 Temporal Policy Manager	135
	8.7.2 Policy Weaving	137
8.8	Flex-SwA	138
	8.8.1 PiptCall	138
	8.8.2 FlexSwACall	140
	8.8.3 Description of Flex-SwA Endpoints	141
8.9	Summary	143

9 Evaluation 145

9.1 Introduction 145
9.2 SOAP4PLC 146
    9.2.1 Qualitative Evaluation 146
    9.2.2 Quantitative Evaluation 150
9.3 SOAP4IPC 153
    9.3.1 Real-Time Operating System 154
    9.3.2 Profiling Step I 156
    9.3.3 Profiling Step II 157
    9.3.4 Deadline Calculation 158
    9.3.5 Test Run 159
    9.3.6 Deadline Violation 160
9.4 TiCS Modeler 161
9.5 Summary 169

10 Related Work   171
10.1 Introduction 171
10.2 Service-oriented Architectures in Industrial Automation 172
    10.2.1 SIRENA 172
    10.2.2 IMNP 174
    10.2.3 SOCRADES 175
    10.2.4 Miscellaneous 176
10.3 Web Services on IPCs and PLCs 177
    10.3.1 DPWS and WS4D 177
    10.3.2 Miscellaneous 179
10.4 Composition of Time-Constrained Workflows 180
    10.4.1 GRIDCC 181
    10.4.2 Miscellaneous 182
10.5 Description of Time Constraints 185
10.6 Efficient Data Transmission in Web Service Environments . . . 186
10.7 Real-time Interconnection Networks 188
10.8 Quality-of-Service 189
10.9 Data Stream Processing Using PIPES 190
10.10 Grid Computing 191
10.11 Summary 192

11 Conclusions and Future Work   195
11.1 Conclusions 195
11.2 Future Work 198

List of Abbrevations   203

CONTENTS

List of Figures 207

List of Tables 209

List of Listings 211

Bibliography 213

1
Introduction

Industrial automation is aimed at the monitoring and control of an industrial plant via hard- and software with minimized human intervention during operation. A well-known example for automation is an assembly line in automobile manufacturing that consists of several devices, e.g. industrial robots or conveyor belts.

Independent of the concrete realization, an industrial automation solution always consists of three different components: sensors, actuators, and the processing logic. A *sensor* collects input data from the production process, e.g. temperature, pressure, or humidity. Depending on the technical realization of the sensor used, the input data may be analog or digital values. An *actuator* permits the manipulation of the production process. Examples for actuators are electric motors, solenoids, or conveyor belts. The *processing logic* implements how the automation system works concretely. The processing logic reads input values of several sensors and computes output values for the actuators. Additionally, the processing logic collects information relevant to the documentation of the production process, e.g. data for quality assurance.

For example, consider the control of a heating installation. A thermometer measures the actual temperature within the boiler as an analog value and a valve positioner adjusts the valve for fuel injection. Therefore, the thermometer acts as a sensor whereas the valve positioner acts as an actuator. Since the temperature within the boiler must not fall below a minimum or exceed a maximum temperature, the processing logic computes the actual fuel injection depending on the temperature in the boiler. More precisely, if the actual temperature falls below the minimum threshold, e.g. 200°C, the valve is opened, e.g. to a level of 75%, whereas if the actual temperature exceeds the maximum threshold, e.g. 600°C, the valve is closed, e.g. to a level of 25%. For a medium temperature, e.g. 400°C, the valve is opened, e.g. to a level of 50%.

A main characteristic of industrial automation is the demand for real-time processing [144, 167]. The notion *real-time* neither means that a process is completed "fast" nor that its execution corresponds to the real time. Real-time means that a task is completed correctly within a given time constraint, i.e. it meets its deadline. Therefore, the worst-case execution time to complete a task is important. A task whose execution exceeds a given time constraint is treated as failed. On the other hand, a task that is completed prior to its time constraint has no additional value. Consider an emergency shutdown within the production process caused by a worker entering the area of operation of an industrial robot. To avoid threats to life or the physical condition of the worker, an emergency shutdown has to be performed within a specified time limit. Real-time can be further divided into *hard real-time* (the time constraint must *always* be satisfied) and *soft real-time* (the time constraint is satisfied *most of the time*). Soft real-time is only sufficient if exceeding a deadline does not lead to a disaster, a threat to life and physical condition, or damage of the equipment.

To visualize the properties of non real-time, soft real-time, and hard real-time, a *utility function* is frequently used [165]. The utility function maps the execution time of a task to the utility of its result, as shown in Figure 1.1. Figure 1.1(a) shows the graph for non real-time. Since there is no deadline defined, the utility of the task is always 100%, independent of the execution time. Soft real-time results in a graph as shown in Figure 1.1(b). After exceeding the deadline, the utility of the task result decreases gradually until it reaches 0%. Hard real-time lacks this gradual decrease of utility, as shown in

Figure 1.1(c). After exceeding the deadline, the utility is immediately 0%.

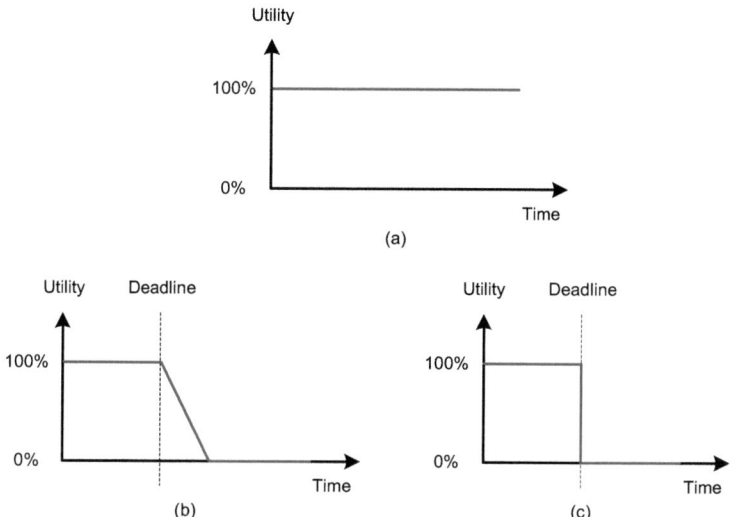

Figure 1.1: Utility function for (a) non real-time, (b) soft real-time, and (c) hard real-time.

The *first generation* of industrial automation was hardware dominated [156]. The processing logic was realized as a hard-wired circuit within a switching cabinet. The main disadvantage of hard-wired processing logic is its inflexibility with respect to changes of the monitored and controlled production process. Even simple changes within the production process may result in a revision of the entire hard-wired processing logic. Another disadvantage is its monolithic nature, i.e. an automation engineer is not able to define reusable modules which implement a part of the processing logic. The monolithic nature finally results in processing logic that is hardly scalable. An extension of the production process often requires a redevelopment of the entire processing logic.

To avoid the inflexibility of hard-wired processing logic and to enable a fast adaptation to changes within the production process, the *second generation* of industrial automation was software-dominated [156]. The software-dominated automation approach results in a distributed, hierarchical monitoring and control of the manufacturing process. The manufacturing process is decomposed in disjunctive steps that are called *production cells*. Each production cell contains several manufacturing devices, which are controlled by a *programmable logic controller* (PLC). Several production cells are monitored by an *industrial PC* (IPC). Figure 1.2 outlines the structure of a production process based on IPCs and PLCs.

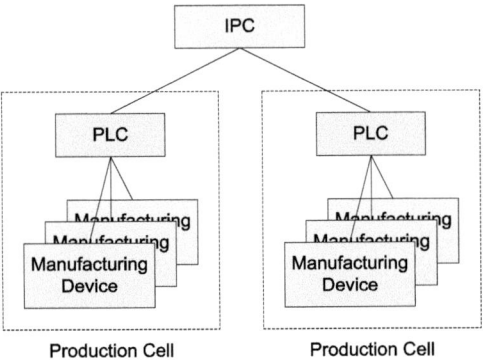

Figure 1.2: Structure of a hierarchical organized production process using IPCs and PLCs.

A PLC is specialized hardware that heavily differs from common desktop PCs. Even though modern PLCs become more and more powerful, they are not comparable to desktop PCs with regard to computing power or main memory. A PLC has several input/output modules that are connected to sensors and actuators, respectively. PLCs operate in a loop according to the input-processing-output (IPO) model where each step is processed in a predetermined time. The PLC reads input data from its sensors, computes the necessary reaction based on a given rule base, and uses its actuators to react. Since each step in an IPO loop can only take a predetermined time, a PLC inherently supports real-time processing. The rule base is set up by a domain expert, namely the automation engineer who maintains the manufacturing process.

An IPC is comparable to a regular desktop PC with respect to computing power and main memory, but the case design is much more robust to resist the hostile physical conditions in the manufacturing layer, e.g. temperature, vibration, or dust and dirt. Often, standardized operating systems like Microsoft Windows or Linux are used to run IPCs.

The main disadvantage of the second generation of industrial automation is the use of a vast number of different interfaces. Both the interface between the IPC and higher layers and the interface between IPCs and PLCs are not standardized but vendor-specific. Additionally, PLCs from different vendors offer different interfaces and protocols for which reason the interconnection is further complicated. Consequently, the interconnection of the production process with higher layers requires expert knowledge from automation engineers and software developers from higher layers which results in additional costs.

The *third generation* of industrial automation is currently investigated and prototypically realized by several research projects [123, 124, 135, 136] and focuses primarily on the use of open, standardized protocols for the interconnection of manufacturing devices and the flexibilization of the entire organization of an industrial enterprise. Consequently, the third generation of industrial automation can be regarded as interaction dominated. Whereas the concrete technical realization is heavily discussed in various interest groups and standardization committees, the fundamental requirements for future industrial automation solutions have been agreed on [163]:

- **Interoperability:**
  All manufacturing devices have to offer a standardized interface based on a common technology to avoid breaks in the communication paradigm.

- **Horizontal Integration:**
  The communication with other enterprises, especially with suppliers and customers, has to be simplified.

- **Vertical Integration:**
  Not only the communication with other enterprises but also the commu-

nication within the enterprise ranging from the shop floor up to the top floor has to be simplified.

- **Agility:**
  The automation system must be easily adaptable to changes within the production process caused by changes of the market situation or the business competition.

Taking the status quo and the requirements into account, the fundamental question for future automation solutions is: *How can future automation solutions be designed and implemented to permit interoperability, integration, and agility?*

1.1 Research Contributions

This thesis suggests the seamless use of *web services as the communication backbone* within industrial enterprises and presents the first realization of the third industrial automation generation. The benefits of using web services as a seamless communication backbone within industrial enterprises [137, 138] meet the identified requirements:

- The increasing proliferation of web services simplifies the interaction with suppliers and customers and fosters the horizontal integration of enterprises. In some branches of industry—especially automotive engineering—the use of web services for business-to-business communication is mandatory to stay competitive.

- The seamless use of web services within an enterprise avoids breaks in the communication infrastructure and therefore the implementation and maintenance of numerous interfaces. This eases vertical integration and enhances the interoperability of software systems within the enterprise by means of open, standardized protocols.

- Today's fast moving market situation requires a flexible adaptation of enterprises. Within an enterprise, the demand for flexibility results in

1.1 Research Contributions

engineering of new business processes and reengineering of existing ones. A business process often consists of several steps, e.g. simple basic tasks or further business processes, which have to be processed in a specific order. This composite nature of a business process is reflected by web services. A web service may implement a basic task or a complex task (by using several other web services).

The envisioned third generation of automation solutions based on web services results in a revision of the entire layered architecture of an industrial enterprise. For the purpose of separation of concerns, most industrial enterprises are—up to now—organized into three vertical layers—business layer, intermediate layer, and manufacturing layer—as shown in Figure 1.3.

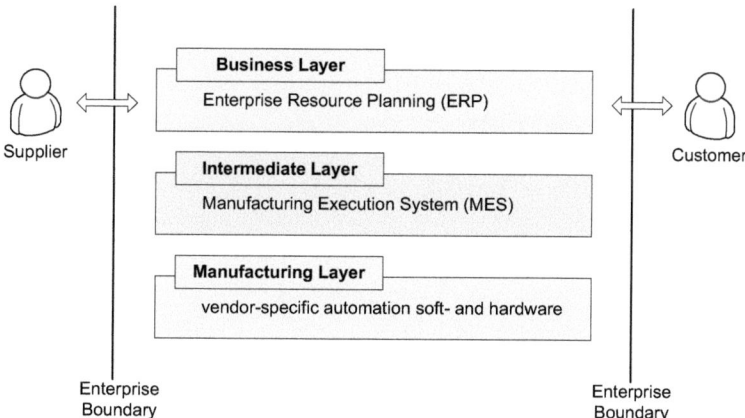

Figure 1.3: Organizational layers of today's industrial enterprises.

The *business layer* of an enterprise contains software functionality for planning purposes, e.g. accounting, administration, or human resources. Large-scale enterprises by the majority and small and medium-sized businesses increasingly use enterprise resource planning (ERP) solutions at the business layer. Current ERP solutions offer a multiplicity of different interfaces for interconnection with suppliers and customers.

The *intermediate layer* acts as a mediator between the business layer and the manufacturing layer. It performs two major tasks:

- Production orders on the business layer are translated into concrete control commands for the manufacturing systems, e.g. throughput increase/decrease, or shutdown for the purpose of service or retooling.

- Manufacturing data from the shop floor, e.g. the system status of an assembly line, already produced units, or error messages, are collected, filtered, merged, and delivered to the business layer.

The intermediate layer uses a so-called manufacturing execution system (MES) to interconnect the business and the manufacturing layer. The main functionalities of an MES are: scheduling of production processes to optimize utilization of the plant, monitoring of resources within the production process, dispatching of production processes, labor and maintenance management, and collecting data about the production process (e.g. data for quality assurance) [91].

At the *manufacturing layer*, the core business of an industrial enterprise is located—the manufacturing process. The manufacturing process is organized using PLCs and IPCs as described above. The software used at the manufacturing layer—especially for PLC programming and maintenance—is highly proprietary and depends on the installed hardware. The hard- and software of the manufacturing layer is normally offered as bundle by the particular vendor.

As a result of this thesis, the intermediate layer—until now realized by an MES—becomes obsolete and is replaced by the web service communication backbone as shown in Figure 1.4. This change is fundamental and comparable with the replacement of hard-wired process control via switching cabinets by soft-wired process control via PLCs in the manufacturing layer. The intermediate layer, which interfaces the business and the manufacturing layer, is not any longer required. Business and production processes are both incorporated in the web service backbone and treated equally.

This thesis presents the *Time-Constrained Services (TiCS)* framework as an architectural and technical foundation to realize the third generation of

1.1 Research Contributions

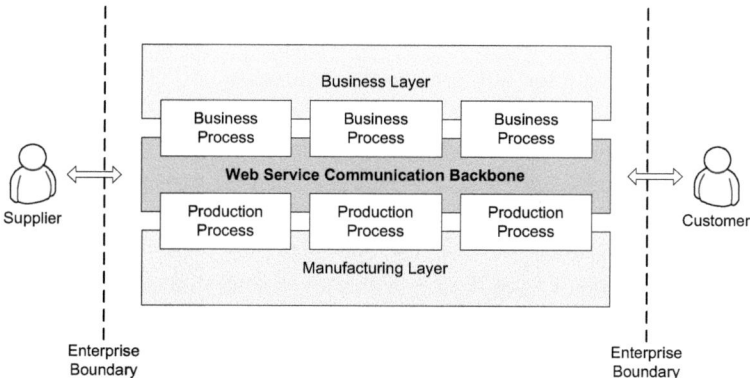

Figure 1.4: The third generation of industrial automation based on a web service communication backbone.

industrial automation. The main research contributions of the TiCS framework are:

- **use of web services at the manufacturing layer:**
  Soft- and hardware used at the manufacturing layer, i.e. manufacturing devices, PLCs, and IPCs, do not innately support communication via web services. Consequently, the first step towards a web service based communication infrastructure is to permit web services at the manufacturing layer. This thesis presents the first SOAP [68] engine for PLCs called *SOAP4PLC*, i.e. PLCs are enhanced with a web service interface.

- **execution of web services within predefined time constraints:**
  Web services come from the Internet domain where time constraints are of little or no importance. Best-effort processing is often sufficient. Consequently, existing web services standards and implementations only support best-effort processing. To permit the use of web services within time-constrained environments like industrial automation, a real-time SOAP engine is required, i.e. a SOAP engine that permits the execution of a web service within a predefined time constraint. This thesis presents the first profiling-and-monitoring based real-time SOAP engine for IPCs

called *SOAP4IPC*.

- **tool support for web service development:**
  Automation engineers are normally novices with regard to web service technologies. Consequently, the basic concepts of web services are often completely unknown to them. The situation is complicated by the fact that it is very challenging to become acquainted with web services, since the learning curve of this technology is very steep. To foster the dissemination of web services within the manufacturing layer, exhaustive tool support for automation engineers is required. More precisely, an automation engineer requires tools to implement, deploy, and invoke time-constrained web services. The TiCS framework offers several wizards to support automation engineers. These *Usability Wizards* permit the easy development and deployment of time-constrained web services.

- **composition of time-constrained workflows:**
  The implementation of production processes using web services requires the composition of simple web services to more complex, value-added, multi-step workflows[1] by automation engineers. For this purpose, an automation engineer needs a workflow composition tool that supports the calculation of time constraints during the composition process. The *TiCS Modeler* presented in this thesis is the first graphical Business Process Execution Language for Web Services (BPEL4WS) [100] workflow editor that automatically calculates the average and worst-case execution time of workflows.

- **description of time constraints:**
  The time constraints of a web service or workflow may vary over time depending on the utilization of the infrastructure. This thesis presents the first policy-based approach to describe the dynamic time constraints of web services named *WS-TemporalPolicy*. WS-TemporalPolicy can be used to describe arbitrary dynamic properties of web services.

---

[1] The notions "workflow" and "business process" are not distinguished within this thesis. Both describe a complex, multi-step working process within an enterprise.

1.1 Research Contributions 11

- **efficient data transmission within web service environments:**
  Web services are not suited for bulk binary input or return parameters. Embedding such data in the SOAP messages used for service invocation is not a reasonable approach, because the Extensible Markup Language (XML) [86] formats that SOAP is built on are not suitable to hold large binary objects. This fact is problematical in the domain of industrial automation, since process data, e.g. status or problem reports, are often bulk binary data. This thesis presents a new approach for flexibly handling bulk binary data in web service environments named *Flex-SwA*.

The research contributions of this thesis have been published in several publications:

1. Markus Mathes, Roland Schwarzkopf, Tim Dörnemann, Steffen Heinzl, Bernd Freisleben: *Composition of Time-Constrained BPEL4WS-Workflows using the TiCS Modeler*, Proceedings of the 13th IFAC Symposium on Information Control Problems in Manufacturing (INCOM), Moscow (Russia), pp. 892–897, Elsevier, 2009

2. Christoph Stoidner, Markus Mathes, Bernd Freisleben: *Sequence-Controlled Web Services for Programmable Logic Controllers*, Proceedings of the 13th IFAC Symposium on Information Control Problems in Manufacturing (INCOM), Moscow (Russia), pp. 2186–2191, Elsevier, 2009

3. Tim Dörnemann, Markus Mathes, Roland Schwarzkopf, Ernst Juhnke, Bernd Freisleben: *DAVO: A Domain-Adaptable, Visual BPEL4WS Orchestrator*, Proceedings of the IEEE 23rd International Conference on Advanced Information Networking and Applications (AINA), Bradford (UK), pp. 121–128, IEEE Computer Society Press, 2009

4. Steffen Heinzl, Markus Mathes, Thilo Stadelmann, Dominik Seiler, Marcel Diegelmann, Helmut Dohmann, Bernd Freisleben: *The Web Service Browser: Automatic Client Generation and Efficient Data Transfer for Web Services*, Proceedings of the 7th IEEE International Conference on

Web Services (ICWS), Los Angeles (USA), pp. 743–750, IEEE Computer Society Press, 2009

5. Markus Mathes, Steffen Heinzl, Bernd Freisleben: *Towards a Generic Backup and Recovery Infrastructure for the German Grid Initiative*, Tagungsband der ITG/GI-Fachtagung Kommunikation in Verteilten Systemen (KiVS), Kassel (Germany), pp. 229–240, Springer, 2009

6. Markus Mathes, Christoph Stoidner, Steffen Heinzl, Bernd Freisleben: *SOAP4PLC: Web Services for Programmable Logic Controllers*, Proceedings of the 17th Euromicro International Conference on Parallel, Distributed, and Network-Based Processing (Euromicro PDP), Weimar (Germany), pp. 210–219, IEEE Computer Society Press, 2009

7. Markus Mathes, Jochen Gärtner, Helmut Dohmann, Bernd Freisleben: *SOAP4IPC: A Real-Time SOAP Engine for Time-Constrained Web Services in Industrial Automation*, Proceedings of the 17th Euromicro International Conference on Parallel, Distributed, and Network-Based Processing (Euromicro PDP), Weimar (Germany), pp. 220–226, IEEE Computer Society Press, 2009

8. Steffen Heinzl, Markus Mathes, Bernd Freisleben: *The Grid Browser: Improving Usability in Service-Oriented Grids by Automatically Generating Clients and Handling Data Transfers*, Proceedings of the 4th IEEE International Conference on e-Science (e-Science), Indianapolis (USA), pp. 269–276, IEEE Computer Society Press, 2008

9. Markus Mathes, Steffen Heinzl, Bernd Freisleben: *Towards a Time-Constrained Web Service Infrastructure for Industrial Automation*, Proceedings of the 13th IEEE International Conference on Emerging Technologies and Factory Automation (ETFA), Hamburg (Germany), pp. 846–853, IEEE Computer Society Press, 2008

10. Markus Mathes, Roland Schwarzkopf, Tim Dörnemann, Steffen Heinzl, Bernd Freisleben: *Orchestration of Time-Constrained BPEL4WS Workflows*, Proceedings of the 13th IEEE International Conference on Emerg-

1.1 Research Contributions 13

ing Technologies and Factory Automation (ETFA), pp. 1–4, Hamburg (Germany), IEEE Computer Society Press, 2008

11. Markus Mathes, Steffen Heinzl, Bernd Freisleben: *WS-TemporalPolicy: A WS-Policy Extension for Describing Service Properties with Time Constraints*, Proceedings of the 1st IEEE International Workshop On Real-Time Service-Oriented Architecture and Applications (RTSOAA) of the 32nd Annual IEEE International Computer Software and Applications Conference (COMPSAC), Turku (Finland), pp. 1180–1186, IEEE Computer Society Press, 2008

12. Steffen Heinzl, Markus Mathes, Bernd Freisleben: *A Web Service Communication Policy for Describing Non-Standard Application Requirements*, Proceedings of the IEEE/IPSJ Symposium on Applications and the Internet (SAINT), pp. 40–47, Turku (Finland), IEEE Computer Society Press, 2008

13. Roland Schwarzkopf, Markus Mathes, Steffen Heinzl, Bernd Freisleben, Helmut Dohmann: *Java RMI versus .NET Remoting – Architectural Comparison and Performance Evaluation*, Proceedings of the 7th International Conference on Networking (ICN), Cancun (Mexico), pp. 398–407, IEEE Computer Society Press, 2008

14. Tim Dörnemann, Steffen Heinzl, Kay Dörnemann, Markus Mathes, Matthew Smith, Bernd Freisleben: *Secure Grid Service Engineering for Industrial Optimization*, Proceedings of the 7th International Conference on Optimization: Techniques and Applications (ICOTA), Kobe (Japan), pp. 371–372, 2007

15. Steffen Heinzl, Markus Mathes, Thomas Friese, Matthew Smith, Bernd Freisleben: *Flex-SwA: Flexible Exchange of Binary Data Based on SOAP Messages with Attachments*, Proceedings of the IEEE International Conference on Web Services (ICWS), Chicago (USA), pp. 3–10, IEEE Computer Society Press, 2006

16. Markus Mathes, Steffen Heinzl, Thomas Friese, Bernd Freisleben: *Enabling Post-Invocation Parameter Transmission in Service-Oriented Environments*, Proceedings of the 2nd International Conference on Networking and Services (ICNS), Silicon Valley (USA), pp. 55–62, IEEE Computer Society Press, 2006

17. Steffen Heinzl, Markus Mathes: *Middleware in Java*, ISBN-10: 3528059125, ISBN-13: 978-3528059125, Vieweg+Teubner, 2005

18. Florian Heidinger, Markus Mathes, Helmut Dohmann: *Java Messaging Service (JMS) – Einsatz in der Industrieautomation*, Automatisierungstechnische Praxis (atp), volume 5, pp. 61–70, Oldenbourg, 2004

Additionally, the TiCS framework received the *IBM Real-time Innovation Award 2008*.

1.2 Organization of this Thesis

The organization of this thesis reflects the components of the TiCS framework via a top-down approach, i.e. starting from a bird's eye view on the entire framework, the details of each component are explained.

Chapter 2 presents an overview of the TiCS framework. After identification of the requirements of a web service based automation solution, the architecture and components of the TiCS framework are discussed. Additionally, the design and implementation principles for the framework are outlined.

Chapter 3 presents the first SOAP engine for PLCs called SOAP4PLC that permits to easily export a PLC function as a web service. A main focus of the SOAP4PLC engine is usability for automation engineers to foster acceptance by the automation community.

Chapter 4 introduces the first profiling-and-monitoring based, multi-purpose, real-time SOAP engine. Although this engine is used for real-time processing of web services at IPC, it is applicable in arbitrary domains where real-time processing of SOAP messages is important.

Chapter 5 demonstrates how the composition of time-constrained workflows

1.2 Organization of this Thesis 15

can be realized. The presented TiCS Modeler is a BPEL4WS workflow editor. It enables the composition of arbitrary time-constrained web services to a manufacturing process. The theoretical foundation for the computation of the worst-case execution time is also derived in this chapter.

Chapter 6 presents WS-TemporalPolicy for the description of dynamic web service properties like time constraints.

Chapter 7 presents a new approach for the efficient transmission of bulk binary data within web service environments called Flex-SwA. Flex-SwA provides functionality for the efficient transmission of the input and return parameters of a web service.

Chapter 8 presents implementation details of the SOAP4PLC engine, the SOAP4IPC engine, the TiCS Modeler, WS-TemporalPolicy, and Flex-SwA.

Chapter 9 evaluates the performance of the SOAP4IPC and SOAP4PLC engine and exemplifies the internal processing of the TiCS Modeler.

Chapter 10 defines the scope of this thesis and discusses related work in the domain of industrial automation, especially with regard to service-oriented architectures and web services for the manufacturing layer.

Chapter 11 summarizes this thesis and outlines directions for future work.

2
Overview of the Time-Constrained Services Framework

2.1 Introduction

This chapter presents an overview of the TiCS framework and its functional components. More precisely, the layered architecture consisting of the hardware layer, the real-time infrastructural layer, the real-time service layer, and the tool support layer and their specific functional components are discussed.

The rest of this chapter is organized as follows: Section 2.2 identifies the requirements for a real-time web service framework for industrial automation. These requirements are the foundation for the layered architecture of the TiCS framework presented in Section 2.3. Section 2.4 outlines general design guidelines for the entire TiCS framework. The chapter is summarized in section 2.5.

Parts of this chapter have been published in [115, 146, 147, 148, 150, 151, 152, 168].

2.2 Requirements Analysis

The design and implementation of the TiCS framework depends on the requirements of a web service based automation infrastructure. The main problem areas are described by the following questions:

How can web services be applied at the manufacturing layer to monitor and control the manufacturing process?

Today's IPCs, PLCs, and manufacturing devices do not offer a web service interface. Typically, IPCs, PLCs, and manufacturing devices offer a vendor-specific interface and therefore are offered as a bundle, i.e. the entire automation solution comes from a single vendor.

Consequence: A technical key requirement of the TiCS framework is a web service interface to the manufacturing layer. More precisely, a SOAP engine tailored to the characteristics of the manufacturing layer is required.

How can a web service be processed within a specific deadline?

Since web service technologies originally have emerged from the Internet domain where time constraints are of little or no importance, existing standards and implementations only support best-effort processing. A direct adoption of these technologies within time-constrained environments like industrial automation is impossible.

Consequence: The TiCS framework must offer a SOAP engine that supports the processing of a web service within a predefined time constraint.

How can the time constraints of a web service be described?

The time constraints of a web service used in industrial automation are determined by the manufacturing device it controls and the production process in which the device is used. Time constraints are not static but may vary over time, e.g. during peak time, lower time constraints can be guaranteed than during off-peak time.

Consequence: The TiCS framework must offer a mechanism to describe the

2.2 Requirements Analysis

dynamic time constraints of web services. Since time constraints are meta-information to a web service, they can be described using policies.

How can web services be composed to model multi-step manufacturing processes? How can the time constraints for multi-step manufacturing processes be calculated?

A production process normally consists of several consecutive steps that are realized by different manufacturing devices. Several web services controlling the functionality of these manufacturing devices have to be composed to a workflow.

Consequence: The TiCS framework needs a component to compose time-constrained web services to a time-constrained workflow. This component must offer the automatic calculation of time constraints.

How can automation engineers be empowered to use web services?

In spite of the euphoria the use of web services in industrial automation produces, one has to keep in mind that web service technologies are completely new for automation engineers who maintain the manufacturing process. Automation engineers rely upon well-known technologies and best-practice solutions to develop and maintain the production process. A switch to web service based automation cannot be realized overnight and requires—first of all—user acceptance.

Consequence: To foster the proliferation of web services within industrial automation, usability is a key enabler. Automation engineers must be supported by sophisticated tools to easily implement, deploy, invoke, and compose time-constrained web services.

How can the input and return parameters of a web service be transferred efficiently?

The execution of web services presumes that all input parameters are available at the service consumer (that may be, for example, an IPC or a PLC). An inefficient transmission of input parameters (and return values) also delays the invocation of a web service.

Consequence: A component enabling efficient data transmission within web service environments is crucial for the TiCS framework.

Taking these central questions into account, the requirements can be distinguished into *usability requirements* (tool support for the automation engineer to ease implementation of time-constrained web services and time-constrained workflows) and *infrastructural requirements* (adoption of web services at the manufacturing layer, web service execution in real-time, description of the time constraints of web services/workflows, efficient data transmission within web service environments). The architectural blueprint of the TiCS framework presented in the following section reflects these requirements.

2.3 Architectural Blueprint

The TiCS framework consists of four functional layers: tool support layer, real-time service layer, real-time infrastructural layer, and hardware layer. Each layer contains several components to meet the demands of a web service based automation infrastructure as identified in the previous section. Figure 2.1 outlines the architectural blueprint of the TiCS framework.

This thesis focuses on the components most relevant from a research perspective: enhancing the manufacturing layer by web service capabilities, processing of web services in real-time, composition of time-constrained workflows, description of time constraints using policies, and efficient data transmission in web service environments.

2.3.1 Hardware Layer

The hardware layer is the basis for the entire TiCS framework and contains only *standardized* automation hardware, i.e. IPCs, PLCs, and arbitrary manufacturing devices, to guarantee backward compatibility with existing automation solutions. The technical details of the automation hardware, e.g. hierarchi-

2.3 Architectural Blueprint

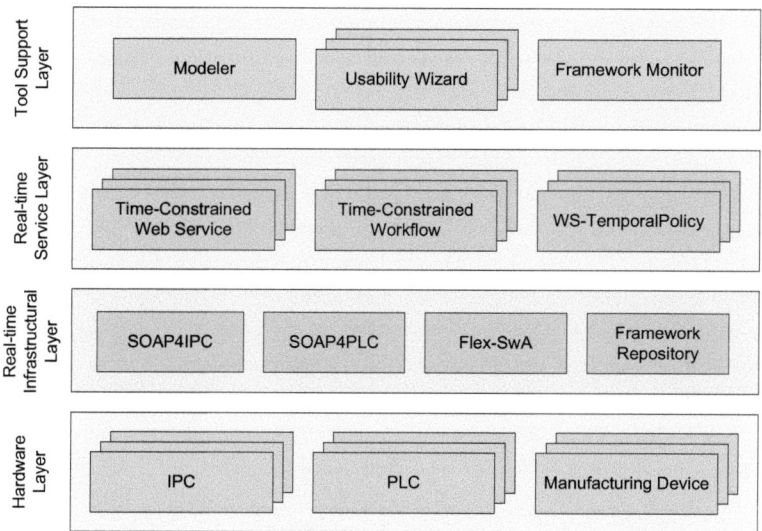

Figure 2.1: Architectural blueprint of the TiCS framework.

cal arrangement or wiring of the manufacturing devices, are hidden by the hardware layer.

A key requirement of the TiCS framework is a web service interface to the hardware layer. This interface does not describe use case dependent protocols or data formats, but how the hard- and software at the manufacturing layer can be empowered with web service functionality. Taking the hierarchical arrangement of production cells into account (see Figure 1.2), there exist three different approaches to realize the web service interface:

1. Only smart devices (web service accessible sensors/actuators) are used at the manufacturing layer.

2. The PLCs are enhanced with web service capabilities.

3. Web services are offered by the IPCs. The invocation of a web service operation results in a call to the corresponding control function at the connected PLCs.

22 2 Overview of the Time-Constrained Services Framework

The first approach requires no additional software, since the smart devices innately contain a web service stack and offer their functionality via web services. The second and third approach require a SOAP engine tailored to the characteristics of PLCs (e.g. low processing power and main memory) and IPCs (e.g. real-time operating system used), respectively.

To clarify the three approaches, consider an industrial robot that supports amongst other things three-dimensional alignment in x-, y-, and z-direction. This functionality should be exported using a web service **Alignment** that offers three operations moveX, moveY, and moveZ.

Using the first approach, the industrial robot is a smart device and offers the web service itself (cp. Figure 2.2). This approach is already discussed in the literature—Gilart-Iglesias et al. call this approach *Industrial Machines as a Service* [122, 123]. This approach currently lacks technical feasibility, since market-ready smart devices are not available up to now.

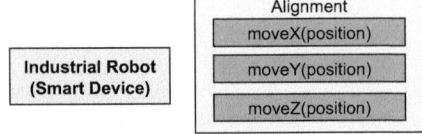

Figure 2.2: Using smart devices to enhance the manufacturing layer with web service capabilities.

The second approach presumes a SOAP engine, since the web service is offered by the PLC (cp. Figure 2.3). The invocation of the **Alignment** web service results in corresponding control commands for the industrial robot. The realization of the second approach is technically challenging due to two reasons: PLCs offer less computational power and the technical details of PLCs differ from vendor to vendor.

The third approach shifts the SOAP engine from the PLC to the IPC (cp. Figure 2.4). IPCs offer more computational power and are more standardized with regard to operating systems and available tools compared to PLCs. The invocation of the **Alignment** web service triggers the corresponding PLC function that again results in control commands for the industrial robot. Therefore,

2.3 Architectural Blueprint 23

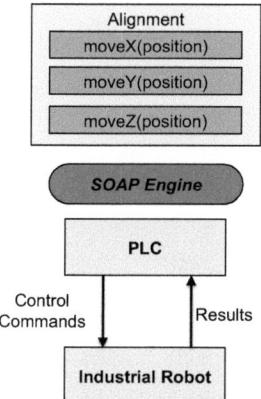

Figure 2.3: Using a SOAP engine for PLCs to enhance the manufacturing layer with web service capabilities.

the IPC acts as a facade for the PLC.

The TiCS framework supports the second *and* third approach, i.e. TiCS offers a SOAP engine for PLCs and a SOAP engine for IPCs. This permits an evolutionary change from the second to the third industrial automation generation (see Section 1) and offers flexibility. Additionally, the existing IPCs, PLCs, and manufacturing devices can be furthermore used and have not to be replaced by new hardware, leading to cost savings.

2.3.2 Real-time Infrastructural Layer

The real-time infrastructural layer contains the SOAP engine for IPCs called *SOAP4IPC* and the SOAP engine for PLCs called *SOAP4PLC*, the *Flex-SwA* data transmission component, and the *Framework Repository*.

A key characteristic of SOAP4IPC is its *generic* design and implementation. The SOAP4IPC core is a time-constrained, multi-threaded server that can be parameterized with an arbitrary processing logic. Consequently, an arbitrary communication protocol and not only SOAP can be processed in real-time. This feature makes SOAP4IPC a development basis for arbitrary

2 Overview of the Time-Constrained Services Framework

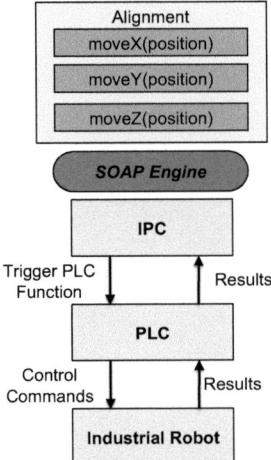

Figure 2.4: Using a SOAP engine for IPCs to enhance the manufacturing layer with web service capabilities.

real-time servers. A key characteristic of the SOAP4PLC engine is *usability* for automation engineers. An automation engineer implements PLC control functions using well-known tools. All web service relevant information is generated automatically with minimal intervention of the automation engineer. Both engines may be adopted separately or in combination within a production process.

The invocation of a web service may require specific input parameters. Within industrial automation, these parameters are often bulk binary data, e.g. status/error reports or parts lists in a proprietary binary format. Embedding such data in SOAP messages used for service invocation is not a reasonable approach, because the XML formats that SOAP is built on are not suitable to hold large binary objects. The Flex-SwA data transmission component offers functionality for the efficient transmission of binary data which permits timely execution of web services.

The Framework Repository stores information concerning the entire TiCS framework: information about all available time-constrained web services and

2.3 Architectural Blueprint

workflows, their average and worst-case execution times, and the IPCs/PLCs where web services are deployed to. The implementation of the Framework Repository can be based on several technologies, e.g. Universal Description, Discovery, and Integration (UDDI) [70]. For performance reasons [160] and for better integration within the entire TiCS framework, the Framework Repository has been implemented with plain web services. To publish and to look up information about time-constrained web services or workflows at the repository, the following interface is offered:

- `publishService`: A new time-constrained web service is stored within the repository and can be retrieved afterwards.

- `lookupService`: This operation can be used to retrieve all information published for a specific time-constrained web service.

- `removeService`: An already published time-constrained web service is removed from the repository. All subsequent lookups for this service will fail.

- `publishWorkflow`: A new time-constrained workflow is stored within the repository and can be retrieved afterwards.

- `lookupWorkflow`: The information stored for the given workflow are returned.

- `removeWorkflow`: The workflow with the given name is removed from the repository. Subsequent invocations of `lookupWorkflow` will fail for this workflow.

- `lookupAllServices`: This operation returns a list of all published time-constrained web services.

- `lookupAllWorkflows`: A list of all published time-constrained workflows is returned.

- `clearServices`: All time-constrained web services are cleared. Subsequent lookups for an arbitrary time-constrained web service will fail.

- `clearWorkflows`: All time-constrained workflows are cleared. Subsequent lookups for an arbitrary time-constrained workflow will fail.

- `clearRepository`: The entire repository is cleared. Subsequent lookups for an arbitrary time-constrained web service or workflow will fail.

The design of the SOAP4PLC engine is presented in Chapter 3. Chapter 4 presents technical details of the SOAP4IPC engine. The Flex-SwA data transmission component is discussed in Chapter 7. Implementation details of all these components are presented in Chapter 8. Chapter 9 presents an evaluation of SOAP4IPC and SOAP4PLC, respectively.

2.3.3 Real-time Service Layer

The real-time service layer contains time-constrained web services, time-constrained workflows, and several temporal policies.

A *time-constrained web service* is a standard web service with additional information concerning the average execution time (aet) and worst-case execution time (wcet). Since time constraints are meta-information from the implementation perspective, annotations are, for example, suitable to describe them. Listing 2.1 shows an example of a Java annotation that describes the average (2.9 msec) and worst-case execution time (6.2 msec).

Listing 2.1: Annotation for a web service operation with time constraints.
```
@TimeConstraintAnnotation(
realtimeDomain = RealtimeDomain.HARD,
worstCaseExecutionTime = 6.2,
worstCaseExecutionTimeUnit = TimeConstraintUnit.MILLI_SEC,
averageExecutionTime = 2.9,
averageExecutionTimeUnit = TimeConstraintUnit.MILLI_SEC
)
```

In principle, there exists a top-down and bottom-up approach to define time-constrained web services. Both approaches are based on the fact that an automation engineer has a priori knowledge about the production process and the required time constraints. Using the top-down approach, the automation engineer firstly defines the acceptable execution time for each web service.

2.3 Architectural Blueprint

After having defined the time constraints, the web services are deployed to a real-time SOAP engine together with the desired time constraints. The real-time SOAP engine measures during web service execution whether the time constraints are kept. Using the bottom-up approach, the automation engineer firstly deploys the web service to the real-time SOAP engine that profiles the average and worst-case execution time of the service. If the profiled average and worst-case execution time are not sufficient, the automation engineer modifies the web service and takes another deployment-profiling-cycle to determine the new average and worst-case execution time.

The top-down approach has the main drawback that an automation engineer may define time constraints that will never be kept by the infrastructure, whereas the bottom-up approach results in technical feasible time constraints only. For these reasons, the TiCS framework supports the bottom-up approach: the automation engineer starts with implementing a web service, deploys this service to the SOAP4IPC engine, and profiles the time constraints of the web service. If the profiled time constraints are sufficient, the web service can be used. Otherwise, the automation engineer modifies the web service and starts another deployment-profiling-cycle, as shown in Figure 2.5.

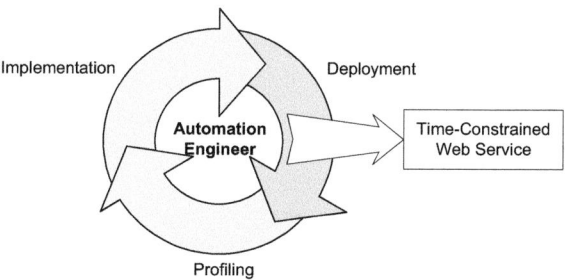

Figure 2.5: Schema of a bottom-up approach to define the time constraints of a web service.

A *time-constrained workflow* is a composition of several time-constrained web services. Within this thesis, the Business Process Execution Language for Web Services (BPEL4WS) [100] is used as workflow composition language due to its proliferation and acceptance in the web service community. Each BPEL4WS workflow encapsulates several web services but is offered as a simple web service. Consequently, a time-constrained BPEL4WS workflow can be handled like a time-constrained web service.

To describe the timing behavior of both time-constrained services and time-constrained workflows, the TiCS framework offers *WS-TemporalPolicy*. WS-TemporalPolicy can be used to describe arbitrary dynamic properties of a web service but was intentionally designed for the description of time constraints.

Chapter 5 derives the timing behavior of BPEL4WS workflows. How WS-TemporalPolicies can be used to describe the timing behavior of time-constrained services and workflows is discussed in Chapter 6. Implementation details of WS-TemporalPolicy are presented in Chapter 8.

2.3.4 Tool Support Layer

Potential users of the TiCS framework are automation engineers who are non web service experts. Therefore, exhaustive tool support is required to ease the implementation, composition, deployment, and publication of time-constrained web services and workflows and the monitoring of the entire TiCS framework. The tool support layer offers these features by means of the TiCS Modeler, several Usability Wizards, and the Framework Monitor.

The *TiCS Modeler* is a workflow editor that permits the composition of time-constrained web services in BPEL4WS and is based on the Domain-adaptable Visual Orchestrator (DAVO) [114]. The automation engineer has expert knowledge about the manufacturing process, e.g. necessary steps in the manufacturing process, required manufacturing devices, worst-case execution time for each step and for the overall process, etc. Equipped with this knowledge, the automation engineer composes a workflow of several time-constrained web services to realize the manufacturing process.

The *Framework Monitor* is a graphical interface to the entire TiCS framework. The current system status is outlined using information provided by the TiCS Framework Repository. This information contains:

2.3 Architectural Blueprint

- overview of deployed and available time-constrained services/workflows (general description of functionality, average execution time, worst-case execution time)

- overview of IPCs/PLCs where SOAP4IPC and SOAP4PLC engines are deployed and their parameterization

- statistical information (number of invocations for each service/workflow, number of successful/erroneous invocations, downtime/uptime information for relevant hosts)

- wiring of IPC, PLC, and manufacturing devices for service deployment

The development process of a time-constrained web service consists of three steps: implementation, deployment, and publication. These tasks are supported by three different *Usability Wizards*, which are implemented as Eclipse [16] plug-ins:

- **Real-time Service Creation Wizard**:
  The implementation of time-constrained web services is supported by a wizard that helps the engineer to define a Java class with several methods. A class template is generated which easily can be completed by the automation engineer.

- **Real-time Service Deployment Wizard**:
  After having implemented a time-constrained web service, the service has to be deployed to a web service engine. The deployment process requires detailed engine-specific knowledge, depending on the web service engine used. To ease the deployment process, the automation engineer is supported by a service deployment wizard.

- **Real-time Service Publishing Wizard**:
  This wizard eases the publication of a time-constrained web service in the Framework Repository for subsequent use.

Chapter 5 derives the time constraints of BPEL4WS workflows. On the basis of this derivation, the TiCS Modeler calculates the execution time of a workflow and assists the automation engineer during the composition process. Implementation details of the TiCS Modeler are presented in Chapter 8. Chapter 9 evaluates the use of the TiCS Modeler by means of a use case.

2.4 Design Considerations

The design of the entire TiCS framework is based on the following principles:

design and development of a common core for the execution of real-time tasks

The SOAP4IPC engine permits processing of SOAP messages in real-time. Since the design and implementation of the engine is generic, an arbitrary protocol and not only SOAP can be processed in real-time. A generic design and implementation offer benefits for future developments, since the implementation need not to start from scratch. Consider, for example, the release of a new SOAP protocol version. The generic design and implementation of the SOAP4IPC engine permits to easily replace the out-dated protocol version.

backward compatibility

The TiCS framework presented in this thesis outlines technologies to realize the third generation of industrial automation. As seen in other domains, the shift from one paradigm to another will not take place overnight but rather gradually. Therefore, it is crucial that all technologies developed within this thesis are adaptable in addition to existing technologies. In other words, the use of the TiCS framework should not interfere or—even worse—conflict with existing, widely-used technologies in industrial automation.

usability

A key requirement for the acceptance and therefore the use of the technologies presented in this thesis is usability. Automation engineers are normally novices with regard to web services and require appropriate tools to cope with this new technology. Consequently, the real-time web service engine for IPCs and the real-time web service engine for PLCs developed and presented in this thesis focus on usability.

2.5 Summary

This section has identified the requirements for a web service based automation solution like a web service interface to the manufacturing layer, usability, or efficient transmission of web service parameters. Motivated by these requirements, the layered architecture of the TiCS framework—manufacturing layer, real-time infrastructural layer, real-time service layer, and tool support layer—and the components of each layer were presented. The main components of the TiCS framework are SOAP4PLC, a SOAP engine to equip PLCs with a web service interface, SOAP4IPC, a real-time SOAP engine for IPCs, the TiCS Modeler, a graphical BPEL4WS workflow editor, WS-TemporalPolicy for the description of time constraints, and Flex-SwA for the the efficient transmission of web service parameters. The subsequent chapters focus on the design, implementation, and evaluation of all these components.

3
Web Services for PLCs

3.1 Introduction

The use of web services in the manufacturing layer is complicated by two main challenges. First, the hardware/software used at this layer differs from hardware/software used at other layers. Second, the manufacturing layer is maintained by automation engineers who are not familiar with web services.

This chapter presents the first SOAP engine for PLCs called *SOAP4PLC* to advance the use of web services in the manufacturing layer. SOAP4PLC offers a low memory footprint due to the low computational power of PLCs and permits to export web services automatically without intervention of an automation engineer. The automation engineer develops the PLC control software in a well-known development environment. The corresponding web services are generated and deployed automatically in the background.

The rest of this chapter is organized as follows: Section 3.2 explains the processing and internal structure of PLC control applications based on the IEC 61131-3 standard. Equipped with this knowledge, the benefits and challenges to use web services on PLCs are explained in Section 3.3. The identified challenges motivate the design objectives of the SOAP4PLC engine as explained in Section 3.4: embedding the event-driven processing of web service invocations in the cyclic processing paradigm of PLCs and usability for automation engineers. Section 3.5 summarizes this chapter.

Parts of this chapter have been published in [152, 168].

3.2 Industrial Automation—Status Quo

Conventional automation solutions subdivide the entire manufacturing process into several disjunctive manufacturing steps that are called *production cells*. Each production cell contains several manufacturing devices, e.g. industrial robots or hoisting platforms, which are controlled by a PLC.

A PLC is a specialized automation hardware which differs heavily from common desktop PCs. A PLC has several input/output modules, which are connected to sensors and actuators, respectively. A sensor collects (often analog) input data from the shop floor, e.g. temperature, pressure, or humidity, whereas an actuator allows to manipulate the production process. Examples for actuators are electric motors, solenoids, or conveyor belts.

To control the manufacturing devices, the PLC reads the data from the sensors, computes the necessary reaction using a so-called PLC application, and uses its actuators to react. The PLC application is set up by a domain expert, namely the automation engineer who maintains the production process. Most PLC vendors provide a proprietary integrated development environment allowing to implement the PLC application with respect to the IEC 61131-3 [65] standard.

An IEC 61131-3 compatible PLC application is organized in several modules, which are called *program organization units* (POUs). A POU consists of multiple expressions of one of the following programming languages: Function Block Diagram (FBD), Instruction List (IL), Ladder Diagram (LD), Structured Text (ST), or Sequential Function Chart (SFC). A POU may also contain calls to other POUs. Three types of POUs can be distinguished:

- A *function* is comparable with functions known from other programming languages like C. A function is defined by a unique name, several input

3.2 Industrial Automation—Status Quo

variables (the arguments) and a return type. Furthermore, a function consists of local variables and some instructions. The instance of a function is allocated on the callers stack and exists only during its execution. When the function terminates, its instance is destroyed.

- A *function block* is similar to a C++ or Java class containing only one method. Like a function, it is defined by a unique name and several input variables (the arguments), local variables and some instructions. A function block has no return type but may consist several output variables. The caller has to create an instance manually, thus the instance exists beyond its execution.

- A *program* is similar to a singleton, i.e. only one instance of the program exists. It may contain local variables which are allocated statically. Consequently, the instance of a program exists during the complete runtime of the PLC application.

A PLC application operates in a loop called *input-processing-output cycle* (IPO cycle). Such an IPO cycle is called a PLC task. Since each step in an IPO cycle can only take a predetermined time, a PLC inherently supports hard real-time processing. A PLC application consists of one or more PLC tasks. Each task is responsible for the execution of a dedicated program POU defined by the automation engineer. Figure 3.1 outlines the logical structure of a PLC application.

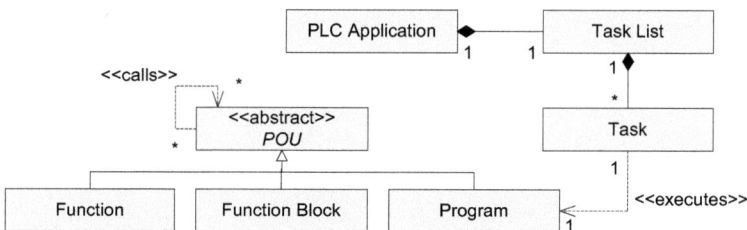

Figure 3.1: Logical structure of PLC applications.

3.3 Benefits and Challenges of Web Services for PLCs

The key benefits of using web services on PLCs are standardization and saving of costs. In a conventionally organized industrial enterprise, a business engineer designs and maintains business processes whereas the automation engineer designs and maintains the production processes. For these purposes, the business engineer requires input from the manufacturing layer, e.g. already produced number of units, and—vice versa—the automation engineer requires input from the business layer, e.g. next planned maintenance shutdown. The business engineer and the automation engineer have to collaborate to define an interface to exchange the required information. Since there exist no standardized formats and patterns for such interfaces, they are often proprietary and must be re-designed if the exchanged information change. This results in recurrent, unnecessary costs. The use of web services as standardized interface on PLCs results in a separation of concerns between the business layer and the manufacturing layer. The automation engineer may define a web service that provides all production-relevant information of the PLC. The business engineer uses this web service to query the current production state. On the other hand, the business engineer may define a web service which provides all business-relevant information. This web service is used by the automation engineer to query current business orders. Figure 3.2(a) illustrates the interconnection of the business and the manufacturing layer using a proprietary interface. Figure 3.2(b) shows the use of web services to interconnect the business and the manufacturing layer.

However, there are some important challenges that have to be considered if web services should be used as standardized interface to the manufacturing layer.

- The use of web services in combination with PLC applications is complicated by the fundamentally different processing paradigms of both technologies. A PLC application consists of several PLC tasks, i.e. infinitely running IPO cycles that are scheduled by a real-time operating

3.4 Design Considerations

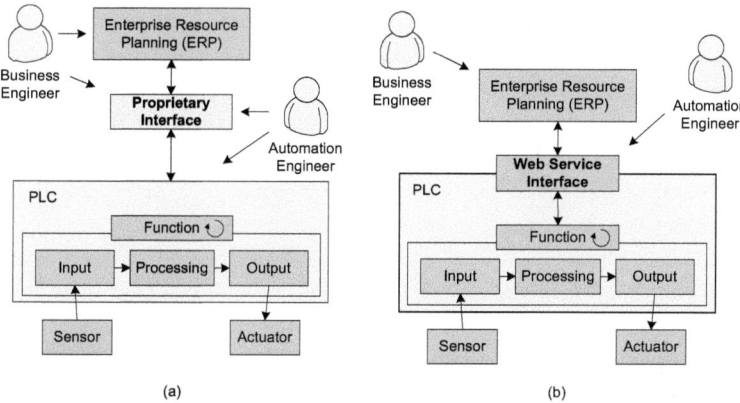

Figure 3.2: Separation of concerns by using a web service interface.

system. In contrast, a web service offers several operations that can be invoked at an arbitrary time, i.e. web services are processed event-driven.

- Automation engineers are normally not familiar with service-oriented architectures in general and web services in particular. Consequently, the use of web services as an interface to PLCs is completely novel to the automation community and there exist no well-established design patterns.

- PLC applications are implemented using an IEC 61131-3 based development environment. These development environments are well-known to automation engineers and cannot be replaced easily by service-oriented development environments since this will result in remarkable education costs for automation engineers.

3.4 Design Considerations

The challenges identified in the previous section—processing paradigms of PLC applications and web services differ significantly, automation engineers are unfamiliar with web service technologies, replacement of widely-used IEC 61131-3 development environment results in remarkable costs—motivates the design objectives of the SOAP4PLC engine.

To align the cyclic and event-driven processing paradigms of PLC applications and web services, a SOAP engine for PLCs must embed the execution of the web service operations into the corresponding IPO cycle. This thesis introduces so-called *sequence-controlled web services* for this purpose.

To improve usability for automation engineers and to avoid the introduction of new development environments, a SOAP engine for PLCs must extend the existing IEC 61131-3 based development environments by functionality that permit the automatic export of POUs as web services. More precisely, the following functionality is required:

- The automation engineer must be empowered to deploy/undeploy PLC functions as web services.

- WSDL descriptions of already deployed web services have to be generated automatically.

- The PLC has to listen for incoming SOAP request messages and has to interpret them.

- A SOAP invocation message must result in a call to the corresponding PLC function.

- After the call of a PLC function, a SOAP response message has to be generated and sent.

These functions are encapsulated in four core components of the SOAP4PLC engine: WS-Infobase, WSDL-Generator, SOAP-Handler, and SOAP2PLC-Bridge:

- **WS-Infobase:**
  This component stores information relevant for all other components about the deployed web services. It provides an interface to permit the export of a PLC function as a web service by the automation engineer.

3.4 Design Considerations

- **WSDL-Generator:**
  This component dynamically generates WSDL descriptions for already deployed web services.

- **SOAP-Handler:**
  This component implements the SOAP protocol, i.e. it processes incoming SOAP request messages and generates outgoing SOAP response messages.

- **SOAP2PLC-Bridge:**
  This component locates and calls the corresponding PLC function for an incoming web service invocation.

Figure 3.3 illustrates the internal structure of a web service enabled PLC. The SOAP4PLC engine acts as a mediator between the conventional PLC application and the web service interface.

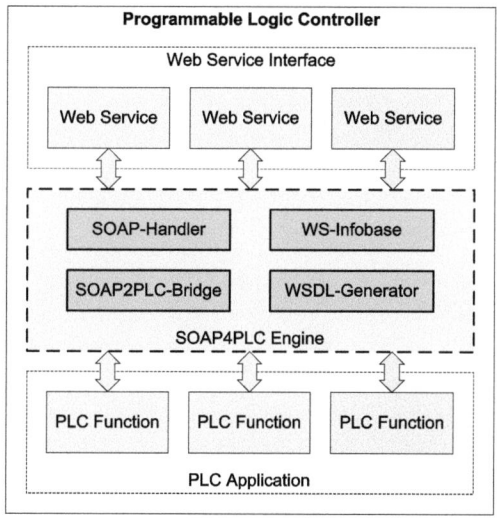

Figure 3.3: Architectural blueprint of the SOAP4PLC engine.

3.4.1 WS-Infobase

The WS-Infobase component implements the *service descriptor table*, a database which holds the metadata of all deployed web services and the related PLC functions. All other components of the SOAP4PLC engine use the WS-Infobase to retrieve required metadata on a specific web service. Each deployed web service is listed in the WS-Infobase with its unique name and a table of provided operations. The unique name will be used to retrieve the web service from the WS-Infobase. The table of operations contains one row for each deployed operation of the web service. One row includes the following information to describe the interface of an operation:

- name of operation: The name is used to determine the operation within the web service.

- reference to the corresponding PLC function: The reference is used to address the PLC function and is realized as a function pointer, a handle, or a unique identifier depending on the used PLC programming system.

- list of input parameters: The input parameter list specifies the number of parameters and the datatype of each one. The order of the parameters in the list specifies the parameter order for an operation call.

- datatype of the operation: The datatype of the operation represents the datatype of its return value.

To the automation engineer, the WS-Infobase provides a user interface to deploy and undeploy web services. More exactly, from the automation engineers point of view, the WS-Infobase provides a user interface to export PLC functions as web service operations. For each exported PLC function, a group name is defined. The group name specifies the web service the PLC function belongs to. That user interface is the only point of contact between the automation engineer and the SOAP4PLC engine.

The WS-Infobase generates all metadata required by the service descriptor table from the input of the automation engineer. The name of the web service as which the PLC function is deployed is derived from the PLC function's

3.4 Design Considerations

group name. Thus, the deployment process will be performed automatically without any interaction of the automation engineer. This will be done at the startup of the PLC application within three steps per web service:

1. All generated metadata will be stored in the service descriptor table.

2. The SOAP-Handler is extended to accept the URI of the newly deployed web service.

3. A new instance of the WSDL-Generator is started offering a WSDL description for the new web service.

3.4.2 SOAP-Handler

The SOAP-Handler component realizes the handling of the SOAP protocol. When the WS-Infobase deploys a web service, the SOAP-Handler will be informed. Upon application startup, it initiates the underlying HTTP protocol handler to listen for the corresponding URI of the web service. After that, the SOAP-Handler is able to handle requests for that web service.

When a request arrives, the SOAP-Handler identifies the target web service via the requested URI and tries to find the corresponding operation interface description using the WS-Infobase. If no matching entry was found, a SOAP fault message is generated. Otherwise, the interface definition is validated, i.e. the operation name, the argument datatypes and the return datatype will be determined and matched with the metadata from the service descriptor table in the WS-Infobase. Additionally, the argument values will be parsed and stored for later usage. Then, the SOAP2PLC-Bridge is used to invoke the PLC function and to pass the argument values.

As soon as the PLC function terminates, the SOAP2PLC-Bridge returns the result to the SOAP-Handler. The result is embedded in a SOAP response message that is delivered to the underlying HTTP protocol handler to complete the web service request.

3.4.3 WSDL-Generator

The WSDL-Generator component provides a WSDL description for each deployed web service. The WSDL description is generated automatically based on the metadata contained in the service descriptor table of the WS-Infobase. When a new web service is deployed via the WS-Infobase, a new instance of the WSDL-Generator will be created. The new instance initiates the underlying HTTP protocol handler to listen for the corresponding URI of the web service. Since all information required for describing the interface of each web service are contained in the WS-Infobase, the generation process could be done completely in background without any attention of the automation engineer.

The URI that provides the WSDL description equals the corresponding web service name extended by the postfix ".wsdl". On an incoming client request, the handler generates the WSDL description dynamically and delivers it to the underlying HTTP protocol handler.

3.4.4 SOAP2PLC-Bridge

The SOAP4PLC engine requires to call a PLC function from outside of the PLC application. It passes the arguments, executes the PLC function and—on return—reads the return value. Since the PLC function is implemented using a PLC development environment, there are several issues to consider:

1. The PLC function is unknown at compile- and link-time of the SOAP4PLC engine, i.e. the PLC function has to be linked dynamically.

2. The PLC function is not located within the context of the SOAP4PLC engine, but within the PLC application. Consequently, a context switch is required before and after the call of the PLC function.

3. PLC functions have specific calling conventions. Thus, a PLC compliant stack frame has to be created for passing arguments, calling the PLC function, and accepting the return value.

4. The PLC application runs in a different task than the SOAP4PLC engine. Hence, the call of a PLC function has to be synchronized to avoid race

3.4 Design Considerations 43

conditions.

All these issues are handled by the SOAP2PLC-Bridge. The used hardware and operating system determine the structure and the implementation of the SOAP2PLC-Bridge. Furthermore, the applied PLC programming system affects the implementation since the IEC 61131-3 standard does not define the low-level details (for example memory layout and structure) of a PLC application.

3.4.5 Sequence-Controlled Web Services

A sequence-controlled web service is a regular web service with a specialized processing flow adapted to the PLC programming paradigm. More precisely, a sequence-controlled web service aligns the cyclic processing paradigm of PLCs and the event-driven processing paradigm of web services. From the client's point of view, a sequence-controlled web service is not distinguishable from a regular web service.

An operation of a sequence-controlled web service is represented by an instance of a function block POU called *SOA function block*. The SOA function block encapsulates the input/output parameters of the SOAP request/response message and maps them to its own inputs/outputs. A SOA function block forwards the input parameters of a SOAP request message to the succeeding POU. Thus, they are mapped to the outputs of the SOA function block. On the other hand, a SOA function block forwards the data from the preceding POU to the SOAP4PLC engine for the use as return parameters within a SOAP response message. Thus, a SOA function block's inputs are mapped to the SOAP return parameters. Figure 3.4 illustrates this novel concept.

The sequence-controlled web services approach permits to select several function blocks of a PLC application for SOA handling, i.e. each instance of a selected function block becomes accessible by a unique web service operation. To enable a function block for SOA handling, some additional handling code is required. This code organizes the interaction with the SOAP4PLC engine and manages the input/output-mapping with the instances of the function blocks. The handling code consists of two components:

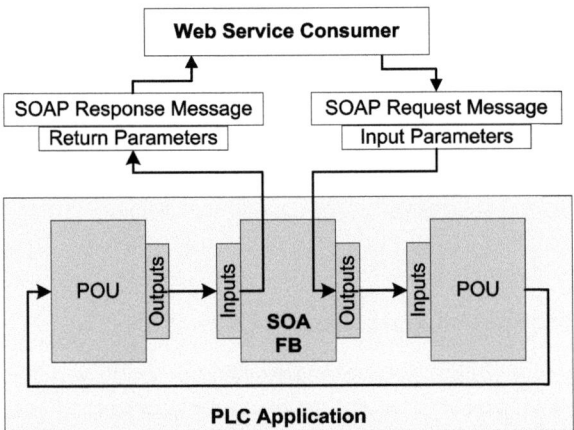

Figure 3.4: Execution of a web service by means of a SOA function block.

- A handler function that will be called on an incoming SOAP request message.

- The SOA function block's implementation that will be triggered by the IPO cycle.

Handler Function

The handler function is a function POU that has to be exported by the SOAP4PLC engine. Thus, the function is executed within the SOAP4PLC's task context. On invocation, it performs the input/output-mapping as discussed before. For this purpose, it writes the values of the SOAP input message to the outputs of the SOA function block instance and sets the chipselect output to TRUE. The chipselect output (`chipselect-out`) is a boolean output that indicates to the PLC application that the output values are valid, i.e. the chipselect output is TRUE while a SOAP invocation message is pending. After that, the handler function waits until the chipselect input (`chipselect-in`)— also a boolean flag—becomes TRUE. The chipselect input indicates that the input values of the SOA function block are valid, i.e. the return parameters

3.4 Design Considerations

for the SOAP response message are available.

The write access to the outputs and chipselect output as well as the read access to the inputs and the chipselect input are enclosed in a binary semaphore (mutex) block. This assures a synchronous access to the PLC task's IPO cycle as described subsequently.

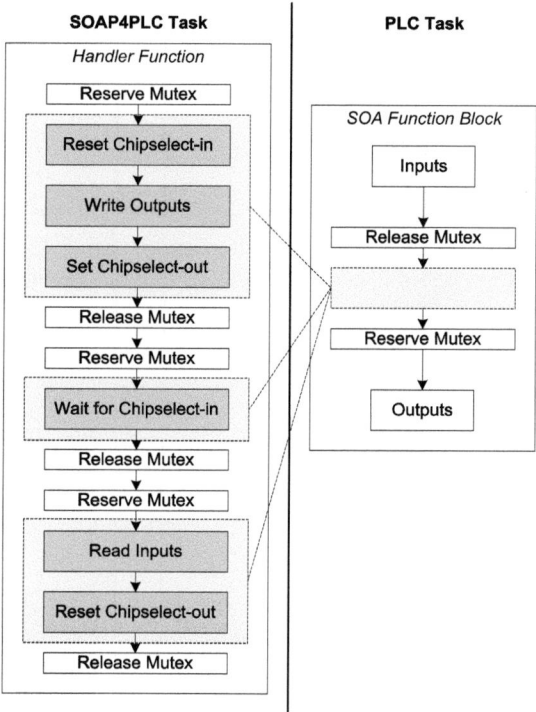

Figure 3.5: Execution of handler code and SOA function block.

SOA Function Block

The SOA function block permits the activation of the handler function at the correct point in time within the IPO cycle. To accomplish this, the same binary semaphore (mutex) block applied by the handler function is also used here. The mutex block is reserved by the SOA function block instance. When it is triggered by the IPO cycle, the implementation releases the mutex block. Thus, the SOA function block permits access to the IPO cycle to the handler function to perform the mapping. Afterwards, the mutex semaphore block is again reserved by the SOA function block instance. Figure 3.5 outlines the execution of the SOAP4PLC task running the handler function and the PLC task running the SOA function block as described above.

3.5 Summary

The use of service-oriented architectures based on web services on PLCs has many advantages. In the industrial automation domain—where software is often proprietary—web service technologies permit the interaction between the manufacturing layer and the business layer without detailed knowledge of the counterpart which leads to a separation of concerns.

Unfortunately, the use of web services on PLCs has several difficulties:

- hard- and software of a PLC is less powerful than hard- and software on workstations and servers
- automation engineers who maintain the PLCs often have less experience in the development and deployment of web services
- web services for the manufacturing layer are completely new within the industrial automation domain, so there are no well-established design patterns

The SOAP4PLC engine presented in this chapter solves these problems. It extends an IEC 61131-3 compliant programming system with an interface for exporting POUs. This interface does not presume any knowledge about web services to the automation engineer. For each exported POU, a corresponding web service will be deployed automatically. All necessary steps from deployment over WSDL generation to verification and execution of requests will be done automatically and completely transparent to the automation engineer.

3.5 Summary

Implementation details of the SOAP4PLC engine are presented in Section 8.4. An evaluation of SOAP4PLC is presented in Section 9.2.

4
Web Services for IPCs

4.1 Introduction

The invocation of web services requires a so-called SOAP engine (web service engine). Popular open-source (e.g. Apache Axis [7, 8]) and commercial SOAP engines (e.g. IBM WebSphere Application Server [27]) stem from the Internet domain where timing requirements are of little interest. Consequently, available SOAP engines operate on a best-effort basis, i.e. their timing behavior is non-deterministic. A non-deterministic timing behavior is insufficient for the use in the context of industrial automation where hard real-time processing is required. Consequently, availability of a real-time SOAP engine is a key requirement for the use of web services in industrial automation.

The TiCS framework fills this gap by means of the first real-time SOAP engine for IPCs called *SOAP4IPC*. SOAP4IPC is a key component of TiCS' real-time infrastructural layer and permits the execution of web services in real-time, i.e. a web service invocation is realized within a predefined time constraint or deadline. SOAP4IPC uses a *profiling-and-monitoring* based approach for this purpose. Additionally, SOAP4IPC offers several functions that ease the work of developers and administrators, such as automated deadline calculation and hot deployment/undeployment of web services.

This chapter discusses relevant design considerations for a real-time SOAP engine in general, motivates the design of SOAP4IPC, and presents an architectural blueprint of the SOAP4IPC engine. Furthermore, it is derived how the execution time of a web service can be calculated, if SOAP4IPC is used. More precisely, this chapter is organized as follows: Section 4.2 discusses the mode of operation and the level of concurrency. Section 4.3 outlines the architecture and important components of the SOAP4IPC engine. Section 4.4 discusses the parameters influencing the execution time of a web service. Section 4.5 summarizes this chapter.

Parts of this chapter have been published in [146].

4.2 Preliminary Design Considerations

Two important characteristics for the design and implementation of a real-time SOAP engine are the *mode of operation*, i.e. how time constraints are guaranteed, and the *level of concurrency*, i.e. how many SOAP messages are processed concurrently. The mode of operation may be either an *analytical* or *profiling-and-monitoring* based approach. The level of concurrency may be either strictly *sequential* or *concurrent* processing of incoming messages.

4.2.1 Mode of Operation

Generally, there are two different approaches to determine the timing behavior of a SOAP engine [116]:

- **analytical approach**:
  The timing behavior of the SOAP engine is determined analytically during the development process, i.e. source code analyzers are used to determine the worst-case execution time for each statement, method, and class within the engine. For example, Bernat et al. [101] developed a tool named *Javelin* that supports worst-case execution time analysis of Java bytecode.

4.2 Preliminary Design Considerations

- **profiling-and-monitoring approach**:
  The timing behavior of the engine is determined experimentally after the development process has taken place. The obtained results are used to monitor the engine during runtime, to notice occurred deadline violations, and to take appropriate actions to log or compensate them. This approach is, for example, used by Lindgren et al. [143] and Petters et al. [157].

The analytical approach totally avoids deadline violations. Since the worst-case execution time is calculated based on each statement, it is impossible to violate the determined deadlines for the overall SOAP engine. Unfortunately, worst-case execution time calculation based on each statement is challenging (consider, for example, the analysis of loops), and often technically impossible for large software systems like a SOAP engine. The use of virtual machine based programming languages like Java and closed-source operating systems complicates the analysis additionally. The profiling-and-monitoring approach determines information about feasible platform and use-case dependent deadlines by measurement of each relevant configuration. These deadlines are used during runtime to monitor the actual timing behavior of the engine. Deadline violations are automatically noticed, logged, and handled. In safety-critical environments like industrial automation, the profiling-and-monitoring approach is more suitable than the analytical approach, since a completely analytical determination of the timing behavior in such domains is either not possible (software systems are much too complex) or not accepted by responsible persons. Provided that the profiling step was performed accurately, almost all deadlines can be met. The missed deadlines are automatically compensated or result in a defined fault.

The SOAP4IPC engine is based on the second approach. After installing the engine on a specific target platform, two profiling steps are necessary to determine the timing behavior of the engine and each deployed web service. The first profiling step—*engine profiling*—determines the latency introduced by the engine, i.e. the worst-case delay until an incoming SOAP invocation is processed. The second profiling step—*service profiling*—determines the worst-case execution time for each web service. Based on the results of both profiling steps, the deadline for each web service depending on the engine configuration and the target platform is calculated (see also Section 4.4).

4.2.2 Level of Concurrency

A SOAP engine may support two different processing modes and therefore two different levels of concurrency:

- **sequential processing**:
  The incoming SOAP messages are processed strictly sequentially, i.e. in the order of their arrival.

- **concurrent processing**:
  The incoming SOAP messages are processed concurrently, i.e. the processing of multiple SOAP messages overlaps.

The main advantage of sequential processing is the avoidance of race conditions. Consider a web service to control a hoisting platform offering two operations: `lower` to lower and `lift` to lift the platform. Using sequential processing, either the invocation message for `lower` is processed prior to the invocation message for `lift` or vice versa. Using concurrent processing may lead to an interleaving of both operations and therefore to undefined behavior of the hoisting platform.

The SOAP4IPC engine implements concurrent processing of incoming SOAP messages for three reasons. First, immediate reaction to important incoming messages is only possible using concurrent processing. Second, concurrent processing results in a higher throughput of SOAP messages and consequently faster invocation of web services from the perspective of the clients. Third, concurrent processing allows to guarantee shorter deadlines by interleaving the processing of multiple web services.

4.3 Architecture

The SOAP4IPC engine is a generic, multi-threaded, real-time enabled queuing system offering *deterministic timing behavior* (real-time processing) and

4.3 Architecture 53

adaptability of an arbitrary processing logic. The engine is logically organized into five functional components:

- profiling
- engine configuration
- connection handling and job management
- job processing and monitoring
- web service management

The *profiling component* contains the engine profiler and the web service profiler. These profilers are used to determine the processing overhead introduced by the SOAP4IPC engine and the worst-case execution time for each operation of each deployed web service. The results of the engine profiling and service profiling runs are used to calculate the deadlines for each web service operation.

The *engine configuration* contains three configuration files: engine.cfg, dependencies.cfg, and profiling.dat. The engine configuration is read only once during engine startup and is offered henceforth as a singleton to all engine components. engine.cfg contains several parameters as name/value-pairs, e.g. a listen port for incoming connections, maximum size of incoming SOAP messages, hot deployment and undeployment delay. dependencies.cfg contains input data for the dependency checker, i.e. a list of competing web service operations that cannot be processed concurrently. profiling.dat contains the results of the engine and service profiling.

The *connection handling and job management component* operates in an event-driven manner, i.e. the entry point waits for new incoming connections and encapsulates them in job objects. Since the engine supports concurrent processing of jobs, the dependencies among the jobs are checked by the dependency checker. If some jobs cannot be processed concurrently, the dependency checker delays their processing by means of an internal buffer whereas the uncritical jobs are put in the job queue. The job queue is a circular queue whose maximum capacity is defined in the engine configuration. The job queue is processed by several workers which are instantiated during engine startup and are passively waiting in a worker pool. When a new job arrives in the job queue, one of the available workers is activated to process the job. The job resides within the job queue, if no worker is available.

The *job processing and monitoring component* permits the processing of an arbitrary high-level transfer protocol. This is realized via replaceable parser, task, and processor objects (shown as dotted lines in Figure 4.1). The incoming data is interpreted by a specific parser that depends on the transfer protocol used. SOAP4IPC uses a SOAP parser to interpret incoming messages as SOAP messages, i.e. the SOAP parser implements the SOAP v1.2 protocol [92, 93, 94], more precisely SOAP over HTTP. Depending on the incoming message, the SOAP parser uses an invocation task (the incoming message contains a web service invocation), WSDL task (the incoming message requests a WSDL description of a web service), or fault task (the incoming message is syntactically incorrect or the target web service/operation is unknown) to encapsulate all relevant information as an object. For each kind of task, there is a specific processor (SOAP processor, WSDL processor, fault processor) which knows how this task is processed. Using the profiling data (worst-case engine delay, worst-case execution time of each web service operation) from profiling.dat, the runtime monitor checks the actual execution time of an invoked web service against the profiling data and takes appropriate actions if a deadline violation occurs.

The *web service management component* permits convenient management, deployment, and undeployment of web services. During test runs, a web service developer may use hot deployment/undeployment of web services, i.e. a new web service can be deployed to the engine and an existing web service can be undeployed from the engine without restarting the engine.

4.4 Execution Time of Web Services

The overall execution time of a web service $t_{execution}$ consists of three different parts, as shown in Figure 4.2:

4.4 Execution Time of Web Services

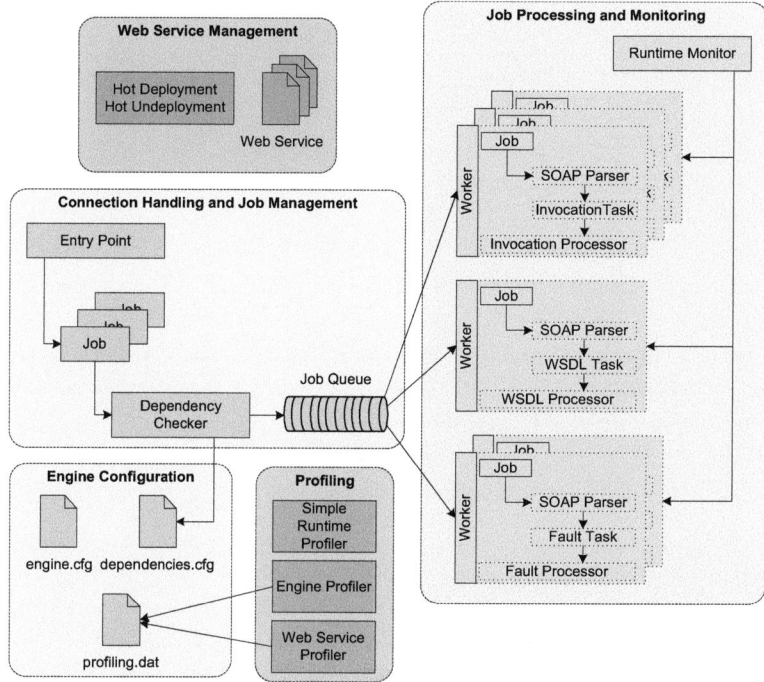

Figure 4.1: Architectural components of the SOAP4IPC engine.

1. time to transfer the SOAP request message from the web service consumer to the IPC and (optionally) the SOAP response message from the IPC back to the web service consumer (t_{transfer})

2. an overhead introduced by SOAP4IPC to prepare the web service invocation (t_{engine})

3. the time required to process the target web service and target operation, respectively (t_{service})

t_{transfer} (Equation (4.1)) is determined by the used interconnection network, the number of messages exchanged (a one-way call results in only one whereas

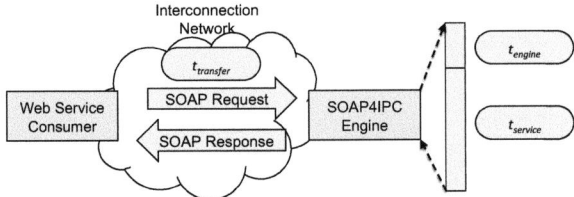

Figure 4.2: Execution time of a web service.

a request/response call results in two messages), and the amount of data (payload) transferred within the SOAP messages (e.g. a simple flag to trigger a process or a complete production order).

$$t_{\text{transfer}} := t_{\text{request}} + t_{\text{response}} \qquad (4.1)$$

To guarantee a worst-case execution time for each web service deployed within SOAP4IPC, two requirements have to be fulfilled: the interconnection network used has to offer deterministic timing behavior and the maximum message size is bounded to limit the time required to transfer the message. There are several interconnection networks with deterministic timing behavior, such as, for example, EtherCAT [20] or Profinet [33]. The selection of an appropriate deterministic interconnection network rests with the automation engineer and is out of scope of this chapter and the entire thesis in general (see also Section 10.7). The maximum feasible message size is a configuration parameter of the engine. If an incoming SOAP over HTTP request message exceeds the maximum message size, it is automatically rejected. Additionally, SOAP4IPC supports Flex-SwA to enhance the transmission of binary parameters within SOAP messages and WS-TemporalPolicy to describe the time constraints of a web service. Since SOAP is an XML-based communication protocol, the use of binary parameters results in a non-negligible overhead, which is avoided by using Flex-SwA as described in Chapter 7. WS-TemporalPolicy is a policy language to define the timing behavior of web services as described in Chapter 6.

4.4 Execution Time of Web Services

t_engine describes the overhead introduced by the engine. More precisely, t_engine is the *latency* between the arrival of a new connection and the call of the corresponding web service operation. The engine overhead depends on the level of concurrency, i.e. the number of concurrent worker threads within the engine.

t_service is the time required for the execution of the target web service (operation). Depending on the web service's functionality, the execution time may range from a few milliseconds (e.g. setting a flag at a manufacturing device) to several seconds (e.g. alignment of an industrial robot).

Since the transfer time of input/output parameters and the processing time of a specific web service operation are depending on each other, t_job is used to describe the job-dependent processing time (Equation (4.2)).

$$t_\text{job} := t_\text{transfer} + t_\text{service} \qquad (4.2)$$

Consequently, the execution time of a web service $t_\text{execution}$ is defined as in Equation (4.3). To determine t_engine and t_job, the engine uses the profiling-and-monitoring approach, as described in Section 4.2.1.

$$t_\text{execution} := t_\text{engine} + t_\text{job} \qquad (4.3)$$

SOAP4IPC processes incoming SOAP request messages concurrently by several worker threads. A round-robin strategy is used to schedule all worker threads within the engine. The worst-case execution time for each service depends on its own execution time and the maximum number of concurrent workers within the engine. Concurrent processing results in a higher throughput compared to sequential processing—especially if the deployed web services' execution times differ significantly—but also causes an additional overhead for thread scheduling which grows with the level of concurrency, i.e. the more concurrent workers exist, the more scheduling overhead is obtained.

Let $S_1, \ldots, S_n$ be the deployed web services, $t_\text{execution}(S_1), \ldots, t_\text{execution}(S_n)$ the execution times of the web services $S_1, \ldots, S_n$ and J the maximum number of concurrent workers within the engine. The worst-case execution time wcet for an arbitrary web service $S_i \in \{S_1, \ldots, S_n\}$ is calculated as shown in

Equation (4.4).

$$\text{wcet}(S_i) := J \cdot t_{\text{execution}}(S_i), 1 \leq i \leq n \qquad (4.4)$$

For example, consider three web services S_1, S_2, and S_3 with the execution times $t_{\text{execution}}(S_1) = 10\,\text{msec}$, $t_{\text{execution}}(S_2) = 20\,\text{msec}$, and $t_{\text{execution}}(S_3) = 30\,\text{msec}$ and three concurrent worker threads. Due to round-robin scheduling and three worker threads, the worst-case execution time for each service results in:

$$\text{wcet}(S_1) = 3 \cdot 10\,\text{msec} = 30\,\text{msec}$$
$$\text{wcet}(S_2) = 3 \cdot 20\,\text{msec} = 60\,\text{msec}$$
$$\text{wcet}(S_3) = 3 \cdot 30\,\text{msec} = 90\,\text{msec}$$

The deadline D that can be guaranteed for the entire engine, i.e. for all deployed services within the engine, is the maximum of the service-specific worst-case execution times, as defined in Equation (4.5).

$$\text{D} := \max_{i \in \{1...n\}} \{\text{wcet}(S_i)\} \qquad (4.5)$$

In the example above, the deadline for all services is 90 msec.

4.5 Summary

This chapter has presented the first real-time SOAP engine for IPCs called SOAP4IPC. SOAP4IPC is part of the real-time infrastructural layer of the TiCS framework and bases on a profiling-and-monitoring approach to determine the worst-case execution time of a web service. Even though SOAP4IPC is designed and developed for the use on IPCs and the processing of SOAP over HTTP, the engine offers general-purpose applicability. For example, SOAP4IPC may be used on a common desktop PC for processing an arbitrary transfer protocol in real-time.

The execution of web services with time constraints is not only of inter-

4.5 Summary

est in industrial automation. There are several other application domains, for example online brokering systems, which require timely processing of web services. Since the TiCS SOAP4IPC engine is designed and implemented in a generic way, it can be used in several other application domains.

Implementation details of the SOAP4IPC engine are presented in Section 8.5 whereas an evaluation is presented in Section 9.3.

5

Composition of Time-Constrained Workflows

5.1 Introduction

Industrial manufacturing processes generally consists of several consecutive production steps or vice versa, several production steps are composed to realize the entire manufacturing process. Consequently, a single time-constrained web service is not suitable to model the entire manufacturing process. Consider, for example, the manufacturing process of a car. The car passes through several stations within an assembly line, e.g. car body installation, surface cleaning, wiring, painting, and drying. Even though each station can be represented as a time-constrained web service, the description of the entire manufacturing process requires a workflow.

For the composition of web services to a workflow, the Business Process Execution Language for Web Services (BPEL4WS) [100] is widely accepted and therefore used by the TiCS framework. Due to the fact that BPEL4WS is an XML-based workflow description language, the composition of several web services to a workflow is quite error-prone without appropriate tool support, especially for automation engineers. Furthermore, BPEL4WS lacks functionality to describe the timing behavior of a workflow. For the adoption of workflows modeled with BPEL4WS within industrial automation, it is vitally important to describe the timing behavior of the entire workflow. Consider again the example of a car manufacturing process. Since in the automotive industry often—if not always—just-in-time production is used, the entire car manufacturing workflow has to meet predefined time constraints.

This chapter presents the *TiCS Modeler*, a graphical workflow editor that permits the assisted composition of time-constrained web services to value-added time-constrained workflows. The main focus of this chapter is on the formal derivation of time constraints for BPEL4WS workflows, since the time constraints of a workflow are not simply the sum of the time constraints of each step within the workflow.

This chapter is organized as follows: Section 5.2 gives an overview of the characteristics of BPEL4WS. The time behavior of BPEL4WS activities is derived in Section 5.3. Section 5.4 discusses the design considerations of the TiCS Modeler. The chapter is summarized in Section 5.5.

Parts of this chapter have been published in [115, 150, 151].

5.2 Characteristics of BPEL4WS

BPEL4WS has emerged from Microsoft's XLANG [52] and IBM's Web Services Flow Language (WSFL) [63], the first initiatives for combining several web services to a business process. Today, Microsoft, IBM, Siebel Systems, BEA, and SAP collaboratively work on BPEL4WS.

The composition of web services to business processes can be generally distinguished into orchestration and choreography. *Orchestration* is a fine-grained view on a business process regarding its internal structure. Often, orchestration describes a business process from the point of view of one participant. *Choreography*, on the other hand, is a coarse-grained view on a business process regarding the message exchange between several participants, e.g. an enterprise and its suppliers. BPEL4WS supports choreography via so-called *abstract business processes* and orchestration via so-called *executable business*

5.3 Time Behavior of BPEL4WS Activities

processes. From the industrial automation's point of view, only executable business processes are of interest to model manufacturing processes.

In principle, BPEL4WS is comparable to a simple procedural programming language and offers several basic and structured activities to model workflows. A *basic activity* is used, for example, to invoke a web service or to copy the value of one variable to another. A *structured activity* contains an arbitrary set of basic or structured activities and is used to model the control flow within a workflow. BPEL4WS offers 8 basic activities and 7 structured activities, as shown in Table 5.1. Additionally, BPEL4WS permits the definition of variables to store and exchange data within a workflow.

Table 5.1: Basic and structured BPEL4WS activities.

Basic Activities	receive	reply	invoke	assign
	throw	terminate	wait	empty
Structured Activities	sequence	switch	while	pick
	flow	scope	compensate	

BPEL4WS is based on WSDL v1.1 [64] for the interface description of web services, XML Schema v1.0 [73, 74, 75] for the definition of datatypes, and XPath v1.0 [61] for the manipulation of variables. For the execution of BPEL4WS workflows, a so-called *BPEL4WS engine* (e.g. ActiveBPEL [2]) is required.

5.3 Time Behavior of BPEL4WS Activities

For industrial automation purposes, the worst-case execution time (wcet) of each BPEL4WS activity is of particular interest. The average execution time (aet) of a BPEL4WS activity is also interesting, since it indicates which time constraints can be realized. Therefore, the wcet and aet of each BPEL4WS activity are derived in this chapter. The derivation of the time behavior is based on the following considerations:

- The average and worst-case execution time can only be defined directly for basic activities. Structured activities can be regarded as containers for basic or further structured activities. Consequently, the average and worst-case execution time for each basic activity are derived first. Subsequently, the average and worst-case execution time for each structured activity are derived recursively.

- There are several activities to handle errors during the execution of a workflow. The `throw` activity is used by a workflow to signal a fault, while the `compensate` activity realizes an error compensation for an inner scope. Since the average and worst-case execution times are only relevant if a workflow is processed without any errors, the timing behavior of these activities is not derived.

- BPEL4WS also supports a feature named `links` which permits to model execution dependencies within a `flow` activity. The same functionality can be realized using nested structured activities (e.g. `sequence`). Therefore, links are not considered within this derivation.

5.3.1 The Receive and Reply Activities

A `receive` activity is used to initially trigger workflow execution, i.e. the `receive` activity waits for an incoming message, afterwards the workflow is started. A `receive` activity can also be used to wait for an input message for an arbitrary duration. The `reply` activity is used to send an answer for a previously received message.

In the context of industrial automation, where soft and hard real-time processing is a fundamental requirement, it is unacceptable to wait for input messages for an arbitrary, potentially infinite, duration. Therefore, the use of a `receive` activity for waiting purposes is prohibited. Instead of `receive`, the `pick` activity should be used to wait for an incoming message. The `pick` activity permits to wait for a given maximum duration.

Both activities may define variables for input and output data, respectively. Since the execution time of `receive` and `reply` activities depends on the size of input/output data, the average and worst-case execution time are defined using a function rcv which maps the input data size to a duration and a function

5.3 Time Behavior of BPEL4WS Activities

snd which maps the output data size to a duration as shown in Equations (5.1) and (5.2). The rcv and snd functions are arbitrary functions (e.g. linear, quadratic, exponential) that depend on the specific BPEL4WS engine and the interconnection network used.

$$\begin{aligned} \text{wcet}\,(\texttt{receive}) &:= \text{rcv}_{\text{wcet}}\,(\text{input data size}) \\ \text{aet}\,(\texttt{receive}) &:= \text{rcv}_{\text{aet}}\,(\text{input data size}) \end{aligned} \quad (5.1)$$

$$\begin{aligned} \text{wcet}\,(\texttt{reply}) &:= \text{snd}_{\text{wcet}}\,(\text{output data size}) \\ \text{aet}\,(\texttt{reply}) &:= \text{snd}_{\text{aet}}\,(\text{output data size}) \end{aligned} \quad (5.2)$$

5.3.2 The Invoke Activity

An `invoke` activity is used to invoke a web service in a synchronous request/response or an asynchronous one-way fashion. To send input data to and to receive output data from the invoked web service, an input and output variable can be defined, respectively.

The average/worst-case execution time for a successful synchronous `invoke` is the sum of the transmission time of the input parameters, the processing of the called target web service, and the transmission of the return value back to the web service caller. Therefore, a function snd that maps the input parameters to a duration, and a function rcv that maps the return value to a duration, for both average and worst-case execution time are used (cp. Equation (5.3)). Obviously, the execution time of the web service also depends on the input parameters. The worst-case execution time for an asynchronous invoke—only consisting of the transmission time of the input parameters—is defined using the snd function only.

$$\text{wcet}(\texttt{invoke}) := \begin{cases} \text{snd}_\text{wcet}(\text{input parameters}) + \\ \text{wcet}_\text{service}(\text{input parameters}) + \\ \text{rcv}_\text{wcet}(\text{return value}) & \text{, synchronous invoke} \\ \text{snd}_\text{wcet}(\text{input parameters}) & \text{, asynchronous invoke} \end{cases}$$

$$\text{aet}(\texttt{invoke}) := \begin{cases} \text{snd}_\text{aet}(\text{input parameters}) + \\ \text{aet}_\text{service}(\text{input parameters}) + \\ \text{rcv}_\text{aet}(\text{return value}) & \text{, synchronous invoke} \\ \text{snd}_\text{aet}(\text{input parameters}) & \text{, asynchronous invoke} \end{cases}$$
(5.3)

5.3.3 The Assign Activity

The `assign` activity is used to copy the value of one variable to another variable. An `assign` activity may contain an arbitrary set of copy commands.

The average and worst-case execution time depends on the number and size of variables copied within this activity. Therefore, a function assign that maps the size of the variable to a duration is used for both average and worst-case execution time (cp. Equation (5.4)).

$$\begin{aligned} \text{wcet}(\texttt{assign}) &:= \text{assign}_\text{wcet}(\text{variable}) \\ \text{aet}(\texttt{assign}) &:= \text{assign}_\text{aet}(\text{variable}) \end{aligned}$$
(5.4)

5.3.4 The Wait Activity

With the `wait` activity, a business process can be delayed for a given period of time or until a deadline expires.

Therefore, the average and worst-case execution time depend on the defined period or deadline, which—for simplicity—is called *duration*, as shown

5.3 Time Behavior of BPEL4WS Activities

in Equation (5.5).

$$\text{wcet}(\texttt{wait}) = \text{aet}(\texttt{wait}) := duration \qquad (5.5)$$

5.3.5 The Empty Activity

An empty activity does nothing within a workflow and is used where an activity is syntactically required.

Therefore, the average and worst-case execution time of this activity is always zero (cp. Equation (5.6)).

$$\text{wcet}(\texttt{empty}) = \text{aet}(\texttt{empty}) := 0 \qquad (5.6)$$

5.3.6 The While Activity

The while activity permits to loop a basic or structured activity until the given boolean expression evaluates to false.

Let k be the number of iterations of the while activity which may depend on the input data. Let bool-expr be the boolean expression of the while activity, aet(bool-expr) the average and wcet(bool-expr) the worst-case evaluation time, respectively. The average and worst-case execution time are defined as in Equation (5.7).

$$\begin{aligned}\text{wcet}(\texttt{while}) &:= (k+1) \cdot \text{wcet}(\text{bool-expr}) + k \cdot \text{wcet}(\text{activity}) \\ \text{aet}(\texttt{while}) &:= (k+1) \cdot \text{aet}(\text{bool-expr}) + k \cdot \text{aet}(\text{activity}) \end{aligned} \qquad (5.7)$$

5.3.7 The Pick Activity

A pick activity is used to wait for one of several messages to arrive. For each of these messages a specific activity is defined which will be executed on arrival of this message. Therefore, a pick activity may block infinitely. To avoid an infinite blocking, an alarm containing an activity can be specified which goes off after a given duration.

Consider a `pick` activity that waits for n different messages $\text{msg}_1, \text{msg}_2, \ldots, \text{msg}_n$. The worst-case execution time is the sum of the duration and the maximum of the execution times for each activity (cp. Equation (5.8)). The average execution time depends on the probability of arrival for each message which is normally unknown. Therefore, the average execution time is defined similarly to the worst-case execution time.

$$\begin{aligned}\text{wcet}\,(\texttt{pick}) &:= \text{duration} + \max_{i\in\{1,\ldots,n\}}\left\{\text{wcet}\,(\text{activity for msg}_i)\right\} \\ \text{aet}\,(\texttt{pick}) &:= \text{duration} + \max_{i\in\{1,\ldots,n\}}\left\{\text{aet}\,(\text{activity for msg}_i)\right\}\end{aligned} \quad (5.8)$$

5.3.8 The Flow Activity

A `flow` activity is used to model concurrency within a workflow. A `flow` contains several (basic or structured) activities which are processed concurrently.

The average/worst-case execution time of a `flow` with n activities is therefore defined as the average/worst-case execution time of all activities contained within the `flow` (cp. Equation (5.9)).

$$\begin{aligned}\text{wcet}\,(\texttt{flow}) &:= \max_{i\in\{1,\ldots,n\}}\left\{\text{wcet}\,(\text{activity}_i)\right\} \\ \text{aet}\,(\texttt{flow}) &:= \max_{i\in\{1,\ldots,n\}}\left\{\text{aet}\,(\text{activity}_i)\right\}\end{aligned} \quad (5.9)$$

5.3.9 The Terminate Activity

The `terminate` activity is used to stop the processing of a workflow.

The average/worst-case execution time of this activity is an engine-dependent, constant value (cp. Equation (5.10)).

$$\text{wcet}\,(\texttt{terminate}) = \text{aet}\,(\texttt{terminate}) := c_{\text{terminate}} \quad (5.10)$$

5.3.10 The Scope Activity

The `scope` activity is used to define a block within a workflow that contains own variables, fault handlers, compensation handlers, and exactly one inner

5.3 Time Behavior of BPEL4WS Activities

activity.

The average and worst-case execution time are defined recursively as shown in Equation (5.11).

$$\begin{aligned}\operatorname{wcet}(\textbf{scope}) &:= \operatorname{wcet}(\text{inner activity}) \\ \operatorname{aet}(\textbf{scope}) &:= \operatorname{aet}(\text{inner activity})\end{aligned} \quad (5.11)$$

5.3.11 The Sequence Activity

A sequence activity contains an arbitrary set of activities which are processed in the given order.

The average and worst-case execution time of a sequence activity with n nested activities are defined as the sum of the average and the sum of the worst-case execution times of all these activities, respectively (cp. Equation (5.12)).

$$\begin{aligned}\operatorname{wcet}(\textbf{sequence}) &:= \sum_{i=1}^{n} \operatorname{wcet}(\text{activity}_i) \\ \operatorname{aet}(\textbf{sequence}) &:= \sum_{i=1}^{n} \operatorname{aet}(\text{activity}_i)\end{aligned} \quad (5.12)$$

5.3.12 The Switch Activity

A switch activity permits to branch between several alternative activities.

The worst-case execution time for a switch activity with n alternative activities is the maximum of the sums of each evaluation time of a specific boolean expression bool-expr and the execution time of the corresponding activity (cp. Equation (5.13)). Since the average execution time depends on the probability to take a specific branch—which is often unknown—the average execution time is defined similarly to the worst-case execution time.

$$\text{wcet}\,(\texttt{switch}) := \max_{i\in\{1,\ldots,n\}} \left\{ \left(\sum_{j=1}^{i} \text{wcet}\,\left(\text{bool-expr}_j\right) \right) + \text{wcet}\,(\text{activity}_i) \right\}$$
$$\text{aet}\,(\texttt{switch}) := \max_{i\in\{1,\ldots,n\}} \left\{ \left(\sum_{j=1}^{i} \text{aet}\,\left(\text{bool-expr}_j\right) \right) + \text{aet}\,(\text{activity}_i) \right\}$$
(5.13)

5.4 Design Considerations

The primary design objectives for the TiCS Modeler are usability and standard conformance with regard to BPEL4WS, i.e. the composition of several time-constrained web services to a time-constrained workflow should be as simple as possible from the automation engineer's point of view and BPEL4WS should neither be extended nor modified. Usability is achieved since the TiCS Modeler is a completely graphical workflow editor comparable to a flowchart designer like Microsoft Visio. Each BPEL4WS activity is represented by a graphical widget. The automation engineer only needs to drag-and-drop these activities to the BPEL4WS workflow. Standard conformance is achieved by a strict separation of workflow-specific and time constraint specific information, i.e. all time constraint relevant information are written to a separate file, which is attached to the BPEL4WS workflow description.

The TiCS Modeler uses information from the TiCS Framework Repository and expert knowledge from the automation engineer to calculate the time constraints of a BPEL4WS workflow. The TiCS Framework Repository contains the time constraints of all available time-constrained web services. These web services are presented to the automation engineer for composition. The time constraints for the entire workflow are defined by the automation engineer. In principle, an automation engineer may use the TiCS Modeler in assisting or non-assisting mode:

- **assisting mode:**
  The automation engineer wants to model a new workflow using his/her

5.4 Design Considerations

a priori knowledge about the required average and worst-case execution time. For this purpose, the automation engineer defines the average and worst-case execution time at the beginning of the workflow composition process. During the composition process, the TiCS Modeler repeatedly calculates the average and worst-case execution time of the current workflow and advises the automation engineer, if the constraints are violated.

- **non-assisting mode:**
  The automation engineer wants to model a new workflow without a priori knowledge about the required average and worst-case execution time. Consequently, the automation engineer is not able to define the average/worst-case execution time at start of the composition process. In non-assisting mode, the TiCS Modeler equals a plain BPEL4WS workflow editor.

From a technical point of view, the TiCS Modeler is based on the *Domain-Adaptable Visual Orchestrator (DAVO)* [114]. DAVO is a domain-adaptable, graphical BPEL4WS workflow editor. The key benefits that distinguish DAVO from other graphical BPEL4WS workflow editors are the *adaptable data model* and *user interface* which permit customization to specific domain needs and increase usability. This section outlines DAVO's design principles which are also relevant for the TiCS Modeler.

The key requirement of DAVO's architecture is *extensibility*, especially with respect to the data model. The plug-in mechanism of the Eclipse platform [16] provides a very convenient way to develop such extensible software. For example, this mechanism allows to provide features like version control by simply adding a third-party Eclipse plug-in (e.g. Subversive [43] for version control).

Figure 5.1 shows a conceptual overview of the core components of DAVO. The architecture is based on a model-driven approach and follows the *model-view-controller* design pattern [120]. Every element of the process is presented to the user through a view component with a corresponding controller, allowing editing operations. By visually adding elements to a workflow, changing properties and so on, the controller object corresponding to the action performed makes changes to the internal data model. Vice versa, changes to the internal data model trigger controller objects to update the visualization. The mapping from the internal data model to executable BPEL4WS code is performed by a code generation component. It generates at least three files from the internal model: a ".bpel" file that contains the logic of the workflow, a ".wsdl" file containing the workflow's interface description and a (non-standardized) deployment descriptor that contains runtime information like service endpoints. The design of the data model, views, and controllers is described in the following subsections.

5.4.1 DAVO's Data Model

BPEL4WS processes may be composed of basic and structured activities that may be nested. This leads to the obvious decision to represent the internal data model in a tree-like manner. The process itself forms the root of the tree with structured child elements that may themselves contain subtrees. For each activity, the model needs to store its BPEL4WS type, several attributes and possibly child elements. The data model must be extensible in two ways:

(1) the model must allow to add new activities

(2) existing elements must be extensible

While (1) might be realized using the standard Eclipse mechanism of extension points, the data model must innately support the extensibility of existing elements (2). In this case, extensibility may mean adding, modifying or removing attributes. To assure the validity of the model, an extensible validation mechanism is needed. DAVO provides a factory component to instantiate activities. These activities may be extended or changed by implementations using an element extender that registers extensions and is able to remove existing ones.

Furthermore, there is a need for an event mechanism that automatically updates, for instance, an element's visual representation whenever an external event occurs. DAVO solves these issues without the need for registering listeners for every event (cp. Section 8.6.4).

5.4 Design Considerations

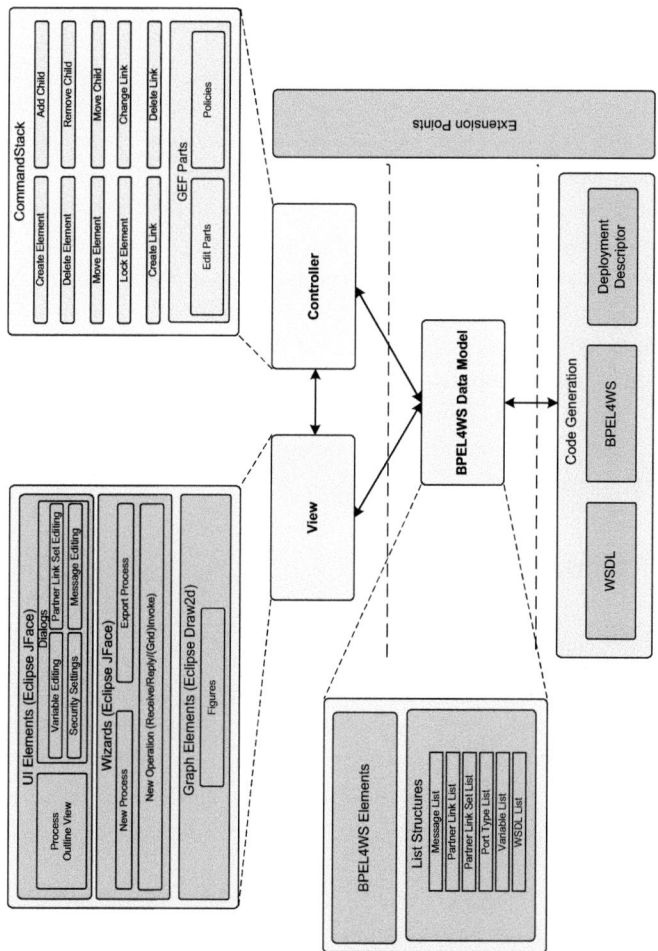

Figure 5.1: Conceptual overview of DAVO's core components.

5.4.2 DAVO's Views and Controllers

In the presented architecture, graphical objects are represented by Eclipse Draw2D [14] objects, whereas controllers are represented by corresponding Eclipse GEF [15] edit parts. A factory component allows to register visual representations and controllers for standard and new activities. For every element of the data model, it stores the class name and the corresponding edit part which refers to its corresponding figure.

Typically, Eclipse displays the properties of an object in a property view that tabularly shows properties in key/value manner. It also allows to group elements and add more sophisticated user interface elements to ease editing. Since this is quite complicated to implement and would have to be done for every extension, DAVO provides a much simpler, but powerful mechanism. It automatically creates visual representations of the properties of an activity using the *adapter* design pattern [120].

5.5 Summary

This chapter has presented the basis for time constraint calculation of BPEL4WS workflows. First, the time behavior of basic and structured BPEL4WS activities has been derived. This formal model is used for the implementation of the TiCS Modeler. The TiCS Modeler adapts the Domain-Adaptable Visual Orchestrator (DAVO) to the domain needs of industrial automation. More precisely, the TiCS Modeler supports the automation engineer by the composition of time-constrained web services to time-constrained BPEL4WS workflows.

Implementation details of the TiCS Modeler are discussed in Section 8.6, whereas an evaluation is presented in 9.4.

6
Description of Time Constraints

6.1 Introduction

The Web Service Description Language (WSDL) [64, 89] is used to describe the interface of a web service, i.e. the operations offered and the messages necessary to invoke these operations. Hence, a WSDL document is used to describe the *functional properties* of a web service that normally do not vary over the time. In addition to the functional properties, many web services have additional *non-functional properties*, such as time constraints, quality of service parameters, and security properties. These non-functional properties are often dynamic, e.g. time constraints may vary over time depending on the current workload. Although there are several standards for describing the non-functional properties of web services, it has up to now been challenging for a web service developer to describe non-functional properties with dynamic characteristics.

This chapter introduces *WS-TemporalPolicy*, a policy language extending WS-Policy [96] by temporal aspects to describe the dynamic, non-functional properties of web services. WS-TemporalPolicy empowers a web service developer to attach a validity period to the properties described in a WS-Policy by means of an expiration date, a start and end date, or a duration. Additionally, an event/action-mechanism permits the description of dependencies between several WS-TemporalPolicies and/or WS-Policies.

This chapter is organized as follows: Section 6.2 explains why a standardized mechanism for the description of dynamic, non-functional web service properties is generally required. Section 6.3 formally defines the WS-TemporalPolicy language and its use in combination with WS-Policy for the description of dynamic, non-functional properties. Section 6.4 identifies functional components for the management of WS-TemporalPolicies. Section 6.5 exemplifies the use of WS-TemporalPolicy by means of two use cases from the financial services and industrial automation domain. Section 6.6 summarizes this chapter.

Parts of this chapter have been published in [129, 148].

6.2 Dynamic, Non-Functional Web Service Properties

There exist several web service specifications that provide a rich, well-defined set of features for loosely-coupled and standardized applications. These specifications are highly extensible to cover requirements that the authors of the specifications could not anticipate. Up to now, many different web service properties can be described by using these specifications:

- bindings, port types, operations, messages, and message parts by WSDL [64, 89],
- quality-of-service parameters by a QoS-policy [121],
- security configurations by a WS-SecurityPolicy [77],
- endpoints of web services by WS-Addressing [87, 88, 95],
- semantics of a service by a WS Modeling Ontology [79],
- protocols for complex interactions by a WS-CommunicationPolicy [129]

6.3 Using WS-Policy and WS-TemporalPolicy

For the description of arbitrary web service properties, the WS-Policy [96] language is of particular importance. WS-Policy is a *generic* policy language permitting the description of the behavior of a web service by specifying several properties that can be associated with the web service's WSDL description. Using WS-Policy, it is possible to define a wide range of web service properties. New policies can be defined for specific domain needs if these have not been addressed yet. All of these properties have one thing in common: they are *static properties*. When the web service is defined, it is assumed that these properties will never change. However, this does not hold for properties concerning, for example, the timing behavior of a web service. Since the workload of the infrastructure directly influences the timing behavior of the web services, these properties may vary over the time. Consequently, there is a need to describe the *dynamic properties* of a web service. Up to now, these properties can only be provided in the functional layer of the web service by an operation, i.e. an operation is used by a consumer to retrieve the current timing behavior. However, conceptually, the timing behavior of a web service should be provided as part of the web service's metadata, i.e. using an appropriate policy language. To describe those dynamic properties, a new policy language called *WS-TemporalPolicy* is proposed in this thesis. A WS-TemporalPolicy extends a WS-Policy by temporal aspects and permits to describe dependencies between several WS-TemporalPolicies and/or WS-Policies.

6.3 Using WS-Policy and WS-TemporalPolicy

This section explains how WS-TemporalPolicies are defined and can be used to describe dynamic properties like the timing behavior of a web service. For this purpose, a short introduction into WS-Policy is given. Subsequently, it is shown how WS-Policy is used in combination with a WS-TemporalPolicy.

6.3.1 WS-Policy

The WS-Policy language enables the definition of policies for web services. A policy is used to describe the properties, i.e. capabilities and requirements, of a web service and is attached either to its WSDL document or exposed as a separate file. Based on the properties defined in a WS-Policy, a potential web service requestor can decide whether this web service satisfies its requirements or not. With WS-Policy, only *static properties*, i.e. properties that do not vary during runtime, can be defined.

Within a WS-Policy, an `ExactlyOne` element can be used to define a set of alternatives from which exactly one can be chosen by the web service requestor. To define a list of mandatory properties, the `All` element can be used. An arbitrary nesting of `ExactlyOne` and `All` elements is possible to describe complex structures of alternative and mandatory properties. Listing 6.1 and Listing 6.2 show the use of the `ExactlyOne` and `All` elements, respectively (namespaces are omitted for simplicity).

Listing 6.1: Example of a WS-Policy using `ExactlyOne`.
```
<Policy Name="http://fb12.de/sampleWSPolicy1">
  <ExactlyOne>
    <!-- alternative property 1 -->
    <!-- ... -->
    <!-- alternative property n -->
  </ExactlyOne>
</Policy>
```

Listing 6.2: Example of a WS-Policy using `All`.
```
<Policy Name="http://fb12.de/sampleWSPolicy2">
  <All>
    <!-- mandatory property 1 -->
    <!-- ... -->
    <!-- mandatory property n -->
  </All>
</Policy>
```

6.3.2 WS-TemporalPolicy

The WS-TemporalPolicy language proposed in this thesis permits to define the validity period of a WS-Policy or another WS-TemporalPolicy. This can be done by using the elements

- expires,

6.3 Using WS-Policy and WS-TemporalPolicy

- `startTime` and `endTime`, or
- `duration`.

The `expires` attribute defines how long a WS-TemporalPolicy is valid by providing an end time (via XML Schema's [73, 74, 75] `dateTime` data type), whereas the `startTime` and `endTime` attributes define a time slot during which the policy is valid. The `duration` attribute is used to specify a relative amount of time for the validity of the policy (via XML Schema's `duration` data type). Each WS-TemporalPolicy has a `name` attribute that defines the unique name of this policy (via XML Schema's `anyURI` data type) and an optional `keywords` attribute that eases the retrieval of a WS-TemporalPolicy from a policy repository. A WS-TemporalPolicy is linked to a WS-Policy or another WS-TemporalPolicy using the `policyRef` attribute and to a WSDL description of a service using the `serviceRef` attribute. A formal schema definition of a WS-TemporaPolicy using XML schema is shown in Listing 6.3.

Listing 6.3: XML Schema for the WS-TemporalPolicy language.

```
<?xml version="1.0"?>
<xs:schema xmlns:xs="http://www.w3.org/2001/XMLSchema"
  targetNamespace="http://fb12.de/temporalPolicy"
  xmlns="http://fb12.de/temporalPolicy"
  elementFormDefault="qualified">

  <!-- definition of actions -->
  <xs:complexType name="actionType">
    <xs:sequence>

      <!-- activate action -->
      <xs:element name="activate" minOccurs="0"
        maxOccurs="unbounded">
        <xs:complexType>
          <xs:attribute name="ref" type="xs:anyURI"
            use="required"/>
        </xs:complexType>
      </xs:element>

      <!-- renew action -->
      <xs:element name="renew" minOccurs="0"
        maxOccurs="unbounded">
        <xs:complexType>
          <xs:choice>
```

```
          <xs:element name="expires" type="xs:dateTime"/>
          <xs:sequence>
            <xs:element name="startTime" type="xs:dateTime"/>
            <xs:element name="endTime" type="xs:dateTime"/>
          </xs:sequence>
          <xs:element name="duration" type="xs:duration"/>
        </xs:choice>
        <xs:attribute name="ref" type="xs:anyURI"
           use="required"/>
      </xs:complexType>
    </xs:element>

    <!-- deactivate action -->
    <xs:element name="deactivate" minOccurs="0"
      maxOccurs="unbounded">
      <xs:complexType>
        <xs:attribute name="ref" type="xs:anyURI"
           use="required"/>
      </xs:complexType>
    </xs:element>

  </xs:sequence>
</xs:complexType>

<xs:element name="temporalPolicy">
  <xs:complexType>

    <!-- child elements of a temporal policy -->
    <xs:sequence>
      <xs:choice>
        <xs:element name="expires" type="xs:dateTime"/>
        <xs:sequence>
          <xs:element name="startTime" type="xs:dateTime"/>
          <xs:element name="endTime" type="xs:dateTime"/>
        </xs:sequence>
        <xs:element name="duration" type="xs:duration"/>
      </xs:choice>

      <xs:element name="onActivation" type="actionType"
        minOccurs="0" maxOccurs="1"/>
      <xs:element name="onRenewal" type="actionType"
        minOccurs="0" maxOccurs="1"/>
      <xs:element name="onExpiration" type="actionType"
        minOccurs="0" maxOccurs="1"/>
      <xs:element name="onDeactivation" type="actionType"
        minOccurs="0" maxOccurs="1"/>
    </xs:sequence>
```

6.3 Using WS-Policy and WS-TemporalPolicy

```
      <!-- attributes of a temporal policy -->
      <xs:attribute name="name" type="xs:anyURI"
        use="required"/>
      <xs:attribute name="keywords" type="xs:string"/>
      <xs:attribute name="serviceRef" type="xs:anyURI"/>
      <xs:attribute name="policyRef" type="xs:anyURI"/>
    </xs:complexType>
  </xs:element>
</xs:schema>
```

It is possible to activate/renew/deactivate a WS-TemporalPolicy depending on another WS-TemporalPolicy using *actions* and *events*, e.g. a WS-TemporalPolicy is activated when another WS-TemporalPolicy is deactivated or vice versa. Dependencies between WS-TemporalPolicies are described by the definition of an **event** element and a corresponding **action** element. Table 6.1 gives an overview of possible events, whereas Table 6.2 gives an overview of possible actions.

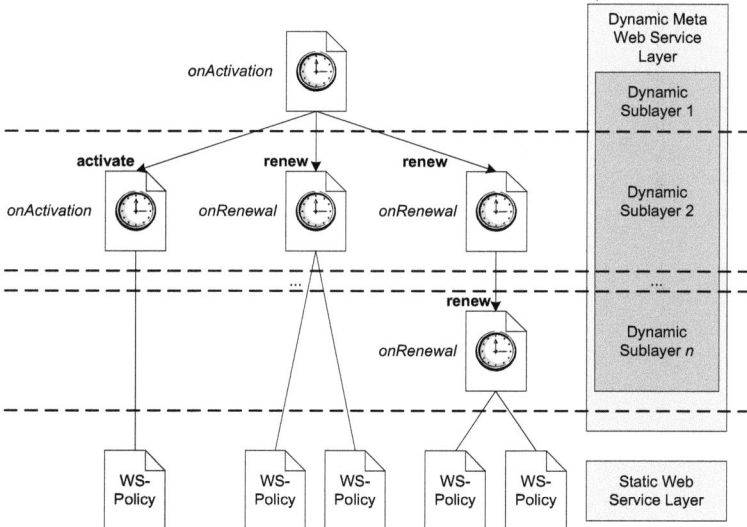

Figure 6.1: Dependency tree for several WS-TemporalPolicies and WS-Policies.

Table 6.1: Overview of events concerning WS-TemporalPolicy.

Event	Description
onActivation	The onActivation event occurs when a WS-TemporalPolicy is activated. The referenced policies are attached to the WSDL description of the referenced web service.
onExpiration	The onExpiration event occurs when the validity period of a WS-TemporalPolicy expires.
onRenewal	The onRenewal event occurs when a WS-TemporalPolicy is renewed, i.e. its validity period is modified.
onDeactivation	This event occurs when a WS-TemporalPolicy is deactivated. As a result, the referenced WS-Policy is detached from the referenced WSDL description.

Table 6.2: Overview of actions concerning WS-TemporalPolicy.

Action	Description
activate	A WS-TemporalPolicy is activated, i.e. an onActivation event occurs.
renew	The validity period of a WS-TemporalPolicy is modified, i.e. an onRenewal event occurs.
deactivate	A WS-TemporalPolicy is deactivated, i.e. an onDeactivation event occurs.

The event/action-mechanism enables the definition of complex policy dependencies that can be visualized via a dependency tree. An example tree that contains five WS-TemporalPolicies and five WS-Policies is shown in Figure 6.1. The events are written in *italics*, whereas the corresponding actions are written in **bold**. As shown in the dependency tree, the use of WS-TemporalPolicy induces several logical layers ranging from static to dynamic with regard to the validity period. In the static web service layer, the operations are located. Above the static web service layer, the dynamic meta web service layer is located, which can be divided into n sublayers. Each sublayer handles a different temporal dimension. At the top layer, there might

6.3 Using WS-Policy and WS-TemporalPolicy

be a WS-TemporalPolicy which defines its (long-lasting) validity period by referencing itself and handles other WS-TemporalPolicies. These again could manage other WS-TemporalPolicies/WS-Policies that are, for example, valid for months, weeks, days and so on. In this way, different layers can be built to enable a fine-grained (hierarchical) management of the validity of policies.

Examples

Listing 6.4 and Listing 6.5 show a WS-TemporalPolicy that defines the validity period for a WS-Policy named `wsPolicy1` by using the `expires` element and a WS-TemporalPolicy which defines the validity period for a WS-Policy named `wsPolicy2` using the elements `startTime` and `endTime`. The first temporal policy additionally attaches the WS-Policy to a concrete web service, since the `serviceRef` attribute is given and defines three keywords to easily retrieve it.

Listing 6.4: Example of a WS-TemporalPolicy using the `expires` element.

```
<temporalPolicy
  name="http://fb12.de/sampleTemporalPolicy1"
  keywords="keyword1 keyword2 keyword3"
  serviceRef="http://fb12.de/exampleService"
  policyRef="http://fb12.de/wsPolicy1">
  <expires>2009-01-01T00:00:00</expires>
</temporalPolicy>
```

Listing 6.5: Example of a WS-TemporalPolicy using the `startTime` and `endTime` elements.

```
<temporalPolicy
  name="http://fb12.de/sampleTemporalPolicy2"
  policyRef="http://fb12.de/wsPolicy2">
  <startTime>2009-01-01T00:00:00</startTime>
  <endTime>2009-07-01T00:00:00</endTime>
</temporalPolicy>
```

The use of events and actions is exemplified in Listing 6.6. The defined `sampleTemporalPolicy3` does not influence a concrete WS-Policy or web service (though this would be possible as well), but the WS-TemporalPolicies `sampleTemporalPolicy1` and `sampleTemporalPolicy2`. It defines that on its activation the `sampleTemporalPolicy1` is also activated, whereas the `sample-`

TemporalPolicy2 is deactivated. On its deactivation, the sampleTemporal-Policy1 is also deactivated, whereas the sampleTemporalPolicy2 is activated. Furthermore, a modification of the validity period of this WS-TemporalPolicy results in a modification of the validity period of sampleTemporalPolicy1 and sampleTemporalPolicy2.

Listing 6.6: Example of a WS-TemporalPolicy which affects other WS-TemporalPolicies.

```
<temporalPolicy name="http://fb12.de/sampleTemporalPolicy3">
  <expires>2009-01-01T00:00:00</expires>

  <onActivation>
    <activate ref="http://fb12.de/sampleTemporalPolicy1"/>
    <deactivate ref="http://fb12.de/sampleTemporalPolicy2"/>
  </onActivation>

  <onRenewal>
    <renew ref="http://fb12.de/sampleTemporalPolicy1">
      <expires>2009-07-01T00:00:00</expires>
    </renew>
    <renew ref="http://fb12.de/sampleTemporalPolicy2">
      <startTime>2009-07-01T00:00:00</startTime>
      <endTime>2009-09-01T00:00:00</endTime>
    </renew>
  </onRenewal>

  <onDeactivation>
    <activate ref="http://fb12.de/sampleTemporalPolicy2"/>
    <deactivate ref="http://fb12.de/sampleTemporalPolicy1"/>
  </onDeactivation>
</temporalPolicy>
```

6.4 Management of WS-TemporalPolicies

The management of WS-TemporalPolicies involves validation, storage, discovery, and weaving/unweaving to/from the WSDL description of the referenced web service. These tasks are realized by several functional components that are identified in this section.

In principle, a WS-TemporalPolicy is simply an XML document. Since real-world applications may use a multiplicity of WS-TemporalPolicies that have to be organized, a *temporal policy repository* is required to store the WS-TemporalPolicies, e.g. in a database or as flat files within a directory. To retrieve a particular WS-TemporalPolicy, the repository should permit to search by name or keyword.

The event/action-mechanism of WS-TemporalPolicy permits the definition of arbitrarily complex dependency trees including countless policies. Consequently, it is very challenging to have an overview if a new WS-TemporalPolicy collides with existing ones. Consider, for example, two WS-TemporalPolicies that activate/deactivate each other alternately. For this reason, a *validator* is required that checks whether a new WS-TemporalPolicy is valid.

During runtime the WS-TemporalPolicy and WS-Policy dependency tree has to be mapped to a concrete web service, i.e. all WS-Policies that reference a specific web service have to be woven to its WSDL description. On the other hand, WS-Policies that are not active any longer, have to be unwoven from the WSDL description. The weaving/unweaving process is realized by a *weaver* component.

The collaboration of the temporal policy repository, validator, and weaver is coordinated by the *temporal policy manager*.

6.5 Use Cases

This section describes two use cases from the financial services and real-time processing domains where WS-TemporalPolicies enable the time-dependent pricing of IT services.

6.5.1 Use Case I: Financial Services

The following use case stems from the Financial Business Grid (FinGrid) project [13] that is part of the German Grid Initiative (D-Grid) [46] and that aims to develop Grid-based solutions for financial service providers to enable easy reorganization and improvement of IT processes within the financial services sector.

Often, the IT infrastructure in the banking sector is organized in a centralized manner: the main IT infrastructure and services are located at the headquarters, whereas branch offices only maintain a small IT infrastructure to save costs. All value-added services are purchased by the branch offices at the headquarters on an on-demand basis.

Service-oriented Grid computing permits financial service providers to purchase computing power on an on-demand basis at in-house or external processing service centers. These processing service centers offer their computing power at different costs and different quality of service levels. The costs of a compute service are determined by several properties, e.g. time of execution (peak time or off-peak time), number of reserved processors, amount of allocated primary and secondary memory, volume of input data, and contractually defined in a service level agreement (SLA). To easily attach dynamic properties relevant for pricing to a Grid service (i.e. a web service according to the Web Service Resource Framework (WSRF) [31]), a WS-TemporalPolicy can be used.

Suppose that the headquarters of the financial service provider offers compute services with different QoS parameters. The key QoS parameters are the number of reserved processors (`processors`), the reserved primary memory (`primaryMemory`), and the input data volume (`dataVolume`). The QoS parameters for peak time and for off-peak time are defined using a WS-Policy. Listing 6.7 and Listing 6.8 show WS-Policies named http://example.com/qosPolicy1 respectively http://example.com/qosPolicy2 that define four alternative QoS parameter sets within an `ExactlyOne` element. For simplicity, the number of processors, amount of primary memory, input data volume, and costs are given as `p1`, `mem1`, `d1`, and `c1`. Note that in this example doubling the number of processors, doubling the amount of main memory, and doubling the input data volume, each doubles the costs. Since during off-peak time more resources are available, the basic costs for the off-peak time WS-Policy amounts to half of the basic costs for the peak time WS-Policy (`0.5*c1`).

Listing 6.7: Using a WS-Policy to define QoS parameters for peak time.
```
<Policy Name="http://example.com/qosPolicy1">
  <ExactlyOne>
```

6.5 Use Cases

```
    <qosParameters processors="p1" primaryMemory="mem1"
      dataVolume="d1" costs="c1"/>
    <qosParameters processors="2*p1" primaryMemory="mem1"
      dataVolume="d1" costs="2*c1"/>
    <qosParameters processors="2*p1" primaryMemory="2*mem1"
      dataVolume="d1" costs="2*2*c1"/>
    <qosParameters processors="2*p1" primaryMemory="2*mem1"
      dataVolume="2*d1" costs="2*2*2*c1"/>
  </ExactlyOne>
</Policy>
```

Listing 6.8: Using a WS-Policy to define QoS parameters for off-peak time.

```
<Policy Name="http://example.com/qosPolicy2">
  <ExactlyOne>
    <qosParameters processors="p1" primaryMemory="mem1"
      dataVolume="d1" costs="0.5*c1"/>
    <qosParameters processors="2*p1" primaryMemory="mem1"
      dataVolume="d1" costs="2*0.5*c1"/>
    <qosParameters processors="2*p1" primaryMemory="2*mem1"
      dataVolume="d1" costs="2*2*0.5*c1"/>
    <qosParameters processors="2*p1" primaryMemory="2*mem1"
      dataVolume="2*d1" costs="2*2*2*0.5*c1"/>
  </ExactlyOne>
</Policy>
```

Now assume that the service provider wants to offer its services at peak time and off-peak time. For this purpose, the administrator defines a WS-TemporalPolicy named `peaktimeQoSPolicy` for peak time and a WS-TemporalPolicy named `offPeaktimeQoSPolicy` for off-peak time, which are shown in Listing 6.9 and Listing 6.10.

Listing 6.9: A WS-TemporalPolicy for peak time.

```
<temporalPolicy
  name="http://example.com/peaktimeQoSPolicy"
  serviceRef="http://example.com/exampleService"
  policyRef="http://example.com/qosPolicy1">
  <duration>PT8H</duration>
  <onExpiration>
    <activate ref=
      "http://example.com/offPeaktimeQoSPolicy"/>
  </onExpiration>
</temporalPolicy>
```

Listing 6.10: A WS-TemporalPolicy for off-peak time.

```
<temporalPolicy
  name="http://example.com/offPeaktimeQoSPolicy"
  serviceRef="http://example.com/exampleService"
  policyRef="http://example.com/qosPolicy2">
  <duration>PT16H</duration>
  <onExpiration>
    <activate ref=
      "http://example.com/peaktimeQoSPolicy"/>
  </onExpiration>
</temporalPolicy>
```

The peak time WS-TemporalPolicy is valid for a duration of 8 hours, whereas the off-peak time WS-TemporalPolicy is valid for a duration of 16 hours. As soon as the peak time WS-TemporalPolicy expires, it activates the off-peak time WS-TemporalPolicy and vice versa. Therefore, at a particular time, only one WS-TemporalPolicy is active and determines the current WS-Policy for service pricing.

6.5.2 Use Case II: Real-time Processing

The second use case exemplifies how WS-Policy in combination with WS-TemporalPolicy can be used to describe and price a production process. Consider an enterprise offers its customers either a production process with a strict deadline or with a best-effort deadline. A production process with a strict deadline is more expensive than a production process with a best-effort deadline. A production process with a best-effort deadline is offered at different reliabilities to keep the deadline (a higher reliability results in higher costs).

Listing 6.11 shows a WS-Policy that defines three alternatives for a production process with a best-effort deadline. The average execution time is given with 1 hour at three different reliabilities: 99%, 90%, and 80%. The costs vary depending on the reliability to keep the average execution time (c1, 0.8*c1, 0,6*c1). Listing 6.12 shows a WS-Policy that defines three alternatives for a production process with a strict deadline. The worst-case execution time is given by 42 minutes; the average execution time is given by 21 minutes and 10 minutes, respectively. Since the assurance of a strict deadline is more challenging, such production processes are more expensive.

Listing 6.11: Using a WS-Policy to define costs for a production process with a best-effort deadline.

```
<Policy Name="http://example.com/rtPolicy1">
  <ExactlyOne>
    <rtParameters domain="best-effort" avgExecTime="01:00:00"
      reliability="0.99" costs="c1"/>
    <rtParameters domain="best-effort" avgExecTime="01:00:00"
      reliability="0.90" costs="0.8*c1"/>
    <rtParameters domain="best-effort" avgExecTime="01:00:00"
      reliability="0.80" costs="0.6*c1"/>
  </ExactlyOne>
</Policy>
```

Listing 6.12: Using a WS-Policy to define costs for a production process with a strict deadline.

```
<Policy Name="http://example.com/rtPolicy2">
  <ExactlyOne>
    <rtParameters domain="strict" maxExecTime="00:42:00"
      avgExecTime="00:21:00" costs"2*c1"/>
    <rtParameters domain="strict" maxExecTime="00:42:00"
      avgExecTime="00:10:00" costs"3*c1"/>
  </ExactlyOne>
</Policy>
```

In combination with a WS-TemporalPolicy similar to Listing 6.9 and Listing 6.10 it is possible to enable the soft real-time policy during the working hours when the IT infrastructure is heavily utilized and the hard real-time policy during night time when the infrastructure is underutilized.

6.6 Summary

There is a fundamental need to describe dynamic, non-functional properties in service-oriented environments based on web or Grid services, e.g. to define time-dependent parameters like QoS parameters or real-time parameters. Available standards are not suitable to describe these parameters, since they are designed to describe properties with a static nature.

This chapter has introduced WS-TemporalPolicy, a policy language for describing the validity periods of properties defined via WS-Policy. Validity periods are expressed via an expiration date, start time and end time, or a relative duration. The dependencies among several WS-TemporalPolicies can be defined by means of actions and events leading to complex dependency trees. Additionally, the functional components of an infrastructure supporting WS-TemporalPolicy have been identified.

Even though WS-TemporalPolicy was developed in the context of time-constrained web services for industrial automation, it offers general-purpose applicability to a multiplicity of different areas. This was shown by a use case derived from the service-oriented Grid computing domain.

Implementation details of WS-TemporalPolicy are presented in Section 8.7.

7
Efficient Data Transmission in Web Service Environments

7.1 Introduction

The invocation of a time-constrained web service presumes an efficient transmission of all input parameters from the web service consumer to the web service provider. Within the industrial automation domain, an input parameter may be a primitive datatype (e.g. integer or floating point numbers), a complex datatype (e.g. arrays or lists), or binary data (e.g. production orders). As long as the required parameters are primitive ones, they can be embedded into the SOAP messages [92, 93, 94]. A problem occurs, if binary data have to be transmitted. SOAP is unsuitable to transmit binary data, since the data have to be encoded before being embedded in the SOAP message.

This chapter presents a novel approach for efficient handling of binary web service parameters called *Flex-SwA*. Flex-SwA avoids the drawback that binary data embedded in a SOAP message have to be encoded. Additionally, Flex-SwA offers several communication patterns that permit the description of parameter transmission and web service execution. Since Flex-SwA uses only standardized SOAP messages for the transmission of binary data, it can also be used in other application domains, e.g. service-oriented Grid computing.

This chapter is organized as follows: Section 7.2 discusses the drawbacks of transferring binary data using conventional technologies like SOAP and SOAP Messages with Attachments. Section 7.3 presents the design of the Flex-SwA protocol stack. Section 7.4 describes the different communication patterns supported by Flex-SwA. Section 7.5 summarizes this chapter.

Parts of this chapter have been published in [130, 131, 149].

7.2 Transmission of Web Service Parameters

Web service interaction usually takes place by exchanging SOAP messages. Fundamentally, a SOAP message is a stateless one-way message. By combining one-way message exchanges, more complex interaction patterns can be realized, e.g. request/response interaction. Within industrial automation, these interaction patterns are often based on the client/server-paradigm in which the web service consumer acts as a client whereas the web service provider acts as a server.

The WSDL SOAP binding describes the structure of a SOAP message used for invocation of a web service [26]. There exist two different binding styles (rpc and document) that can be used in two different ways (encoded or literal). Consequently, four different WSDL SOAP bindings can be distinguished:

1. rpc/encoded
2. rpc/literal
3. document/encoded
4. document/literal

The *rpc* binding style indicates that a web service interaction follows the remote procedure call paradigm, i.e. a request message contains input parameters, a response message return values. The *document* binding style indicates that a web service interaction is document-oriented, i.e. a message contains documents like facsimiles. The use of an *encoded* SOAP binding style results in

7.2 Transmission of Web Service Parameters

embedding the XML Schema type definitions of parameters within the SOAP message, whereas the use of a *literal* SOAP binding style omits embedding the type definitions within the SOAP message. Within the industrial automation domain, the rpc/literal binding style is of particular interest, since it introduces a minimal overhead. Consequently, the SOAP4PLC and SOAP4IPC engines support this binding style.

Using the rpc binding style, a web service consumer invokes a web service by passing a SOAP message to the web service provider. This message contains the target web service and operation to invoke, as well as any number of parameters required by the operation. Response messages may be transmitted either synchronously or asynchronously from the provider to the consumer. An example for a SOAP interaction based on the rpc binding style is shown in Figure 7.1. The web service consumer composes a request message containing the remote operation and all necessary parameters and sends it to the web service provider. The web service provider processes the request, i.e. the desired operation is invoked with the received parameters. After processing of the operation is finished, the web service provider composes a response message containing a return value. This response message is sent back to the web service consumer.

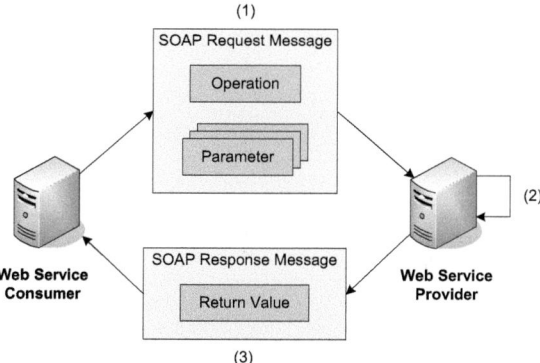

Figure 7.1: An example for a SOAP RPC interaction.

7 Efficient Data Transmission in Web Service Environments

The SOAP protocol defines an XML-based format for the messages used to invoke a web service. This XML format requires an encoding of binary payload prior to embedding it into a message to avoid XML control characters within the payload (e.g. less than (<) or greater than (>) for marking tags). The standard encoding of binary data within SOAP messages is a Base64 encoding [66] which results in an overhead of 33%. Consequently, SOAP is innately *not suitable* for the transmission of binary data due to the additional overhead and enconding/decoding effort [162].

For this reason, SOAP Messages with Attachments (SwA) [62] proposes to transmit binary data objects outside of the SOAP message. To attach binary objects to a SOAP message, SwA uses Multipurpose Internet Mail Extensions (MIME) messages [54, 55, 56, 57, 58]. The SOAP message always resides in the first part of the multipart message. MIME uses a delimiter to separate different message parts from each other. Consequently, the message must be parsed until the delimiter of the desired part of the message is found. For example, a MIME message with a web service invocation and two images as attachments is shown in Listing 7.1. `------=_Part_0_21662929.1130315394983-` is the delimiter that is used for this MIME multipart/related message to separate each message part (another MIME multipart/related message may define another delimiter). The first part of the message is the SOAP request including the operation to invoke (`putFile`). The second and the third part are images in the graphics interchange format sent as attachments. The message ends with the delimiter.

Listing 7.1: Example of a MIME multipart/related message.
```
------=_Part_0_21662929.1130315394983
Content-Type: text/xml; charset=UTF-8
Content-Transfer-Encoding: binary
Content-Id: <ED8BBCB74E9A8832E096679A7B3B2829>
<?xml version="1.0" encoding="UTF-8"?>
<soapenv:Envelope
  xmlns:soapenv=
    "http://schemas.xmlsoap.org/soap/envelope/"
  xmlns:xsd="http://www.w3.org/2001/XMLSchema"
  xmlns:xsi="http://www.w3.org/2001/XMLSchema-instance">
  <soapenv:Body>
    <putFile soapenv:encodingStyle=
      "http://schemas.xmlsoap.org/soap/encoding/"/>
  </soapenv:Body>
```

7.3 Flex-SwA Protocol Stack

```
</soapenv:Envelope>
------=_Part_0_21662929.1130315394983
Content-Type: image/gif
Content-Transfer-Encoding: binary
Content-Id: <CE1E2EF092B98740A3FC5EDF67B1308D>
[...]
------=_Part_0_21662929.1130315394983
Content-Type: image/gif
Content-Transfer-Encoding: binary
Content-Id: <1C4EF7B7D9E0EC61045E3D97744CA0F8>
[...]
------=_Part_0_21662929.1130315394983--
```

A main disadvantage of SwA is the fact that a SOAP engine cannot randomly access an arbitrary attachment but has to receive the entire MIME multipart/related message. Therefore, it is not possible to skip dispensable attachments that may result in an unnecessary consumption of time and memory. Depending on the implementation of the underlying SOAP engine, processing of the SOAP message and invocation of the target operation is often deferred until the entire message containing all attachments has been completely received (compare, for example, Apache Axis [8]).

7.3 Flex-SwA Protocol Stack

Figure 7.2 shows the entire protocol stack from the web service consumer's and the web service provider's point of view. Each layer of the Flex-SwA protocol stack uses lower layers and offers special functionality to higher layers. The web service consumer uses the Flex-SwA layer to invoke remote web services and to transmit required parameters. On top of the web service provider's protocol stack, several web services are offered that are based on the Flex-SwA layer.

To transfer binary data, the Flex-SwA layer uses a *reference builder* to create a reference. A *reference* is an XML description that refers to the locations of the binary data and determines the protocols which can be used to transfer it. A reference is transferred in the body of a SOAP message. An example for a reference is shown in Listing 7.2. The reference must at least identify the resource. In the example given, this is done via a URL pointing to the location from where the resource can be obtained and specifying the protocol to use.

7 Efficient Data Transmission in Web Service Environments

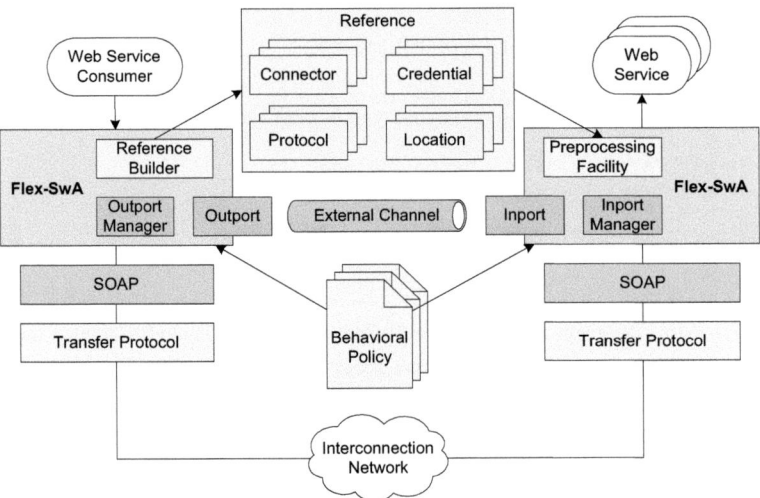

Figure 7.2: The Flex-SwA protocol stack.

Furthermore, it may contain one or more *connectors* that exactly know how to obtain the referenced data and one or more *credentials* for managing security.

Listing 7.2: Example of a Flex-SwA reference.
```
<ref
  xsi:type="ns2:Reference"
  xmlns:ns2="http://infrastructure.flexswa.fb12.de"
  xmlns:soapenc="http://schemas.xmlsoap.org/soap/encoding/">
  <connector xsi:type="soapenc:string" id="4">
    SocketConnector
  </connector>
  <credential xsi:type="ns2:Credential">
    <user xsi:type="soapenc:string">[...]</user>
    <password xsi:type="soapenc:string">[...]</password>
  </credential>
  <resourceUrl xsi:type="soapenc:string">
    [...]
  </resourceUrl>
</ref>
```

If an invocation message containing one or more references arrives, the

7.3 Flex-SwA Protocol Stack

preprocessing facility handles data transmission for the received references. However, the preprocessing facility does not need to handle every reference. The unhandled references can be forwarded to other web service providers. This allows for forwarding messages without additional communication cost, since the reference compared to the referenced data is very small.

Both Flex-SwA layers at the web service consumer's and web service provider's site are communicating via conventional SOAP messages that contain the references. Consequently, Flex-SwA can also be used in application domains where SwA is not supported, e.g. in service-oriented Grid computing based on the Globus Toolkit v4.0.x [22, 118]. For the transmission of the SOAP messages containing Flex-SwA references, an arbitrary transfer protocol can be used, e.g. HTTP.

The concrete behavior of the Flex-SwA layer regarding the handling of data transmission and web service execution can be controlled by specifying a so-called *behavioral policy*. As an additional benefit, web service developers can use the protocol handling capabilities of Flex-SwA to use high performance binary protocols without having to deal with the protocol details in the application code. A behavioral policy can specify a default behavior for the entire platform (e.g. selection of a preferred transport protocol) or a web service specific behavior. Binary protocols can be selected for each reference individually. In contrast to a realization in a more traditional application environment where the developer has to handle every aspect of the communication, most of the functionality needed to handle a specific transport mechanism is realized in the Flex-SwA layer.

Flex-SwA also supports to transfer parameters to a web service after its invocation, which is called *post-invocation parameter transmission*. The consumer retrieves an *outport* from the *outport manager* to repeatedly send data to a web service already invoked. An invoked web service uses the *inport manager* to retrieve an *inport* that is interconnected with the outport of the invoking consumer via an external channel. An *external channel* is an abstraction of a transmission channel which can use arbitrary transfer protocols. Typically, an external channel interconnects inports and outports in a 1 : 1 ratio, since a consumer only invokes one web service. However, it is possible to relate outports and inports $1 : n$, if a consumer wants to invoke n web services concurrently.

7.4 Communication Patterns

Flex-SwA offers different communication patterns describing the transmission of binary data and the execution of web services. These can be distinguished in execution patterns, data transmission patterns, concurrency patterns, and blocking mode patterns:

- **execution patterns:**
  Two possible behaviors exist regarding the handling of data transmission and execution of a web service. In *non-overlapping mode*, the platform performs all data transfers prior to invocation of the web service; in *overlapping mode*, data transmission and web service execution are performed in parallel. If a web service needs to ensure the availability of all data on the web service provider's site before it starts processing, it requests Flex-SwA to handle invocations in non-overlapping mode. If initialization of the web service requires time and is independent of the referenced data resources, a web service developer can specify the web service to use overlapping invocation mode, causing the platform to start data transmission and web service execution in parallel.

- **data transmission patterns:**
  Flex-SwA can be instructed to perform *eager* or *lazy* transmission of referenced data, meaning that references are resolved as soon as possible or only upon a real attempt to access their content. The latter is especially useful when a data resource can be omitted, e.g. if an error during processing has occurred. Additionally, the web service can prioritize referenced data resources that are tagged to be transmitted in eager mode, leading to a transmission plan for these.

- **concurrency patterns:**
  If data resources are transmitted *iteratively*, only one data resource at a

7.4 Communication Patterns

time is retrieved. If the data resources are transmitted *concurrently*, all data resources are retrieved in parallel.

- **blocking mode patterns:**
  Flex-SwA offers a blocking and non-blocking mode. If a web service uses *blocking mode*, it requests the retrieval of a data resource and waits until it is completely available. If a web service is in *non-blocking mode*, web service execution resumes directly after the retrieval request.

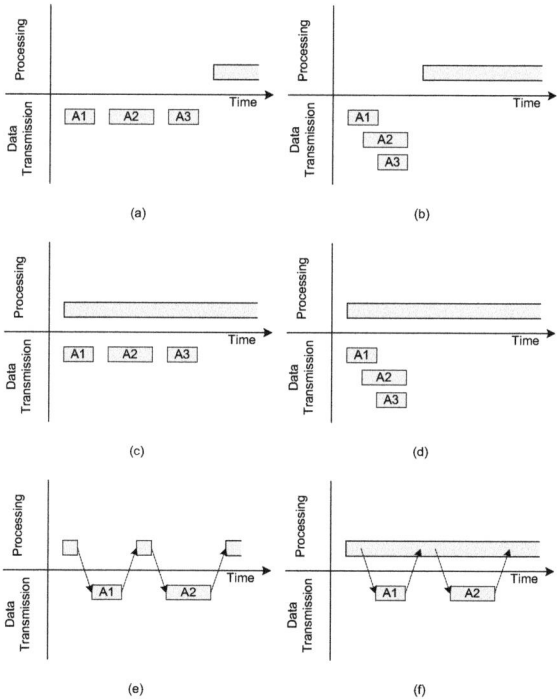

Figure 7.3: Overview of Flex-SwA communication patterns.

For each web service, a combination of these patterns can be chosen by the developer. The reasonable combinations of the execution, data transmission, concurrency, and blocking mode patterns are shown in Figure 7.3. These patterns enable the demand-driven evaluation and transmission of binary data.

A combination of non-overlapping execution and the eager transmission mode (cp. Figure 7.3(a)) results in transferring every data resource before the web service is executed. This scheme is similar to the original transmission via SwA. Transmission of the data resources can also be done concurrently (cp. Figure 7.3(b)), for example by using several threads, thus providing the possibility of improving the transfer rate.

Combining overlapping execution and eager transmission handling (cp. Figure 7.3(c)) results in the immediate start of data transmission and the web service. This mode is useful if the web service has a certain warm-up time or does not need any data resources for startup. Here again, a concurrent transmission of resources (cp. Figure 7.3(d)) possibly provides a better transfer rate than the iterative approach.

Lazy data transmission in combination with overlapping execution results in an on-demand transmission of data resources. If the web service needs a data resource, transmission is triggered at that time. This can be done in a blocking manner (cp. Figure 7.3(e)), i.e. the web service is blocked until data is retrieved from the remote source and stored locally by Flex-SwA or in a non-blocking manner (cp. Figure 7.3(f)), i.e. the web service only triggers the transmission and continues directly. Blocking mode is used if the web service needs the complete data resource before it can resume execution. Non-blocking mode can be used if only a part of the data resource is needed by the web service.

7.4.1 Benefits using Flex-SwA

The Flex-SwA reference system in combination with the different communication patterns offer three main benefits:

1. avoidance of encoding/decoding of binary parameters

2. reduction of data movement

3. simple handling of overload situations and load balancing

7.4 Communication Patterns

Consider a web service consumer invokes a web service on another host and the input parameters are stored on a third host as shown in Figure 7.4(a). Using conventional technologies like SwA, the input parameters have to be transferred twice: from the resource server to the consumer and from the consumer to the provider. Using Flex-SwA, the input parameters have to be transferred only once from the resource server to the provider, since the consumer may use a reference as shown in Figure 7.4(b).

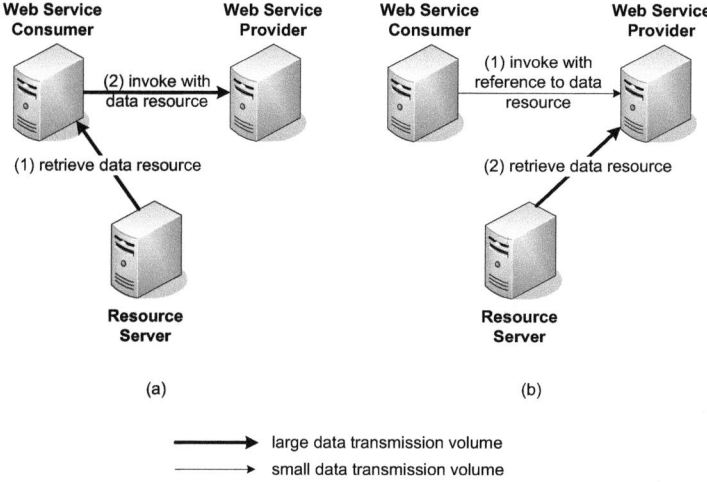

Figure 7.4: Example of data movement reduction.

Flex-SwA easily permits to handle overload situations by forwarding web service invocations to another provider without transferring the input parameters twice. This is realized by forwarding the reference instead of the input parameters. The preprocessing facility may make this decision if an eager pattern is used or the web service itself when a lazy pattern is used. Figure 7.5 shows a client sending multiple references to a web service provider (1). The first web service provider decides to let a second web service provider handle a part of the references (2) and processes the remaining parts itself (3). The second web service provider resolves its references (4) and provides the results for the references handled (5). The first web service provider then returns the collected results (6).

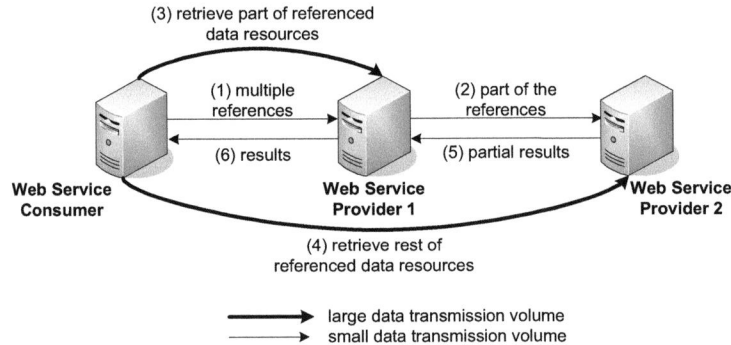

Figure 7.5: Example of simple load balancing using Flex-SwA.

7.5 Summary

This chapter has presented Flex-SwA for the flexible and efficient transmission of binary parameters within web service environments. The key concept of Flex-SwA is the use of references pointing to the location of a binary resource instead of embedding the binary resource in the invocation message directly. In combination with several communication patterns, the reference system avoids the drawbacks of plain SOAP and SwA.

Implementation details of Flex-SwA are presented in Section 8.8.

8
Implementation

8.1 Introduction

The TiCS framework developed in the context of this thesis is based on several technologies, amongst others Java and C as programming languages; J2SE and JamaicaVM as virtual machines; QNX Neutrino and Microsoft Windows as operating systems; Linux shell and Microsoft Windows command prompt as scripting languages; Eclipse, Apache Ant, and Subversion as development environment and tools respectively; IPC@CHIP PLCs and regular desktop PCs as hardware.

This chapter focuses on selected components of the TiCS framework. More precisely, parts of the SOAP4PLC and SOAP4IPC engines, the TiCS Modeler, WS-TemporalPolicy, and Flex-SwA are presented. Since most of TiCS' components are implemented using Java, the challenges to use Java within real-time processing domains like industrial automation are discussed first.

This chapter is organized as follows. Section 8.2 describes the obstacles of using Java for real-time processing and possible solutions. The source code organization of the entire TiCS framework is presented in Section 8.3 by means of a UML package diagram. Section 8.4 outlines the implementation of the

SOAP4PLC engine with focus on several functional components. Section 8.5 presents implementation details of the first real-time SOAP engine for industrial PCs. The implementation details of the TiCS Modeler are discussed in Section 8.6, whereas implementation details of WS-TemporalPolicy are discussed in Section 8.7. Details of Flex-SwA for efficient data transmission are presented in Section 8.8. Section 8.9 gives a summary of this chapter.

Parts of this chapter have been published in [115, 130, 146, 147, 148, 149, 150, 151, 152, 168].

8.2 Java for Industrial Automation

The Java programming language—initially designed and developed for the implementation of consumer electronics software and Web applications—nowadays enjoys great popularity in various domains. The proliferation and popularity of Java is mainly based on its virtual machine concept, comprehensive class library, semi-automatic memory management, inherent security model, and its extensive tool support.

Java is an interpreted language based on the virtual machine concept ("write once, run anywhere" [45]). The Java source code is compiled into a target platform independent bytecode. This bytecode is interpreted by the Java Virtual Machine (JVM). Consequently, only a single Java compiler is required, and a Java program is executable on every platform where a JVM implementation exists.

Java offers a comprehensive class library containing frequently required standard classes, e.g. data structures like linked lists, sets, or hash tables; widgets for programming graphical user interfaces like buttons, menus, text fields; or classes for logging and monitoring purposes. Additionally, there is inherent support for concurrency using threads and several classes for network communication.

Java offers semi-automatic memory management, i.e. objects have to be manually allocated using the **new** operator. This memory is automatically deallocated by the garbage collector (GC) when it is not further used. To decide which memory can be deallocated, the GC repeatedly searches the

8.2 Java for Industrial Automation

JVM heap space to find objects that are no longer referenced.

The Java security model contains platform security (e.g. bytecode verification, secure class loading), cryptographic programming interfaces (e.g. signatures, symmetric/asymmetric ciphers, authentication), secure communication (e.g. Transport Layer Security (TLS), Secure Sockets Layer (SSL)), and a public key infrastructure (e.g. key stores, certificates, and certificate stores).

The number of freely available development tools for Java—integrated development environments (e.g. Eclipse [16], NetBeans [30]), version control systems (e.g. Subversion (SVN) [42], Concurrent Versions System (CVS) [12]), build systems (e.g. Apache Ant [6], Apache Maven [9])—is quite high. A full-fledged development environment is usually available for free.

All these advantages make Java interesting for using it in industrial automation, too. Additionally, vertical integration is eased by the use of Java, since various software systems on the business layer are implemented in Java or offer Java-based interfaces. Unfortunately, the adoption of Java within industrial automation is hindered by four main obstacles:

- **semi-automatic memory management:**

  Semi-automatic memory management—for most developers a main advantage of Java—is problematic for using Java in real-time environments. The memory for an object is manually allocated on the JVM heap using the **new** operator. Once an object is not needed anymore, it is automatically deallocated by the GC. To detect an object that is not further used, the GC searches the JVM heap for objects not referenced anymore. All referenced objects may still be used and therefore remain on the heap. Another function of the GC is the defragmentation of heap space, since by repeated allocation and deallocation of objects, the heap becomes more and more fragmented during runtime. The defragmentation of heap space maximizes free memory at the end of the heap. The GC in Java is realized as an independent thread with highest priority that is automatically started at application start. Therefore, the GC thread is able to interrupt normal program execution arbitrarily. Unfortunately, the amount of time the GC thread works is not deterministic, i.e. the programmer cannot anticipate how long the application will be interrupted as shown in Figure 8.1.

- **scheduling based on the host operating system:**
  Java permits prioritization of threads. Each thread can be assigned a priority from 1 to 10. The Java priorities are mapped to operating system priorities. All Java threads are scheduled by the scheduler of the used operating system. However, most operating systems do not provide support for real-time scheduling.

- **priority inversion:**
  Priority inversion occurs if a high-prioritized thread has to wait until a low-prioritized thread releases a critical section, e.g. write access to a file. This event conflicts with the general requirement that a runnable thread should always be executed if no higher prioritized thread exists. Java does not innately offer functionality to prevent priority inversion amongst threads.

- **interpretation of the Java byte code:**
  Since Java is an interpreted language, the runtime performance of a Java program is smaller than the runtime performance of a program compiled for a specific target platform.

The first three problems are targeted by the Real-time Specification for Java (RTSJ) [47] whereas the last problem is targeted by advanced interpreter/compiler technologies and JVMs realized in hardware.

8.2.1 Real-time Specification for Java

The Real-time Specification for Java (RTSJ) [47] was developed by the Real-time for Java Expert Group. RTSJ extends the Java language specification and the JVM specification to enable analysis, creation, execution, and verification of threads which have to satisfy time constraints. RTSJ defines that thread execution should be deterministic, i.e. the execution time of a thread should be predictable.

To satisfy time-constraints, RTSJ introduces the new thread classes `RealtimeThread` and `NoHeapRealtimeThread`. `RealtimeThread` extends the

8.2 Java for Industrial Automation

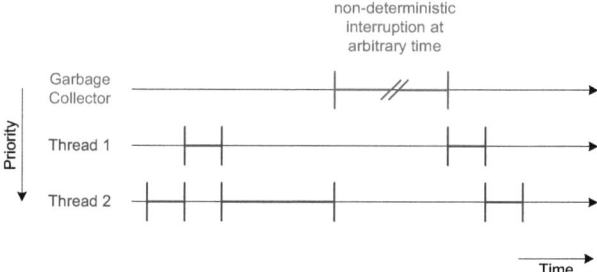

Figure 8.1: Non-real-time garbage collector (cp. [164]).

conventional `Thread` class and implements the `Schedulable` interface that is also defined by RTSJ. The class name `RealtimeThread` is misleading since a `RealtimeThread` also has a lower priority than the GC thread and can therefore be interrupted. The difference between a `RealtimeThread` and a conventional `Thread` is the possibility to assign `SchedulingParameters` and `ReleaseParameters` that define how the `RealtimeThread` is executed. Objects of the `NoHeapRealtimeThread` class have a higher priority than the GC thread. Hence, a `NoHeapRealtimeThread` is able to interrupt the GC and is executed deterministically. To allow this, a `NoHeapRealtimeThread` does not use heap space but the newly introduced `ScopedMemory` or `ImmortalMemory`.

Since RTSJ is only a formal specification of the characteristics of JVMs that support real-time processing, an adequate implementation is required. The reference implementation is offered by TimeSys at the RTSJ project homepage [47]. Within this thesis, aicas' JamaicaVM was used for the implementation of the SOAP4IPC engine (see Section 8.5.1).

8.2.2 Java on Silicon

There exist two main approaches to enhance the runtime performance of Java programs: using advanced just-in-time compilers like LaTTe [177] or using microprocessors that support Java bytecode execution natively like PicoJava [153] from Sun Microsystems or aJ-100 [5] from aJile Systems.

Using the second approach is much more promising from an industrial automation's point of view, since Java processors may be easily integrated in embedded and manufacturing devices. Consequently, the runtime performance of Java programs is boosted dramatically and embedded devices will be programmable using Java in the near future.

8.3 TiCS Source Code Organization

TiCS' source code is organized in several packages, as shown in Figure 8.2. These reflect the key components of the framework and are part of the namespace `de.fb12.tics`. The `services` package contains all time-constrained web services, whereas the `workflows` package contains all time-constrained workflows. The `wizards` package contains TiCS Usability Wizards for the creation/deployment/publication of time-constrained web services. The `modeler` package contains the TiCS Modeler for the composition of time-constrained web services to time-constrained workflows. The `temporalpolicy` package contains and handles WS-TemporalPolicies. These are used for the description of time-constrained web services and workflows. The SOAP4PLC engine is contained within the `soap4plc` package whereas the SOAP4IPC engine is contained within the `soap4ipc` package. Both packages use functionality from the `flexswa` package for the efficient transmission of binary data. The `repository` package contains the Framework Repository to store information about deployed time-constrained web services and workflows. This package is used by the `modeler` and `monitoring` packages. The `monitoring` package contains the Framework Monitor to visualize current runtime information by means of the `repository` package.

8.4 SOAP4PLC

This section discusses the implementation of the SOAP4PLC engine. More precisely, an architectural blueprint of the engine is presented and the implementation of the WS-Infobase, WSDL-Generator, SOAP-Handler, and SOAP2PLC-

8.4 SOAP4PLC

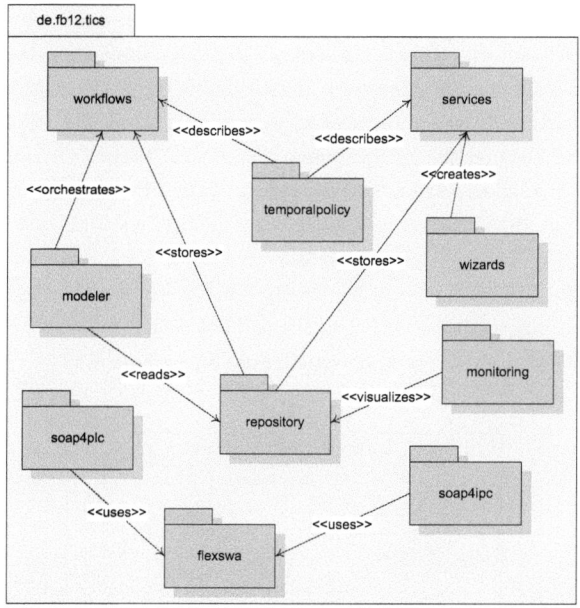

Figure 8.2: Source code organization of the TiCS framework.

Bridge is discussed.

8.4.1 Experimental Soft- and Hardware Environment

The IPC@CHIP PLC from Beck IPC GmbH [11] was used as experimental hardware. All products based on the IPC@CHIP technology contain a full-featured embedded real-time operating system (RTOS) called @CHIP-RTOS. @CHIP-RTOS supports all common features of modern operating systems such as multitasking, support for several network interfaces, TCP/IP protocol stack including IPsec and SSL, and standard transfer protocols like HTTP, FTP, and SSH.

CoDeSys, an IEC 61131-3 compliant programming system developed by 3S Smart Software Solutions [1], is used as PLC development environment. The

CoDeSys programming system consists of two software components. The first one is CoDeSys itself. This is a Microsoft Windows application that realizes the PLC development environment, consisting of editor, compiler, debugger, etc. The second software component is the runtime system called CoDeSys SP. CoDeSys SP runs on the target system (the IPC@CHIP PLC) and manages download, linking, execution, and debugging of the PLC application.

To permit SOAP-based interaction, the IPC@CHIP PLC was extended by the WS-Infobase, WSDL-Generator, SOAP-Handler, and SOAP2PLC-Bridge. The WS-Infobase and SOAP2PLC-Bridge extend the CoDeSys runtime system, whereas the SOAP-Handler and the WSDL-Generator extend the @CHIP-RTOS by SOAP protocol capabilities (cp. Figure 8.3).

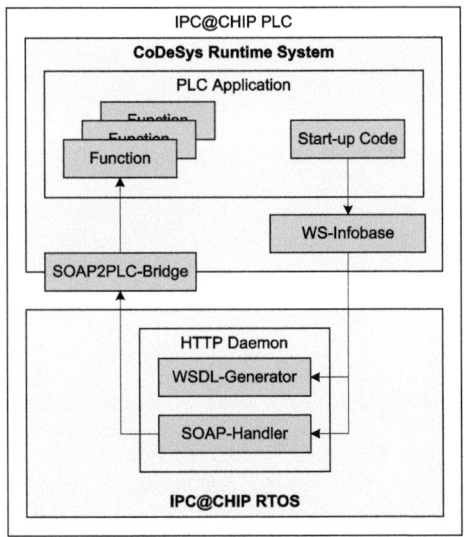

Figure 8.3: Implementation of the SOAP4PLC engine using an IPC@CHIP PLC.

The implementation of the SOAP4PLC engine offers a low memory footprint to respect the restricted computational power of current PLCs. The entire main memory required for engine code and static data are only 7 kByte

8.4 SOAP4PLC 111

approximately. The memory requirement for every exported PLC function depends on the size of its interface description (number of arguments). Typically, a PLC function reserves approximately 40 − 100 byte of main memory.

8.4.2 WS-Infobase

The SOAP4PLC engine is implemented inside the CoDeSys runtime system only. Thus, there is no graphical user interface (GUI), but a simple application programming interface (API). It provides the functions `S4PaddArgument`, `S4PexportPlcFunction`, and `S4PshutDown` to handle the export of PLC functions. These functions are implemented as external functions, i.e. these functions are accessible from the PLC application but are not implemented in a PLC programming language. Instead, the functions are part of the runtime system and are implemented using the programming language C.

The function `S4PexportPlcFunction` is called at the start of the PLC application, once for each PLC function to be exported. The function expects the group name, the PLC function name, a reference to the corresponding PLC function, the interface description (argument list) and the return type as its arguments. The arguments are stored in the service descriptor table. The group name will be used as web service name. If the web service name is unknown (i.e. there was no registration call on that name before), two more steps are necessary:

- The SOAP-Handler is extended to accept the URI of the newly registered web service.

- A new instance of the WSDL-Generator is started that offers a WSDL description for the new web service.

The function `S4PaddArgument` creates an argument list that is required by the function `S4PexportPlcFunction` as described above. To create an argument list, it will be called once for each argument. It expects the argument type of the new argument and the current argument list and returns the current argument list extended with the new argument as its result. To create a complete argument list, the function will be called for the first argument with

S4P_EMPTY (an empty argument list). The next calls will be done with the result of the previous call. Thus, the last call returns the complete list and could be used as input value for S4PexportPlcFunction.

The function S4PshutDown is called once at the shutdown of the PLC application. The function clears the service descriptor table and undeploys all web services, i.e. all web services are deregistered from the SOAP-Handler and all instances of the WSDL-Generator are terminated and removed.

As mentioned before, the S4PexportPlcFunction, S4PaddArgument, and S4PshutDown functions are called at application startup and shutdown, respectively. The CoDeSys programming system provides an event concept that offers several system events. One of these system events—the start event—occurs when the PLC is powered on or when the PLC application was stopped and restarted again. The automation engineer is able to register a PLC function for this event which implements the PLC function export using S4PexportPlcFunction and S4PaddArgument. Similarly, the unregister process is realized using the CoDeSys system events. For this purpose, the system stop event is used to call the S4PshutDown function. This terminates the engine and thus unregisters all functions. The engine will be restarted again on the first S4PexportPlcFunction call automatically.

8.4.3 WSDL-Generator

The IPC@CHIP PLC offers an integrated HTTP server. The implementation of the WSDL-Generator component uses this HTTP server to listen for HTTP requests and to send an HTTP response back to the client. The interaction between the WSDL-Generator component and @CHIP-RTOS' HTTP server is realized using the CGI interface of @CHIP-RTOS. This interface permits to register external handlers for incoming requests on specific URIs. The WSDL-Generator component takes advantage of this feature. Every instance of the component announces its own handler for the WSDL URI of the specific web service. On an incoming client request, the specific handler will be called. Then, the handler creates the WSDL description dynamically and delivers it to the HTTP server. The HTTP server sends it back to the requesting client.

8.4 SOAP4PLC

Listing 8.1 shows the `generateWSDL` function that is called by a handler if a WSDL description is requested. The function takes the name of the target service as input, generates a string representing the WSDL description of the target service, and stores this string in a specific response buffer.

Listing 8.1: Dynamic generation of WSDL descriptions.

```
static int generateWSDL(char *serviceName)
{
  [...]

  // search service in service descriptor table
  i = wsiGetServiceIndex(serviceName);
  if (i<0)
  {
    // service not found, return error
    return -1;
  }

  // write WSDL header in response buffer
  pCur += snprintf(pCur, (int)(pEnd-pCur),
    "<?xml version=\"1.0\" encoding=\"UTF-8\"?>"
    [...]
    "   <types></types>");

  // create WSDL message blocks
  for (i=0; i<gNWebServices; i++)
  {
    if (stricmp(gWebServiceList[i].webServiceName,
      serviceName) == 0)
    {
      // create request messages
      [...]

      // create response message
      [...]
    }
  }

  // create WSDL portType block
  pCur += snprintf(pCur, (int)(pEnd-pCur),
    "<portType name=\"%s\">",
    serviceName);

  for (i=0; i<gNWebServices; i++)
  {
    if (stricmp(gWebServiceList[i].webServiceName,
```

```
      serviceName) == 0)
    {
      // create operation
      pCur += snprintf(pCur, (int)(pEnd-pCur),
        "<operation name=\"%s\" parameterOrder=\"",
        gWebServiceList[i].functionName);

      [...]

      // close operation
      pCur += snprintf(pCur, (int)(pEnd-pCur),
        "\">"
        "<input message=\"tns:%sRequest\"></input>"
        "<output message=\"tns:%sResponse\"></output>"
        "</operation>",
        gWebServiceList[i].functionName,
        gWebServiceList[i].functionName);
    }
  }

  // close portType block
  pCur += snprintf(pCur, (int)(pEnd-pCur),
    "</portType>");

  // create WSDL binding block
  pCur += snprintf(pCur, (int)(pEnd-pCur),
    "<binding name=\"%sPortBinding\" type=\"tns:%s\">"
    [...]
    serviceName,
    serviceName);

  // create operations
  [...]

  // close binding block
  pCur += snprintf(pCur, (int)(pEnd-pCur),
    "</binding>");

  // create WSDL service block
  pCur += snprintf(pCur,(int)(pEnd-pCur),
    "<service name=\"%sService\">"
      "<port name=\"%sPort\" binding=\"tns:%sPortBinding\">"
        "<soap:address location=\"http://%s:%s/%s\">"
        "</soap:address>"
      "</port>"
    "</service>",
    serviceName,
```

8.4 SOAP4PLC

```
        serviceName,
        serviceName,
        host,
        port,
        serviceName);

    // close WSDL description
    pCur += snprintf(pCur, (int)(pEnd-pCur),
        "</definitions>");

    // WSDL description available in response buffer

    return 0; // success
}
```

8.4.4 SOAP-Handler

Just like the WSDL-Generator component, the SOAP-Handler uses @CHIP-RTOS' HTTP server for HTTP protocol handling. Therefore, it registers an external handler for every deployed web service URI using the @CHIP-RTOS CGI interface. As soon as a request for a specific web service arrives, @CHIP-RTOS' HTTP server triggers the external handler. The external handler implements the SOAP parser and interacts with the other required components.

8.4.5 SOAP2PLC-Bridge

The SOAP2PLC-Bridge handles low-level functionality to permit sequence-controlled web services. This functionality depends on the used processor architecture and operating system. Since the IEC 61131-3 standard does not define the low-level layer of a PLC application (memory layout and structure), the used PLC programming system also affects the implementation of that component.

Listing 8.2 shows the function `s2pInvokePlcFunction` implemented in C and assembler that calls a PLC function as result of a web service invocation. For this purpose, the following steps are necessary:

- retrieving a function pointer to the target PLC function
- creating the stack frame required by the PLC function

- saving the current SOAP4PLC process context on the stack
- loading the process context of the PLC application
- restoring the SOAP4PLC process context

Listing 8.2: Calling a PLC function.
```
unsigned long s2pInvokePlcFunction(
    char *pArgumentStack,
    int argumentStackSize,
    unsigned long pouIndex)
{
  // local variables (located on stack)
  unsigned int oldDataSegment;
  void far *pFunction;
  unsigned int resulthigh;
  unsigned int resultlow;

  // retrieve function pointer to given PLC function
  pFunction = (void far *) CodeManGetFunctionPointer(pouIndex);

  // create stack frame required by the PLC function
  asm sub sp, 4        // space for a 16bit return value
  pArgumentStack -= 2; // step back to last argument
  // push arguments onto stack
  for (int i=0; i<argumentStackSize; i+=2)
  {
    asm les bx, pArgumentStack
    asm mov ax, word ptr es:[bx]
    asm push ax
    pArgumentStack -= 2;
  }
  asm mov ax, sp    // save stack pointer
  asm sub sp, 1     // insert dummy value
  asm push ss       // instance pointer (segment)
  asm push ax       // instance pointer (offset)

  // save SOAP4PLC context onto stack
  asm mov ax, ds                // move context to accu
  asm mov oldDataSegment, ax    // move accu to local variable

  // load context of PLC application
  CmGetDataArea(); // puts PLC application context in accu
  asm mov ds, ax   // switch context to PLC application

  // call PLC function
```

8.5 SOAP4IPC

```
    asm call pFunction

    // restore SOAP4PLC stack
    asm add sp, 5    // remove dummy value and instance pointer
    asm add sp, argumentStackSize   // remove argument values

    // restore SOAP4PLC context
    asm mov ax, oldDataSegment
    asm mov ds, ax

    // remove return value of PLC function from stack
    asm pop resultlow    // read and remove lower 16bit
    asm pop resulthigh   // read and remove higher 16bit

    // return result to SOAP-Handler
    return ((unsigned long) resulthigh<<16) |
       (unsigned long) resultlow;
}
```

8.5 SOAP4IPC

This section presents implementation issues of the SOAP4IPC engine. More precisely, the entry point which handles incoming SOAP over HTTP messages, the dependency checker which synchronizes competing web services invocations, the hot deployment/undeployment functionality, the simple, engine and web service profiler, the runtime monitor, the engine configuration, and the parameterization of the different engine threads are presented. The section starts with a short description of the RTSJ-compliant JVM used to implement SOAP4IPC.

8.5.1 JamaicaVM

aicas' JamaicaVM [4] is a JVM implementation compatible with J2SE v1.2 [45] and supports RTSJ v1.0.2 [47]. It is a cross-platform development environment, i.e. a real-time application is implemented on a development operating system (e.g. Linux, Solaris, or Windows) and built for a specific target operating system (e.g. VxWorks, Real-time Linux, INTEGRITY, or Windows) and processor architecture (e.g. PowerPC, x86, or Sparc). Depending on the target operating system, soft real-time constraints (using a non real-time operating system) or hard real-time constraints (using a real-time operating system) can be guaranteed.

aicas offers several development tools to ease the development of real-time applications. *jamaicac* is the source-to-bytecode compiler which takes ".java" files as input and produces ".class" files as output. *jamaicavm* is aicas' implementation of a JVM with RTSJ support. *jamaica* implements the Jamaica Builder which produces a stand-alone executable for a desired target platform. For this purpose, *jamaica* produces portable code written in C that is compiled to a platform-specific executable. To easily determine the memory utilization of an application, JamaicaVM offers a memory analyzer tool.

Using JamaicaVM, there is no difference between conventional Threads, RealtimeThreads, and NoHeapRealtimeThreads. All threads within the JamaicaVM are treated like real-time threads and share the same priority range. This means that there are no restrictions for memory allocations, i.e. a NoHeapRealtimeThread may also allocate memory on the normal heap. This feature depends on the fact that JamaicaVM implements a real-time garbage collector.

8.5.2 EntryPoint

The EntryPoint is an aperiodic real-time thread that handles new incoming connections. If the utilization of the engine is 100%, i.e. the current number of utilized worker threads equals the maximum number of worker threads given in the engine configuration, a new connection is immediately rejected. Otherwise, the new connection is encapsulated in a Job object and enqueued in the JobQueue. Listing 8.3 shows an excerpt of the EntryPoint.

Listing 8.3: Processing logic of the EntryPoint.

```
[...]
while(true) {
  // wait for incoming connection
  Socket socket = serverSocket.accept();

  // encapsulate new connection in a job
  Job job = new Job(socket, startEngine);
```

8.5 SOAP4IPC

```
    // exceeded maximum number of jobs
    if(!jobQueue.addJob(job)) {
      socket.close();
    }
  }
[...]
```

8.5.3 DependencyChecker

The `DependencyChecker` uses information from dependencies.cfg to check whether jobs depend on each other, i.e. whether their processing may lead to a race condition. One line in dependencies.cfg defines a group of competing operations. Listing 8.4 gives an example for a dependency configuration which defines two groups: `group1` prohibits that operation `op1` of web service `service1` is processed concurrently with operation `op2` of the same web service; `group2` prohibits that the operations `op1`, `op2`, and `op3` of web service `service2` are processed concurrently.

Listing 8.4: Example of dependencies.cfg.
```
[...]
group1=service1.op1,service1.op2
group2=service2.op1,service2.op2,service2.op3
[...]
```

8.5.4 Hot Deployment and Hot Undeployment

The `HotDeployerUndeployer` thread—a periodic real-time thread—searches a local directory for new Java classes to export as web services. Internally, the `HotDeployerUndeployer` uses a `FilenameFilter` for ".class" files to consider Java class files only. As soon as the `HotDeployerUndeployer` discovers a new Java class, it uses reflection to determine the internal structure of this class. The period of the `HotDeployerUndeployer` thread and the directory to search for new web services are given via the engine configuration engine.cfg.

8.5.5 Profiling Modes

SOAP4IPC supports two different profiling modes: service profiling by the ServiceProfiler and engine profiling by the EngineProfiler. If the profiling.mode in engine.cfg is set to service, the ServiceProfiler is used to measure the execution time for each web service operation, whereas if the profiling.mode in engine.cfg is set to engine, the EngineProfiler is used to measure the engine overhead. If the profiling.mode is neither set to engine nor to service, the SimpleProfiler is used to collect statistical information about all processed SOAP messages. This information is merged and output at engine shutdown. Listing 8.5 shows an example output of the SimpleProfiler.

Listing 8.5: Example output of the SimpleProfiler.
```
PROFILING INFORMATION

  Total processed tasks:    10000
    Invocation tasks:       10000 (0.00% exceeded deadline!)
    WSDL tasks:             0
    Fault tasks:            0

  Average processing time:  47578717 nanosec
  Standard deviation:       2163928 nanosec
  Min. processing time:     41993000 nanosec
  Max. processing time:     99985000 nanosec
```

To recognize engine shutdown, a ShutdownHandler is bound to the SIGINT signal, i.e. as soon as the keystroke [CTRL]+[C] appears, the handleAsyncEvent method of the ShutdownHandler is called (cp. Listing 8.6) and the statistical data is written to the console.

Listing 8.6: The handleAsyncEvent method of ShutdownHandler.
```
public void handleAsyncEvent() {
  String profile;
  Profiler profiler = SimpleProfiler.getInstance();
  engineCfg = EngineConfiguration.getInstance();

  if(engineCfg.engineProfilingEnabled()) {
    profiler = EngineProfiler.getInstance();
  }
  else if(engineCfg.serviceProfilingEnabled()){
```

```
    profiler = ServiceProfiler.getInstance();
  }

  profile = profiler.getProfile();
  System.out.println("Shutting down...");
  System.out.println(profile);
  System.out.println("Bye!");
  System.exit(0);
}
```

8.5.6 Monitoring of Job Execution Time

The execution time of each job within the engine has to be monitored to guarantee its worst-case execution time. In general, there are three possible strategies to realize execution time monitoring:

1. The execution time of each job is monitored at specific locations within the SOAP engine, e.g. before and after web service invocation.

2. In addition to the worker threads which process jobs, another high-prioritized monitoring thread exists that knows each worker thread and its worst-case execution time. The monitoring thread controls each worker thread and handles deadline violations.

3. For each job, an alarm is set. As soon as the actual execution time exceeds the worst-case execution time, the alarm is raised.

The first strategy can be implemented easily, but may result in a delayed detection of deadline violations. Consider that the current execution time is measured before and after service invocation that detects a deadline violation by the web service. Although the deadline violation is detected—provided that the web service terminates and does not run indefinitely—the detection may take an arbitrary duration, which is unacceptable in the real-time processing domain. Execution time measurement at further locations, i.e. insertion of additional measuring statements within the engine, does not solve the problem. In contrast, the insertion of further execution time measurements leads to a mixup of functional engine/web service and monitoring code.

The second strategy results in a clear design. Only one additional thread is required to monitor the execution time of each job thread within the engine. As soon as a new job enters the engine, this job is registered at the monitoring thread. The monitoring thread works periodically, i.e. it checks the execution time of each registered worker thread in equidistant time intervals for time constraint violations. If a time constraint violation has occurred, the monitoring thread stops the corresponding worker thread. The implementation of this strategy within Java is problematic, since a thread cannot innately be safely stopped by another thread [128].

This thesis introduces a third strategy called *piggybacking of time constraints* that leads to a clear design and implementation of execution time monitoring. The SOAP4IPC engine utilizes this strategy by means of a `OneShotTimer` (part of the RTSJ specification) that internally uses the system clock. A `OneShotTimer` takes a deadline and an `ExceededHandler`. The `ExceededHandler` is an `AsyncEventHandler` whose `handleAsyncEvent` method is called as soon as the deadline is violated. When the job is successfully processed within its deadline, the `OneShotTimer` is deactivated and detached from the `Task` object. Listing 8.7 exemplifies the use of a `OneShotTimer` to monitor the execution time of tasks.

Listing 8.7: Adding a `OneShotTimer` to a `Task` object.

```
[...]
// calculate deadline
AbsoluteTime deadline = new AbsoluteTime(entryTime.add(
   services.getAllowedTime(service),0));
// configure ExceededHandler
exceededHandler = new ExceededHandler(this);
exceededHandler.setSchedulingParameters(engineConfiguration.
   getParameterSet().getExceededSchedParams());
exceededHandler.setReleaseParameters(engineConfiguration.
   getParameterSet().getExceededRelParams());
// start OneShotTimer
oneShotTimer = new OneShotTimer(deadline, exceededHandler);
oneShotTimer.start();
[...]
```

8.5.7 Engine Configuration

The configuration of SOAP4IPC is given as a Java properties file, i.e. a flat text file with name/value-pairs. Important parameters and their meanings are shown in Table 8.1.

Table 8.1: Excerpt of the engine configuration parameters.

Parameter	Meaning
max.size	Maximum size of a SOAP request message in kilobytes.
concurrency.level	Number of concurrent worker threads.
profiling.mode	Selects engine-profiling or service-profiling mode.
hot.deployment.delay	Period between two hot deployment or undeployment runs in milliseconds.
hot.deployment.path	Search directory for class files for hot deployment/undeployment.

8.5.8 Parameterization of Engine Threads

The engine contains four different thread types: the EntryPoint thread handles incoming connections, the JobWorker threads process jobs, the HotDeployerUndeployer thread handles the deployment/undeployment of Java classes as web services, and the ExceededHandler thread handles logging of a deadline violation.

These thread types are scheduled by the operating system on the basis of SchedulingParameters and ReleaseParameters. SchedulingParameters are used to define the priority of a thread, whereas ReleaseParameters are used to define the scheduling strategy in general. Since SchedulingParameters and ReleaseParameters are realized as abstract classes, they cannot be used directly.

A concrete implementation of ReleaseParameters are AperiodicParameters and PeriodicParameters. AperiodicParameters are used for threads that should be scheduled aperiodically, e.g. if an event occurs. On the other hand, `PeriodicParameters` are used for threads that should be scheduled periodically, e.g. every 3 seconds. `PeriodicParameters` are specified by *start*, *period*, *cost*, *deadline*, *overrun handler*, and *miss handler*. *start* defines the first activation of the corresponding thread, whereas *period* defines the time between two activations. The *cost* parameter restricts the maximum CPU time the thread is permitted to consume. The *deadline* defines the maximum execution time of the corresponding thread. The *overrun handler* and the *miss handler* are used to define reactions for cost and deadline violations, respectively.

A concrete implementation of the abstract `SchedulingParameters` class is `PriorityParameters`. The constructor of `PriorityParameters` takes an integer value as priority. Valid priority values can be obtained from the `PriorityScheduler`. The priority hierarchy within the engine is

$$\text{prio}(\texttt{HotDeployerUndeployer}) < \text{prio}(\texttt{JobWorker})$$
$$\text{prio}(\texttt{JobWorker}) < \text{prio}(\texttt{EntryPoint})$$
$$\text{prio}(\texttt{EntryPoint}) < \text{prio}(\texttt{ExceededHandler})$$

i.e. the highest priority is reserved for deadline violation handling.

To ease the definition of appropriate scheduling and release parameters, the engine uses a `ParameterSet` to encapsulate the scheduling and release parameters for each thread type and a `ParameterSetGenerator` to automatically fill the `ParameterSet`.

8.6 TiCS Modeler

Since the implementation of the TiCS Modeler is based on the Domain-Adaptable Visual Orchestrator (DAVO) [115], this section is organized as follows: First, implementation details of DAVO relevant to the TiCS Modeler are discussed. Second, equipped with this knowledge, implementation details of the TiCS Modeler are presented.

8.6.1 Data Model

The internal data model of DAVO represents a workflow in a tree-like model. Each of the activities used within a workflow is defined by its *type*, a specific set of *attributes* (e.g. name), and specific nested elements (e.g. for exception handling) according to the BPEL4WS standard. In the case of structured activities, the nested elements can be other activities as well. In DAVO, the activities are represented using objects of the class hierarchy shown in Figure 8.4. Element is the parent class for all activities, whereas ContainerElement is the parent class for all structured activities. The actual class hierarchy is more sophisticated than the one outlined in Figure 8.4. It contains two additional abstractions that are omitted for simplicity since they are not relevant to the data model:

- ConnectedElement contains several attributes referring to other web services (e.g. port types and operation names) and is the parent class of the invoke, receive, and reply activities.

- A SequentialContainer is a container whose nested activities are executed in the given order. For example, SequentialContainer is the parent class of sequence and while.

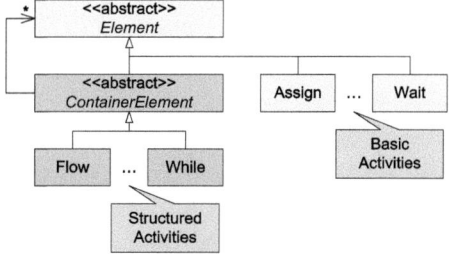

Figure 8.4: A simplified Element class hierarchy.

While it is sufficient for a standard BPEL4WS workflow editor to use a simple data model like fields to store the process's information, i.e. information for elements and attributes, this approach is not feasible with regard to extensibility. For the use of BPEL4WS within and the adaptation of DAVO to specific domains (e.g. industrial automation), it is necessary to associate additional information with an activity (e.g. the average and worst-case execution time). DAVO uses named properties to associate arbitrary information with activities.

The properties not only consist of a name and a value, but also of an `IValidator` that can be used to check validity when `setValue` is called. Additionally, the properties itself have various meta-properties like the exemplary ones shown in Figure 8.5 that can be queried with the corresponding getter: `persistent` determines if the property value is stored together with the DAVO data model; `readOnly`, `visible`, and various other meta-properties are used to control the automatic creation of property views as described in Section 5.4.2. There may be various dependencies between the properties of an `Element`. For instance, an operation name depends on the port type. Additionally, there may also be dependencies to external events. For instance, a list of variables shown in the property view needs to be updated whenever the variable set of the process or scope changes. All these dependencies are automatically managed by the `PropertySet`. For internal dependencies a property just needs to implement an interface giving the `PropertySet` access to the the names of the properties it depends on and providing a callback method that will be invoked automatically. For external dependencies a similar interface exists that gives access to a list of events that the property needs to be notified about. The external events will be automatically propagated through the workflow by the `ContainerElement`s. With this design it is not necessary for `Property` objects to register themselves as listeners. Since an `Element` is a set of properties plus additional information, an `Element` inherits from `PropertySet`.

The extension mechanism is illustrated in Figure 8.6. The core of each DAVO extension is an implementation of the `IModelExtender`. A specific `IModelExtender` implementation knows the `ElementExtension` for each `Element`. After the `ElementFactory` has created the `Element` (1), it passes it to the `ElementExtender` (2). The `ElementExtender` asks the `IModelExtender` for extensions for the given `Element` (3). After the `IModelExtender` has created the extension for the given `Element` (4), it is added (5). The `Element`-

8.6 TiCS Modeler

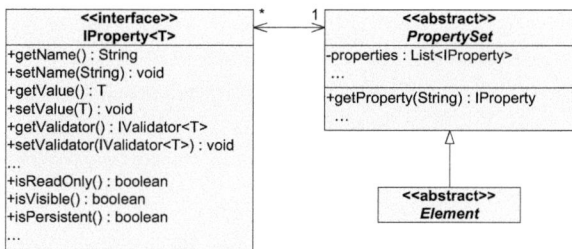

Figure 8.5: The property model of DAVO.

`Extension` can modify the `Element` in many ways. For example, it can add new `Property` objects or hide existing ones.

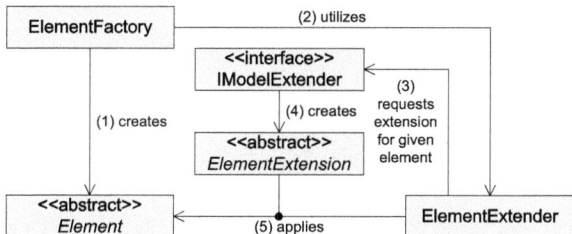

Figure 8.6: The `Element` extension mechanism.

New activities can be added by simply inheriting from an arbitrary class from the hierarchy and registering the new activity using one of DAVO's extension points. As a consequence, the new activity is added to DAVO's graphical user interface.

8.6.2 Views and Controllers

The abstractions realized by the data model are reused to create a minimal hierarchy of view and controller implementations. The controller hierarchy shown in Figure 8.7 is very similar to the data model. Analogously, it contains the same main abstractions `ElementEditPart` and `ContainerElementEdit-Part`, a concrete controller for basic activities (`BasicElementEditPart`), and two controllers for structured activities (`SequentialElementEditPart` and `NonSequentialElementEditPart`). The hierarchy of view classes is organized similarly. In both cases, a factory is used to create instances of views and controllers. It automatically chooses the concrete type according to the activity's type. An extension may register new views or controllers with the factories and associate them with the `Elements`.

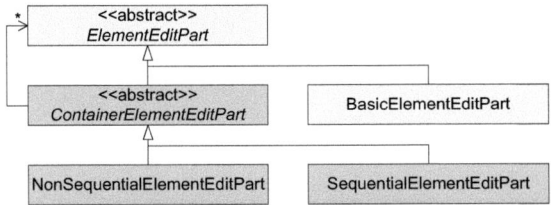

Figure 8.7: The `EditPart` type hierarchy.

In DAVO, activities are represented by graphical widgets containing the name of the activity and an icon to easily distinguish the different activities. Additionally, one or more status icons can be added to the activities. Together with new properties, DAVO extensions may also add corresponding status icons to the activities.

Apart from the graphical workflow view, the most important part of DAVO is the property view that allows to assign values to the properties of an activity. The property view is one of Eclipse's core views. It contains a table of property names and values that can either be directly entered or selected from a list of possible values. Additionally, groups of user interface controls—so-called sections—can be added to the property view to edit a group of properties in a more sophisticated way. In that case, the property view uses tabs to switch between the basic property view and the other sections. Because detailed knowledge of the Eclipse Standard Widget Toolkit (SWT) [17] is required to create such sections, an easy way to use the standard property view is desirable.

Eclipse defines two interfaces that have to be implemented to edit properties of any object: `IPropertySource` and `IPropertyDescriptor`. `IPropertySource` contains methods to read and change the values of properties and to

8.6 TiCS Modeler

return a list of `IPropertyDescriptor` objects. An `IPropertyDescriptor` object describes one of the available properties. The adapter pattern [120] is used to dynamically create wrapper objects for `Element`s of the data model if they are selected. This process is shown in Figure 8.8. When an activity is selected—more precisely, the `EditPart` belonging to its graphical representation is selected—Eclipse tries to update the properties view. It discovers that the `EditPart` does not implement `IPropertySource` and uses an adapter factory to create a valid adapter that is an instance of `PropertySetAdapter` in this case. This instance will create the list of `IPropertyDescriptor`s using the meta-properties mentioned earlier. For instance, properties having their `visible` meta-property set to `false` will not be shown, whereas properties having their `readOnly` meta-property set to `false` will be shown but will not be editable. Calls to read or change the value of a property are delegated to a `PropertyAdapter` that wraps the property and is responsible for value conversion, since the property view only accepts strings.

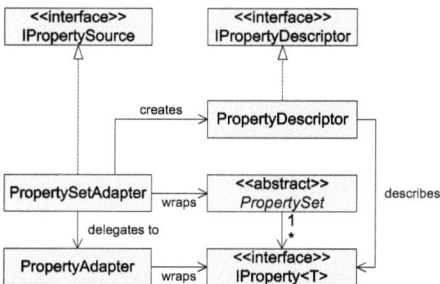

Figure 8.8: The `Property` adapter model.

8.6.3 Shadow Model

The translation of the workflow from the data model to actual BPEL4WS code is done by the so-called *shadow model*, a second class hierarchy equivalent to the data model. The use of a separate model for translation purposes prevents that changes to the translation process may influence the data model. The model contains an `ElementShadow` class for every `Element`, whose sole purpose is the conversion of the values stored in the properties of its associated `Element` to an XML element representing the corresponding BPEL4WS activity. The translation process is coordinated by the `Exporter` that is responsible for the generation of the BPEL4WS document. The document contains the activities and other meta-information as well as auxiliary files needed to deploy the workflow. All classes involved in the conversion process are shown in Figure 8.9.

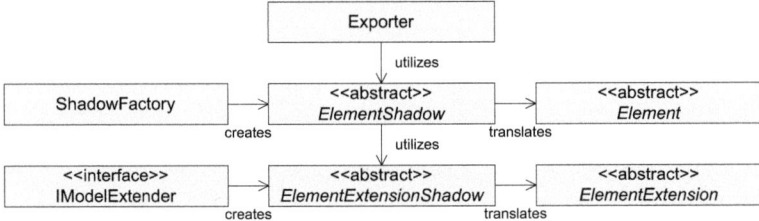

Figure 8.9: A BPEL4WS translation process using the shadow model.

A DAVO extension that adds new `Element`s to the data model must register the corresponding `ElementShadow`s with the `ShadowFactory`. If the extension does not add new `Element`s, but instead modifies existing ones by means of an `ElementExtension`, it is required to provide an appropriate `ElementExtensionShadow` that is capable of translating the auxiliary information.

8.6.4 Adapting DAVO to Real-time Processing

The TiCS Modeler extends each BPEL4WS activity with a property that stores the worst-case execution time and the average execution time, respectively. For basic activities, the values of these properties depend on the action realized by this activity. For a structured activity, on the other hand, the values of these properties depend on the property values of the child activities contained in the structured activity and has to be calculated individually for different activities as discussed in Section 5.3.

8.6 TiCS Modeler

To be able to extend the data model, an implementation of the `IModelExtender` interface has to be provided by the TiCS Modeler. It is used to create the `ElementExtensions` for given `Elements` as shown in Listing 8.8. There are different properties for basic and structured activities, thus different `ElementExtensions` are used. For the basic activities, a further distinction is made between `ConnectedElements` related to a specific operation of a web service and other `Elements`.

Listing 8.8: The implementation of the `IModelExtender` interface.
```java
public class ModelExtender implements IModelExtender {
    @Override
    public ElementExtension createExtension(
        Element targetElement, ProcessContext context) {
            if (targetElement instanceof ContainerElement) {
                return new ContainerElementExt();
            } else if (targetElement instanceof ConnectedElement) {
                return new ConnectedElementExt();
            } else {
                return new ElementExt();
            }
    }
}
```

The three `ElementExtensions` are almost identical, thus only one is exemplified in Listing 8.9. The most interesting method of this class is `applyExtension` that modifies the actual element. In this case, it creates two new properties, an instance of `ElementWCETProp` and `ElementAETProp` respectively, adds these properties to a newly created `PropertyGroup` that again is added to the `Element`. A `PropertyGroup` is just a collection of properties to simplify their handling, i.e. it is possible to remove multiple properties at once by the `removeExtension` method. Additionally, a `PropertyGroup` permits reuse when the group is not created on thy fly like in the example, but as a stand-alone class. In this latter case, the group may also provide additional initialization code. `Activator.PLUGIN_ID` is the plug-in ID of the specific DAVO extension, as specified in the plug-in manifest. It is used as ID for the `ElementExtension` as well as for the `PropertyGroup`. Although the use of this ID is not required, it is recommended because it prevents namespace clashes between properties of different extensions.

Listing 8.9: The `ElementExtender` for plain `Elements`, that are neither containers nor connected elements.
```
public class ElementExt extends ElementExtension {

  public ElementExt() {
    super(Activator.PLUGIN_ID);
  }

  @Override
  protected void applyExtension() {
    PropertyGroup group =
      new PropertyGroup(Activator.PLUGIN_ID);
    group.add(new ElementWCETProp());
    group.add(new ElementAETProp());
    getExtendedElement().addPropertyGroup(group);
  }

  @Override
  protected void removeExtension() {
    getExtendedElement()
      .removePropertyGroup(Activator.PLUGIN_ID);
  }
}
```

Listing 8.10 exemplifies the worst-case execution time property in its simplest form. It has an ID to address it, a description and category used to identify it within the property view and is of the type `Integer`. After its creation, it is initialized with the value 0. By default, this value is editable in the property view.

Listing 8.10: The worst-case execution time property, that is applied to all `Elements`, that are neither containers nor connected elements.
```
public class ElementWCETProp extends Property<Integer> {
  public static final String
    ID = "de.fb12.tics.modeler";
  public static final String
    DESCRIPTION = "worst-case execution time";
  public static final String
    CATEGORY = "TiCS";

  public ElementWCETProp() {
    super(ID, DESCRIPTION, CATEGORY, Integer.class);
    setValue(0);
  }
```

8.6 TiCS Modeler

}

The `ConnectedElement`s are extended with another property, that is shown in Listing 8.11. Because the worst-case execution time of a `ConnectedElement` depends on the specific operation it is connected to, this property is dependent on the operation name and therefore also transitively on the port type property. This dependency is modeled by the implementation of the `IPropertyValue-Dependent` interface, which consists of the two public methods `getProperty-ValueDependencyIDs` and `relevantPropertyValueChange`. The first method returns a list of the properties this property is depending on. This list is stored as a static array here. The second method is invoked when the value of one of the depending properties is changed. Because the value of the property is determined automatically, it is not editable.

Listing 8.11: The worst-case execution time property, that is applied to all `ConnectedElement`s.

```
public class ConnectedElementWCETProp extends ElementWCETProp
  implements IPropertyValueDependent {

  public ConnectedElementWCETProp() {
    setEditable(false);
  }

  private final static String[] PROP_DEP_IDS =
    new String[] {ConnectedElement.OPERATION_NAME_PROP};

  @Override
  public String[] getPropertyValueDependencyIDs() {
    return PROP_DEP_IDS;
  }

  @Override
  public void relevantPropertyValueChange(
    ValueChangeEvent event) {
    /* retrieve worst-case execution time */
  }
}
```

The `ContainerElement`s are also extended with a specific property that is shown in Listing 8.12. The worst-case execution time of a `ContainerElement` depends on the type of the container (e.g. `flow`, `sequence`, `switch`, etc.) and the worst-case execution times of its children. Consequently, this property does not depend on the values of other properties in the same `Element`, but on property values of other `Elements`. This is called an *external dependency* in DAVO and realized by implementing the interface `IExternalEventDependent`. This interface defines the methods `getExternalEventDependencies` and `relevantExternalEvent`. The first method returns a list of event classes that this property needs to be notified about. The latter method is invoked when an event is fired. In this case, some further tests are necessary to determine if the value of the property has to be updated. The actual calculation is done by an implementation of the `IContainerCalculator` interface that is provided by a special factory (not shown here), depending on the type of the container.

Listing 8.12: The worst-case execution time property, that is applied to all `ContainerElements`.

```
public class ContainerElementWCETProp extends ElementWCETProp
  implements IExternalEventDependent {

  [...]

  @SuppressWarnings("unchecked")
  private final static
  Class<IExternalEvent>[] EXT_EVT_DEP_CLS =
    (Class<IExternalEvent>[])
      new Class[] { ContainerChangeEvent.class };

  @Override
  public Class<IExternalEvent>[]
  getExternalEventDependencies() {
    return EXT_EVT_DEP_CLS;
  }

  @Override
  public void relevantExternalEvent(IExternalEvent event) {

    [...]

    if (update) {
      setValue(getContainerCalculator()
        .calculateWCET(getContainerElement()));
      System.out.println("[" + getPropertySet() +
        "] updated, new value == " + getValue());
```

```
      }
    }
}
```

As an example of such a calculator, the `FlowCalculator` is shown in Listing 8.13 that calculates the worst-case execution time according to Equation (5.9).

Listing 8.13: The calculator for `flow` activities.
```
public class FlowCalculator implements IContainerCalculator {
  @Override
  public Integer calculateWCET(
    ContainerElement containerElement) {
    Integer result = 0;
    for (Element child : containerElement.getChildren()) {
      Integer childWCET =
        (Integer) child.getPropertyValue(ElementWCETProp.ID);
      if (result < childWCET) {
        result = childWCET;
      }
    }
    return result;
  }
}
```

8.7 WS-TemporalPolicy

This section presents realization details of WS-TemporalPolicy. The section focuses on the temporal policy manager that holds an in-memory model of active temporal policies and the weaver which attaches a valid temporal policy to a web service description.

8.7.1 Temporal Policy Manager

The temporal policy manager `TempPolManager` is part of the TiCS SOAP4IPC engine and uses an internal model to represent all WS-TemporalPolicies used. The `TempPolManager` offers two different modes of operation for test and productive operation. In test operation, the `TempPolManager` is realized as a thread with lowest priority and repetitive reads WS-TemporalPolicies from a directory. This directory is specified in the engine configuration file. If any changes are found during test operation, i.e. policy files were modified, added, or removed, their corresponding model representation are reloaded, newly loaded, or removed. In productive operation, the `TempPolManager` reads the temporal policies only once at engine startup. The two different modes of operation permit the modification of WS-TemporalPolicies during test operation and saves resources during productive operation.

The WS-TemporalPolicy files are represented by a Java class named `TemporalPolicy` that contains several attributes: `name`, `keywords`, `policyRef`, `serviceRef` `activated`, `activatedOnce`, `expires`, `startTime`, `endTime`, `duration`, `activationAction`, `renewalAction`, `expirationAction`, and `deactivationAction`. Furthermore, a `TemporalPolicy` has the four methods `onActivation`, `onRenewal`, `onExpiration`, and `onDeactivation` that execute the corresponding actions.

The `name` attribute holds the name of the WS-TemporalPolicy. The `keywords` attribute is an array of strings that holds the keywords of the policy. The `policyRef` and `serviceRef` attributes hold a reference to a WS-TemporalPolicy/WS-Policy and WSDL description, respectively. The `activated` attribute is a boolean that indicates whether the policy influences on other policies. The `expires` attribute always holds the current time when the policy's influence will end. When a policy is activated for the first time due to its start time or because it has been newly loaded, the `activatedOnce` attribute is set to `true`. If the policy was activated by setting the `activatedOnce` attribute, it will never be activated again due to the start of its validity period.

The four action attributes each contain a list of action objects that can be an `ActivateAction`, `DeactivateAction` or `RenewAction`. The `ActivateAction`/`DeactivateAction` just contains a reference to the policy to activate/deactivate. The `RenewAction` is more complex and again contains the fields `expires`, `startTime`, `endTime` and `duration` like the `TemporalPolicy` and a reference to the policy to renew. `OnExpiration` is the last action in the lifetime of a policy. For example, clean-up operations can be conducted within this operation.

8.7 WS-TemporalPolicy

8.7.2 Policy Weaving

The weaving and unweaving of WS-Policies to the WSDL description of a web service is realized by the `TempPolWeaver`. Whenever a web service's WSDL description is requested, the SOAP4IPC engine generates the WSDL document on the fly. Therefore, the `TempPolWeaver` just has to ask the `TempPolManager` which policies to weave into the WSDL description at the moment of the WSDL request. Figure 8.10 outlines the policy weaving process.

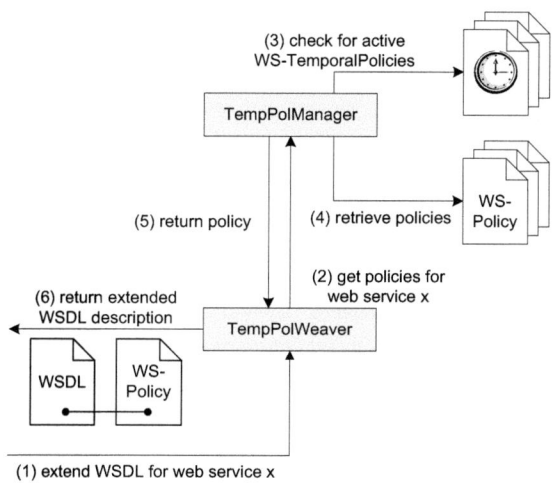

Figure 8.10: An example for policy weaving.

(1) The `TempPolWeaver` is instructed to extend the WSDL description of the given web service.

(2) The `TempPolWeaver` asks the `TempPolManager` for all active WS-Policies for the given web service.

(3) The `TempPolManager` searches for all active WS-TemporalPolicies.

(4) The `TempPolManager` selects only those WS-Policies that are referenced by an active WS-TemporalPolicy and concern the given web service. These WS-Policies are returned to the `TempPolWeaver`.

(5) The `TempPolWeaver` takes the WS-Policies, links them to the WSDL description and returns the extended description.

8.8 Flex-SwA

Flex-SwA was initially developed for use in combination with Apache Axis v1.2.1 [8] (or newer) and either Tomcat v5.5.9 [10] (or newer) or Jetty v5.1.10 [28] (or newer) but can also be used in combination with SOAP4PLC and SOAP4IPC or an arbitrary SOAP engine. This section presents selected implementation details of Flex-SwA. Figure 8.11 gives an overview of Flex-SwA's client and server components for post-invocation parameter transmission and reference handling.

From the user's perspective, the `PiptCall` and the `FlexSwACall` are of particular interest and discussed in this section. A web service consumer can either use a `PiptCall` or a `FlexSwACall` if it wants to use functionality of the Flex-SwA layer. A `PiptCall` can be used to send parameters to a web service after its invocation using an external channel, whereas a `FlexSwACall` is used when large amounts of data should be transferred in a flexible manner.

8.8.1 PiptCall

The `PiptCall` registers type mappings for a specific `Outport` at the (Axis) type mapping registry, acquires the WSDL description from the target web service and retrieves the locations where data should be repeatedly sent to. For each of these locations, the consumer has to provide an `Outport` as a parameter when calling the `PiptCall`'s `invoke` method. Via these `Outport`s, the consumer is able to send data to the web service after web service invocation.

After calling the `invoke` method, the `PiptCall` initializes the `Outport`s with the locations extracted from the WSDL and hands the provided parameters to the corresponding serializers. For each `Outport`, a connection is opened

8.8 Flex-SwA

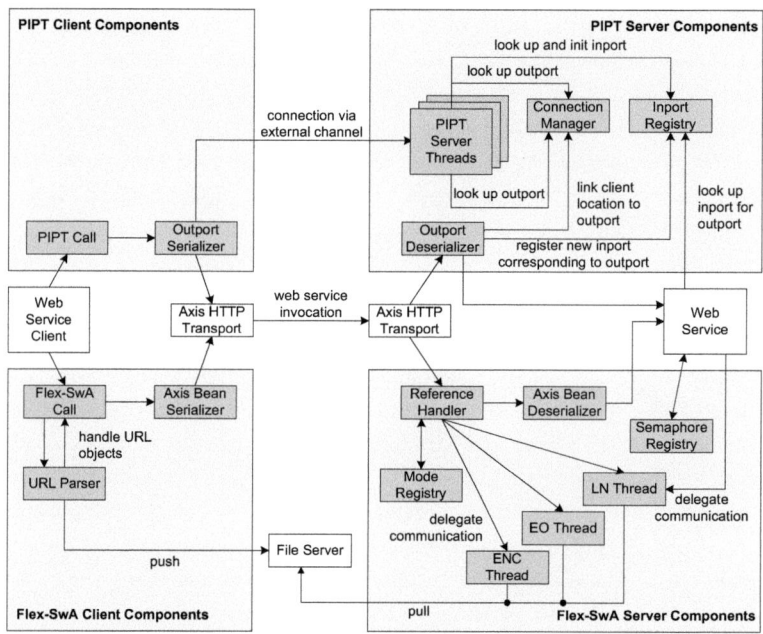

Figure 8.11: Implementation overview of the Flex-SwA data transmission component. (ENC=eager, non-overlapping, concurrent; EO=eager, overlapping; LN=lazy, non-overalpping)

to the corresponding location. Afterwards, the client is able to send data to the web service. As soon as the serialization is finished, the Axis HTTP transport component sends the SOAP message to the target web service.

At the server, each Outport connection request is handled by a PiptServerThread. The server thread blocks at a semaphore until the Axis HTTP transport component has received the SOAP message, has handed it to the corresponding deserializers of which the OutportDeserializer has deserialized the corresponding Outport and has registered it with the ConnectionManager and InportRegistry. Then, the Inport is initialized, such that the web service is able to read from the Inport. If the web service is started before the external channel is established between the consumer's `Outport` and the provider's `PiptServerThread`, the web service will block when calling the `read` method.

After the `OutportDeserializer` has finished, the actual web service is invoked. The web service then takes the received `Outport` and queries the `InportRegistry` for the corresponding `Inport`. The `Inport` also provides a `read` method by which the web service can read data sent via the corresponding consumer `Outport`.

8.8.2 FlexSwACall

The `FlexSwACall` registers type mappings for the `Reference` and the `Credential` at the (Axis) type mapping registry upon creation. If the client wants to directly send data to the target web service, it can use a URL object. If the `URLParser` finds a URL object as a parameter, it streams the data the URL points to directly to the target web service. If another protocol should be used, it is possible to make the `FlexSwACall` use another parser. Otherwise, the client calls the `invoke` method with a `Reference` object (instead of an URL object) for each resource. Each `Reference` is then serialized by the standard Axis bean serializer and the resulting SOAP message is handed to the HTTP transport which transfers the data to the target web service. At the server, the HTTP transport receives the SOAP message and hands it to the `ReferenceHandler`. The `ReferenceHandler` looks up the execution, data transmission, concurrency, and blocking mode pattern of the web service and handles the `Reference`s accordingly. If the transmission mode is eager, the `ReferenceHandler` will either itself acquire the referenced data resources from the server or delegate the acquisition to one or more threads depending on the processing and concurrency mode. In lazy mode, the web service itself can use the `Reference` object to retrieve the data resource. In detail, for an eager, non-overlapping, iterative web service, the `ReferenceHandler` itself acquires the data resource. For an eager, non-overlapping, concurrent web service, the `ReferenceHandler` instantiates an `ENCThread` (eager, non-overlapping, concurrent) for each `Reference` and then waits for the threads to finish. In over-

8.8 Flex-SwA

lapping mode, an `EOThread` (eager, overlapping) is started that retrieves all the referenced files one after the other (iteratively) or that starts a thread for each `Reference` (concurrently). Directly after delegating the communication to the `EOThread`, the web service is started. If the web service wants to access the file, it can retrieve a semaphore from the `SemaphoreRegistry` that blocks the web service if the acquisition of the file has not yet been completed. For a lazy web service, the `ReferenceHandler` does nothing, since it leaves the handling of the communication to the web service itself. The web service can use the `Reference` object to retrieve the referenced file. In blocking mode, the `Reference` retrieves the file itself and the web service waits for the `Reference` object to finish. In non-blocking mode, the `Reference` delegates the communication to the `LNThread` (lazy, non-overlapping), which retrieves the file, while the web service proceeds with execution.

8.8.3 Description of Flex-SwA Endpoints

To create an outport for the consumer, the Flex-SwA layer needs to know the endpoint where the web service waits to receive the parameters. The consumer needs to know which parameters to embed in the request message and which parameters to send via an external channel. All necessary information to invoke a web service are normally described within a WSDL document. Consequently, also the Flex-SwA protocol information should be embedded within the WSDL description. A simple approach to embed the information in the WSDL description is to use the `documentation` element. A `documentation` element is used to embed human readable information in a WSDL description. The content of this element may be arbitrary data or XML elements. Hence, it can be used to embed endpoint information. A main advantage of this approach is compatibility with consumers not aware of post-invocation parameter transmission. A consumer aware of post-invocation parameter transmission parses the web service description, encounters the `documentation` element and uses the specified endpoint to establish the external channel. All consumers not aware of post-invocation parameter transmission simply ignore the element. Listing 8.14 shows the WSDL description of an `ExampleService`. The

ExampleService offers an operation echo, which takes two parameters: an integer and a string. Each parameter sent via an external channel is marked with a documentation element. The integer parameter i is sent via an external channel to the endpoint defined in the location attribute. The string parameter str is not marked with a documentation tag and is therefore embedded in the SOAP message.

Listing 8.14: Using the documentation element for Flex-SwA.

```
<wsdl:definitions targetNamespace="...">
  [...]
  <wsdl:message name="echoRequest">
    <wsdl:part name="i" type="xsd:int"/>
    <wsdl:documentation>
      <param name="i" location="uri"/>
    </wsdl:documentation>
    <wsdl:part name="str" type="xsd:string"/>
  </wsdl:message>
  <wsdl:message name="echoResponse">
    <wsdl:part name="echoReturn" type="xsd:string"/>
  </wsdl:message>
  [...]
</wsdl:definitions>
```

The re-use of the documentation element violates its intentional semantics to encapsulate human readable information. Therefore, this thesis proposes an extension of WSDL to specify whether a parameter is embedded into the SOAP request message or sent via an external channel. If the parameter is sent via an external channel, an endpoint must be provided. Hence, a location attribute is introduced for each parameter sent via an external channel. Listing 8.15 shows the proposed extension. The integer parameter i is still sent via an external channel. The location attribute added to the part element specifies the endpoint.

Listing 8.15: An extension to WSDL to describe Flex-SwA parameters.

```
<wsdl:definitions targetNamespace="...">
  [...]
  <wsdl:message name="echoRequest">
    <wsdl:part name="i" type="xsd:int" location="uri"/>
    <wsdl:part name="str" type="xsd:string"/>
  </wsdl:message>
  [...]
```

```
</wsdl:definitions>
```

8.9 Summary

This section has presented selected implementation details of the TiCS framework. Firstly, it was motivated why Java is an interesting programming language also for the industrial automation domain and how the TiCS' source code is organized. Subsequently, implementations details of the SOAP4PLC and SOAP4IPC engine were discussed. SOAP4PLC is the first SOAP engine for PLCs whereas SOAP4IPC is the first profiling-and-monitoring based, general-purpose real-time SOAP engine at all. Additionally, a novel approach for execution time monitoring called time constraint piggybacking is implemented by SOAP4IPC. The implementation of the TiCS Modeler is discussed in detail, with special focus on the extensible data model. The handling of WS-TemporalPolicies for the description of time constraints and Flex-SwA for the efficient data transmission in service-oriented environments are also discussed on implementation level.

9
Evaluation

9.1 Introduction

This chapter presents a qualitative and quantitative evaluation of selected parts of the TiCS framework.

At first, by means of an experimental setup, it is demonstrated that web service based access to the manufacturing layer is technically feasible by using the SOAP4PLC engine. In the following, the performance of the SOAP4PLC engine is evaluated.

The use of the SOAP4IPC engine is presented in detail, i.e. the profiling-and-monitoring approach is exemplified on different real-time operating systems. Additionally, the performance of the SOAP4IPC engine is evaluated.

Finally, the TiCS Modeler is evaluated by means of an example workflow that describes one step in a production process. It is shown which information is required from the automation engineer and how the internal calculation of the time constraints is realized.

Parts of this chapter have been published in [146, 147, 150, 151, 152].

9.2 SOAP4PLC

9.2.1 Qualitative Evaluation

In this section, it is demonstrated that web service based access to the manufacturing layer is technically feasible by using the SOAP4PLC engine. For this purpose, an experimental setup is realized that uses a PLC to move a carriage from left to right and vice versa on an axis. This functionality is exported as a web service with several operations using SOAP4PLC.

Sample Application

Figure 9.1 outlines the automation example that consists of three main components:

1. an one-dimensional axis on which a carriage is installed (the carriage can be moved from left to right and vice versa)

2. a PLC that controls the movement of the carriage

3. a lamp

The PLC used for control has two physical inputs `in1` (triggers new positioning of the carriage) and `in2` (defines the new position) and one physical output `out1` (lamp for signaling that new position has been reached).

Figure 9.2 shows a conventional PLC control program for the example. The program POU `Axis` is implemented using the IEC 61131-3 function block diagram. The POU consists of one instance of the function block `TON` named `tonPos` and one instance of the function block `FBAxisControl` named `axisControl`. `TON` implements an on-delay timer, i.e. on a rising edge on its input `IN` it delays for the time given on input `PT`. The POU `tonPos` between `in1` and the input `startPositioning` of `axisControl` realizes a delay of 500 msec to assure that the analog value on `in2` has a stable state when the process starts. After the delay the output `Q` becomes `TRUE`. The function block `FBAxisControl` controls the axis. On a rising edge on `startPositioning`, it moves the carriage to the position given on `newPosition`. While the positioning is

9.2 SOAP4PLC

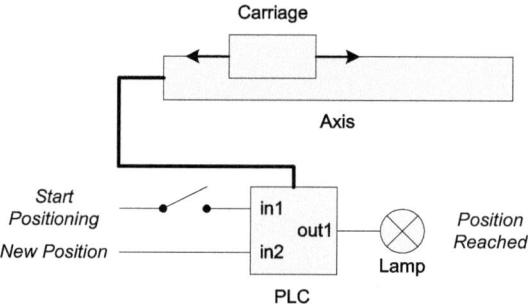

Figure 9.1: Carriage movement using a PLC.

active, the output `ready` is `FALSE`. When the new position has been reached, `FBAxisControl` sets `ready` to `TRUE`. The program POU `Axis` in Figure 9.2 uses the physical input `in1` of the PLC to start a new positioning process. The physical input `in2` takes the new position for the carriage. The physical output `out1` signals the state of the axis since it is connected to `ready` of `axisControl`.

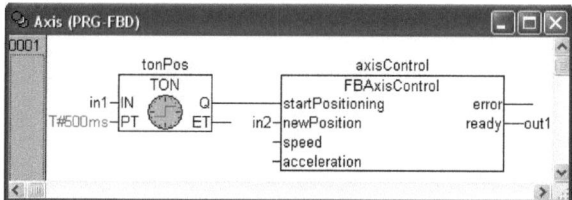

Figure 9.2: A PLC control program for carriage movement.

The program POU `Axis` is attached to a PLC task of the PLC application. The PLC task executes the attached POU cyclically with a defined interval time. In every cycle all concerned functions blocks (`tonPos` and `axisControl`) are executed to read their inputs, do some processing and write their outputs.

This sample application has been realized using the SOAP4PLC engine to export the carriage movement functionality as web service.

Experimental Setup

Figure 9.3 shows a photography of the test installation consisting of:

(1) a PLC (based on Beck IPC@CHIP SC143 [11])

(2) a servo controller (Festo SEC-AC-305-PB [21])

(3) a toothed belt axis (Festo DGE-ZR)

The carriage will be driven by a high voltage servo motor. The servo controller that manages the power supply is connected to the PLC via Profibus [33]. The software that realizes the control has to verify the accurate function of the whole device permanently and must stop the carriage and switch-off the power supply if an exception occurs to avoid damages to the hardware.

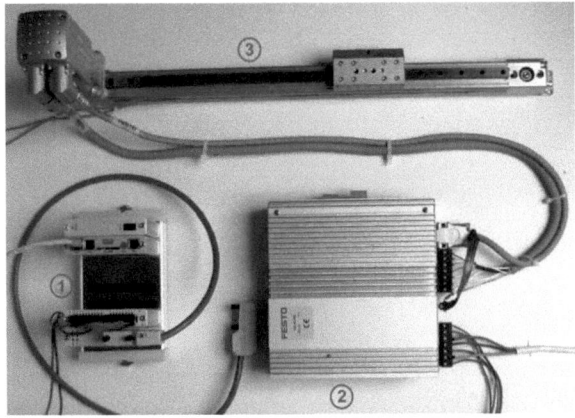

Figure 9.3: Overview of the experimental setup.

The control software is implemented as a PLC application. The axis control is encapsulated in a function block called **SEC_AC**. The function block contains several inputs and outputs to control the axis and to determine its current state. Some of these inputs and outputs will be controlled by SOA function blocks to permit control of the carriage using web services. Figure 9.4 shows a

9.2 SOAP4PLC

screenshot of the CoDeSys development environment with the PLC application code.

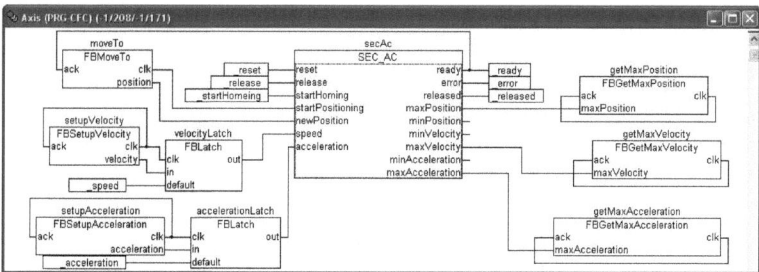

Figure 9.4: Web service enabled carriage control application.

To move the carriage, the inputs `startPositioning` and `newPosition` are used. First, the new position is defined using `newPosition`. After that, the boolean input `startPositioning` has to go from `FALSE` to `TRUE` (high edge triggered). When `SEC_AC` has recognized the high edge, the output `ready` becomes `FALSE` and the positioning process starts. When the new position has been reached, the output `ready` becomes `TRUE` again.

The positioning process using a web service is provided by the SOA function block `FBMoveTo`. `FBMoveTo` consists of a chipselect-out (`clk`), a chipselect-in (`ack`) and an integer output (`position`). When the corresponding web service invocation arrives, chipselect-out is set to high level and the positioning process is triggered via `startPositioning`. When the positioning process has been finished, a high edge on the `ready` output of `SEC_AC` acknowledges this to the web service via the chipselect-in of `FBMoveTo`. `FBMoveTo` is accessible via the operation `moveTo` of the web service `Axis`.

Besides the operation `moveTo`, the PLC application supports further web service operations. Two of them—the function blocks `FBSetupVelocity` and `FBSetupAcceleration`—support the configuration of the carriage's velocity and acceleration. Their outputs (`velocity` respectively `acceleration`) are connected to the corresponding inputs of `SEC_AC`. To buffer the input value for `velocity` and `acceleration`, a latch is used. This is required since the ouput of the `FBSetupVelocity` and `FBSetupAcceleration` is only valid during the corresponding web service invocation.

The last three web service operations return the values of the outputs `max-Position`, `maxVelocity` and `maxAcceleration` of `SEC_AC`. Thus, the outputs are connected to the corresponding function blocks' inputs.

All SOA function blocks' chipselect-outputs except for those of `FBMoveTo` are connected to their own chipselect-inputs, i.e. the web service operations are returning immediately.

9.2.2 Quantitative Evaluation

The quantitative evaluation of the SOAP4PLC engine was realized on an IPC@CHIP PLC similar to the one used for the qualitative evaluation in the previous section. To derive a deadline for a service, three steps are necessary:

1. determine the latency introduced by the engine

2. determine the worst-case execution time of each service

3. calculate the deadline

These steps are exemplified in the following by means of three simple web services: `EchoService`, `PowService`, and `MathService`. The `EchoService` offers an operation `echo` that takes a plain string as input parameter and immediately returns this string as return parameter. The `PowService` takes the three input parameters `basis`, `exponent`, and `cnt`, calculates $cnt \cdot basis^{exponent}$, and subsequently returns `"Done!"`. The `MathService` offers the operations `add` that returns the sum of its two input parameters and `sub` that returns the difference of the two input parameters.

Profiling Step I

The latency L to invoke a web service depends on the complexity of the target web service. The more operations a web service offers or arguments are required, the higher is the latency introduced by the engine. As a consequence, the latency has to be measured individually for each deployed web service. To

9.2 SOAP4PLC

achieve statistical significance, the measurements were repeated 10,000 times. For the three example services, the *maximum* measured latencies are identical:

$$L\,(\texttt{EchoService}) = 1.8\,\text{msec}$$
$$L\,(\texttt{MathService}) = 1.8\,\text{msec}$$
$$L\,(\texttt{PowService}) = 1.8\,\text{msec}$$

Profiling Step II

In general, the execution of a web service S by the SOAP4PLC engine consists of two steps:

1. transferring the input parameters from the SOAP request message to the SOA function block

2. waiting for results from the SOA function block and transferring the results to the SOAP response message

The worst-case execution time wcet of both steps is deduced from the cycle time t_{cycle} of the PLC task that processes the corresponding SOA function block. For the first step, the engine needs to wait until the PLC task is in a valid state for parameter transmission—this occurs once in every cycle. For the second step, the engine waits until the SOA function block signals that the result of the target operation is available. The required time for this step is defined by the number of cycles (#cyc) needed to process the service. Consequently, the worst-case execution time is defined as in Equation (9.1).

$$\text{wcet}\,(S) := 1 \cdot t_{\text{cycle}} + \#\text{cyc} \cdot t_{\text{cycle}} = (1 + \#\text{cyc}) \cdot t_{\text{cycle}} \tag{9.1}$$

In this experimental setup, the SOA function blocks of the services are implemented in a PLC task with 10 msec cycle time. The `EchoService` and the `MathService` require only 1 cycle to be processed. The number of cycles required by the `PowService` depends on the `cnt` argument.

$$\text{wcet}\,(\texttt{EchoService}) = 1 \cdot 10\,\text{msec} + 1 \cdot 10\,\text{msec} = 20\,\text{msec}$$
$$\text{wcet}\,(\texttt{MathService}) = 1 \cdot 10\,\text{msec} + 1 \cdot 10\,\text{msec} = 20\,\text{msec}$$
$$\text{wcet}\,(\texttt{PowService}) = 1 \cdot 10\,\text{msec} + \texttt{cnt} \cdot 10\,\text{msec} = (1 + \texttt{cnt}) \cdot 10\,\text{msec}$$

Deadline Calculation

The deadline D of a web service is the worst-case delay between the request and the corresponding response, i.e. the sum of the latency and the worst-case execution time. Using the results of profiling step I and profiling step II, the deadline can be calculated. This results in the following deadlines:

$$D\,(\texttt{EchoService}) = L\,(\texttt{EchoService}) + \text{wcet}\,(\texttt{EchoService}) = 21.8\,\text{msec}$$
$$D\,(\texttt{MathService}) = L\,(\texttt{MathService}) + \text{wcet}\,(\texttt{MathService}) = 21.8\,\text{msec}$$
$$D\,(\texttt{PowService}) = L\,(\texttt{PowService}) + \text{wcet}\,(\texttt{PowService}) =$$
$$1.8\,\text{msec} + (1 + \texttt{cnt}) \cdot 10\,\text{msec}$$

Test Run

By means of a test run of the `EchoService`, it is demonstrated that the calculated deadlines are met by the SOAP4PLC engine. Therefore, monitoring code was added at important locations (called test points) of the SOAP4PLC engine. The first test point records the time stamp of incoming SOAP requests. The second test point records the time stamp of the corresponding SOAP responses. The difference between these two time stamps represents the time needed by the service. A third test point records the time stamp when the PLC task was triggered. This allows to measure the PLC task jitter while service processing, i.e. the time when the PLC task is triggered within the cycle time (since the PLC task is configured with 10 msec cycle time, the task has to be triggered once within every 10 msec interval). Figure 9.5 shows the measured values of the first 10,000 msec of the `EchoService` test. The service consumer starts to send SOAP requests after 2,000 msec from test beginning.

9.3 SOAP4IPC

The lower graph shows the PLC task jitter. The worst-case jitter is 3 msec, which does not violate the 10 msec task cycle. The scatterplot above represents the execution time of processed invocations. All requests are processed within the calculated deadline.

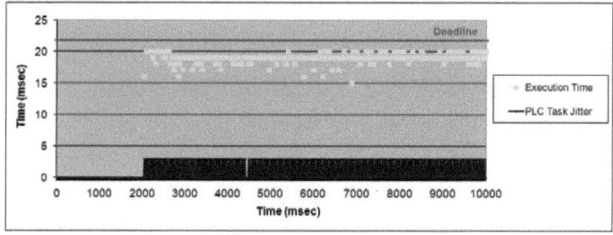

Figure 9.5: Test run of the `EchoService` on the SOAP4PLC engine.

9.3 SOAP4IPC

Bringing the SOAP4IPC engine into service usually takes 4 steps:

1. selecting an appropriate real-time operating system
2. profiling of the overhead introduced by the engine
3. profiling of the worst-case execution time of each web service operation
4. calculating deadlines

This section exemplifies the steps above by means of the `EchoService`, the `PowService`, and the `MathService` that were already used for the performance evaluation of the SOAP4PLC engine in the previous section.

The overhead of the SOAP4IPC engine profiled in step 2 obviously depends on the concurrency level, i.e. the number of concurrent workers as defined in the engine configuration. The more workers may run concurrently, the higher is the engine overhead. In addition, the engine overhead is determined by the hardware used. The worst-case execution time for each service profiled in step

3 depends on the input parameters. Therefore, this profiling step must reflect realistic operation conditions. Only if both profiling steps are performed under conditions similar to live operation, a realistic deadline for each operation can be calculated.

9.3.1 Real-Time Operating System

The SOAP4IPC engine requires a real-time operating system to guarantee the profiled deadlines. In this evaluation, two different real-time operating systems were used: Ubuntu Studio v8.04 [49] and QNX Neutrino v6.3.2 [34]. Ubuntu Studio is an open-source Linux distribution optimized for the multimedia processing domain. Therefore, Ubuntu Studio offers a real-time kernel (v2.6.24-16-rt in the experimental setup) by default. QNX Neutrino is a micro-kernel operating system offering preemptive thread-based scheduling and mechanisms for priority inversion avoidance to permit hard real-time processing. The use of Ubuntu Studio in combination with JamaicaVM v3.0 (Release 45) reveals two important problems:

- The engine requires round-robin scheduling for threads of the same priority. More precisely, round-robin scheduling is required for the concurrent processing of invocations by several worker threads to guarantee a fair processing of invocations. Although JamaicaVM offers round-robin scheduling, the mapping of the virtual machine's internal scheduling strategy to the operating system's native scheduling strategy fails.

- The mapping of priorities of engine threads to priorities of operating system threads fails. The priority map parameter (`priMap`) of the JamaicaVM builder tool is completely ignored under Ubuntu Studio. Each thread within the engine is mapped to an operating system thread with standard priority. Therefore, threads within the engine cannot be prioritized, and the entire engine is not executed with real-time priority. This may result in violation of time constraints.

In Listing 9.1, a process state dump of engine threads under Ubuntu Studio is shown. The scheduling strategy for each engine thread is time sharing

9.3 SOAP4IPC

(column 3), whereas the priority of each engine thread is 19 (column 4). As a result of these problems, the use of Ubuntu Studio in combination with SOAP4IPC was not further evaluated.

Listing 9.1: Thread scheduling and priorities within Ubuntu Studio.
```
tics@laptop:~$ ps -eLc | grep engine
    [...]
    5776  5776 TS  19 pts/0    00:00:00 engine
    5776  5777 TS  19 pts/0    00:00:00 engine
    5776  5778 TS  19 pts/0    00:00:00 engine
    5776  5779 TS  19 pts/0    00:00:00 engine
    5776  5780 TS  19 pts/0    00:00:00 engine
    5776  5781 TS  19 pts/0    00:00:00 engine
    5776  5782 TS  19 pts/0    00:00:00 engine
    5776  5783 TS  19 pts/0    00:00:00 engine
    5776  5785 TS  19 pts/0    00:00:00 engine
    5776  5786 TS  19 pts/0    00:00:00 engine
    5776  5787 TS  19 pts/0    00:00:00 engine
    5776  5788 TS  19 pts/0    00:00:00 engine
    [...]
tics@laptop:~$
```

These problems do not occur under QNX Neutrino. Listing 9.2 shows a process state dump under QNX Neutrino (details are omitted for simplicity). The thread priority and scheduling strategy are given in the fourth column. Since the priority map parameter prioMap is set to 1...40=161...200, all engine threads are mapped to the native priority range of 161 to 200. The o(ther) flag indicates the scheduling strategy, which means round-robin under QNX Neutrino.

Listing 9.2: Thread scheduling and priorities within QNX Neutrino.
```
# pidin | grep engine
    [...]
    581674     5 ./engine        199o [...]
    581674     6 ./engine        199o [...]
    581674     7 ./engine        199o [...]
    581674     8 ./engine        161o [...]
    581674     9 ./engine        170o [...]
    581674    10 ./engine        161o [...]
    581674    11 ./engine        197o [...]
    581674    12 ./engine        197o [...]
    581674    13 ./engine        198o [...]
    581674    14 ./engine        180o [...]
```

```
[...]
#
```

RT_PREEMPT Patch

To avoid the use of a commercial real-time operating system, it is also possible to run the SOAP4IPC engine under the freely available Real-time Linux [35]. In general, *Real-time Linux* is a conventional Linux distribution extended by the RT_PREEMPT patch. The RT_PREEMPT patch extends a vanilla (standard) Linux kernel to a completely preemptible kernel. A preemptible kernel guarantees a maximum interrupt latency, i.e. a maximum time to call an interrupt handler for an occurred interrupt, and therefore a maximum context switching time for threads (thread latency). A maximum thread latency permits to estimate the maximum execution time of an application for a given payload. After successful installation of the preemptible kernel, a benchmark of the environment helps to determine the maximum thread latency. For comparability reasons, a standard benchmark like `cyclic-test` or `preemption-test` should be used [35]. To guarantee that actually the maximum thread latency is measured, the system should be heavily utilized. A generator for artificial load is, for example, `lookbusy` [29] or `stress` [41].

For example, if a vanilla kernel v2.6.23.11 patched with the corresponding RT_PREEMPT patch v2.6.23.11-rt14 is used on an Intel Pentium 4 with 2.8GHz clock frequency and 1GB main memory, a thread latency of $6\,\mu$sec can be achieved. In this experiment, `lookbusy` was used to generate 100% CPU utilization and `cyclic-test` was used to measure the thread latency.

9.3.2 Profiling Step I

The first profiling step measures the overhead introduced by the SOAP4IPC engine, i.e. the maximum latency until an invocation message is processed. This latency depends on the target platform and the number of concurrent workers in the engine.

The target system was a regular desktop PC with an AMD Athlon XP processor with 1,150MHz actual clock speed, 512MB main memory, and a

9.3 SOAP4IPC

3COM 3C905B network adapter running under QNX Neutrino.

2, 4, 6, and 8 concurrent workers to process incoming messages were evaluated. In general, the number of concurrent workers is a trade-off between latency and throughput of SOAP messages. More concurrent workers result in a higher throughput but also in a higher latency, whereas less concurrent workers result in a lower throughput but also in a lower latency.

The maximum latency for each level of concurrency is shown in Figure 9.6. To achieve statistical significance, each experiment was conducted 10,000 times. For example, a concurrency level of two workers merely introduces a *maximum* additional overhead of only 1 msec.

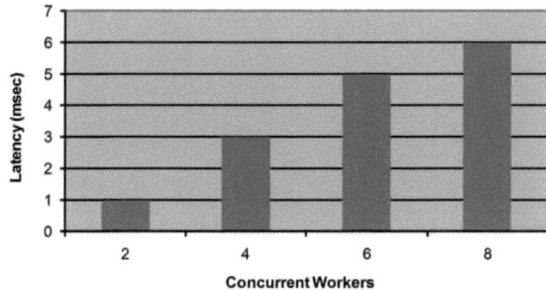

Figure 9.6: Level of concurrency and resulting latency.

9.3.3 Profiling Step II

The second profiling step determines the worst-case execution time for each web service, more precisely for each operation with specific input parameters of each web service. To achieve statistical significance, each experiment was conducted 10,000 times. Table 9.1 and Figure 9.7 show the minimum, maximum, and average execution time, and the standard deviation of the example web service operations in milliseconds. The standard deviation, minimum, and maximum values show that the execution time of each operation does not vary much, i.e. the average execution time is very stable, and the engine works nearly deterministically.

Table 9.1: Evaluation of execution time for each operation.

Operation	Min (msec)	Max (msec)	Avg (msec)	Dev (msec)
echo	53.991	63.991	59.364	2.873
pow	88.986	99.985	94.666	2.907
add	55.991	65.990	61.362	2.860
sub	55.991	65.990	61.157	2.900

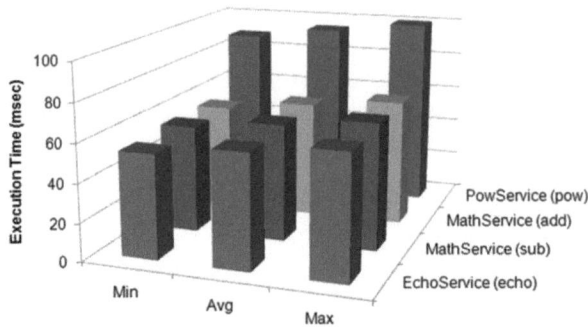

Figure 9.7: Execution time for each service operation.

9.3.4 Deadline Calculation

The results of both profiling steps are written to profiling.dat. For each operation of each web service, profiling.dat contains a line of the structure service.operation=profiling-max, whereas the *maximum* profiled execution time was selected for deadline calculation. Since 3 worker threads were used and the worst-case execution time of the EchoService is 64 msec, the calculated deadline is 201 msec[1].

---
[1] The deadline of 201 msec is only valid, if no other services are deployed.

9.3 SOAP4IPC

9.3.5 Test Run

After both profiling steps and the deadline calculation have been performed, all information necessary for productive operation are available. By means of the EchoService it is shown that the calculated deadlines are met. Therefore, 3 concurrent consumers invoke the echo operation 3,333 times with a 10-character string. The engine is parameterized to use three concurrent worker threads to process incoming messages. Figure 9.8 shows the execution time for each invocation and the calculated deadline. The resulting scatterplots depend on the number of concurrently processed invocations, i.e. the lower scatterplot represents one, the middle scatterplot represents two, and the upper scatterplot represents three concurrently processed invocations.

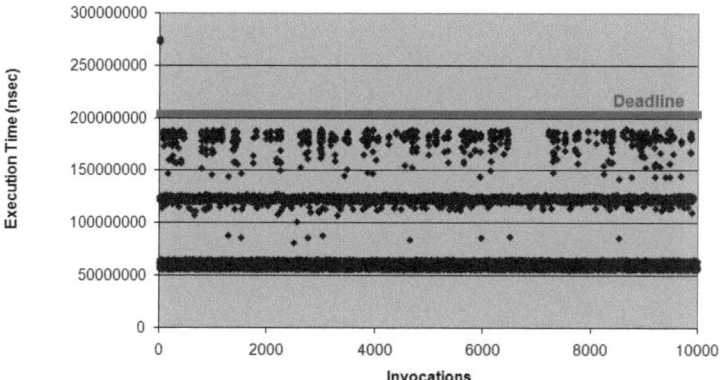

Figure 9.8: Execution times during test run.

Once the engine is shut down, the statistical information shown in Listing 9.3 is output. Three invocations exceeded their deadline (0.03% of all invocations). The deadline violations are caused by class loading if a web service/operation is invoked for the first time. To avoid these deadline violations, the engine may use "dummy" invocations at startup time to trigger class loading.

Listing 9.3: Statistical information of the test run.

```
PROFILING INFORMATION

  Total processed tasks:      9999
     Invocation tasks:        9999 (0.03% exceeded deadline!)
     WSDL tasks:              0 (0.00%)
     Fault tasks:             0 (0.00%)

     Average processing time: 106205852 nanosec
     Standard deviation:      36067708 nanosec
     Min. processing time:    54991000 nanosec
     Max. processing time:    274958000 nanosec
```

9.3.6 Deadline Violation

To provoke deadline violations, the `echo` operation was invoked 100 times, each time with a string with increasing length. As soon as the actual string length exceeds the profiled string length, the `echo` operation violates its deadline profiled before. The SOAP4IPC engine recognizes these deadline violations and dumps the corresponding `Task` objects to the console (cp. Listing 9.4). Figure 9.9 shows the execution times for each invocation of the `echo` operation and marks all invocations that violate the deadline.

Listing 9.4: Example output for deadline violations.

```
[...]
Task@96fe3c0:  63991000
Task@96d5800:  66990000
Task@96b8be0:  63990000
Task@969bce0:  Deadline exceeded!
Task@969bce0:  70990000
Task@967e980:  63991000
Task@96610a0:  Deadline exceeded!
Task@96610a0:  71989000
Task@9643460:  63990000
Task@9625340:  Deadline exceeded!
Task@9625340:  72989000
[...]
```

9.4 TiCS Modeler

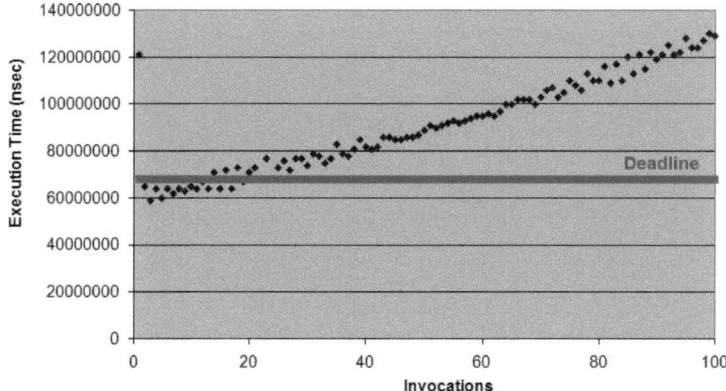

Figure 9.9: Examples for wcet violations.

9.4 TiCS Modeler

This section evaluates the TiCS Modeler by means of an example. More precisely, the TiCS Modeler is used to design a time-constrained workflow for a manufacturing process. The example shows in detail which information must be provided by the automation engineer and how the TiCS Modeler calculates the average and worst-case execution time step by step.

Consider a manufacturing process that consists of n independent production steps. In each step, the processing may be successful or erroneous depending on the result of the manufacturing device. If the addressed device does not signal success or failure within a process-specific deadline, it is assumed that a non-recoverable error has occured, and the entire process has to be halted. A generic example for a processing step within such a manufacturing process is shown in Figure 9.10.

A processing step is modeled as a **sequence** activity with several subactivities. The **sequence** starts with a **receive** activity that is used to wait for an incoming message that triggers this processing step. Subsequently, an **invocation** activity is used to asynchronously trigger the service that actu-

Figure 9.10: A generic workflow for a step within a production process.

ally implements this processing step. To wait for several incoming messages simultaneously for a maximum duration, the `pick` activity is used. Depending on the event (arrival of a success message, arrival of an error message, or timer expiration), different actions may occur:

- If a success message arrives, the workflow invokes an operation at the overall manufacturing process to signal successful processing.

- If an error message arrives, the `pick` activity logs the error by invoking a system logger service and reports the error to the overall manufacturing workflow.

- If neither a success nor an error message arrives within the predefined duration, an alarm goes off. Within this alarm, several activities can be specified to react to the deadline violation. To avoid threats to life or physical condition of a production worker and damages to the manufacturing device, the entire manufacturing process is immediately halted by invoking a corresponding shutdown web service. Afterwards, the missed deadline is logged by invoking the system logger service and the error is

9.4 TiCS Modeler

reported to a control room which permits human-in-the-loop processing.

To calculate the average and worst-case execution time of the given example workflow, the formulas of Section 5.3 are used. Equation (9.2) and Equation (9.3) exemplify the successive calculation of the average and worst-case execution time.

$$
\begin{aligned}
&\text{aet}(\texttt{ProcessingStepN}) = \\
&\quad \text{aet}(\texttt{Receive}) + \text{aet}(\texttt{InvokeProcessing}) + \text{aet}(\texttt{Pick:ProcessingResult}) = \\
&\quad \text{aet}(\texttt{Receive}) + \text{aet}(\texttt{InvokeProcessing}) + \text{duration} + \max_{i \in \{1,2\}}\{\text{aet}(\text{activity for msg}_i)\} = \\
&\quad \text{aet}(\texttt{Receive}) + \text{aet}(\texttt{InvokeProcessing}) + \text{duration} + \\
&\quad \max\{\text{aet}(\text{activity for }\texttt{SuccessMessage}), \text{aet}(\text{activity for }\texttt{ErrorMessage})\} = \\
&\quad \text{aet}(\texttt{Receive}) + \text{aet}(\texttt{InvokeProcessing}) + \text{duration} + \\
&\quad \max\{\text{aet}(\texttt{InvokeStepSuccessful}), \\
&\quad (\text{aet}(\texttt{InvokeSystemFailureLogger}) + \text{aet}(\texttt{InvokeStepFailed}))\}
\end{aligned}
$$
(9.2)

$$
\begin{aligned}
&\text{wcet}(\texttt{ProcessingStepN}) = \\
&\quad \text{wcet}(\texttt{Receive}) + \text{wcet}(\texttt{InvokeProcessing}) + \text{wcet}(\texttt{Pick:ProcessingResult}) = \\
&\quad \text{wcet}(\texttt{Receive}) + \text{wcet}(\texttt{InvokeProcessing}) + \text{duration} + \\
&\quad \max_{i \in \{1,2\}}\{\text{wcet}(\text{activity for msg}_i)\} = \\
&\quad \text{wcet}(\texttt{Receive}) + \text{wcet}(\texttt{InvokeProcessing}) + \text{duration} + \\
&\quad \max\{\text{wcet}(\text{activity for }\texttt{SuccessMessage}), \text{wcet}(\text{activity for }\texttt{ErrorMessage})\} = \\
&\quad \text{wcet}(\texttt{Receive}) + \text{wcet}(\texttt{InvokeProcessing}) + \text{duration} + \\
&\quad \max\{\text{wcet}(\texttt{InvokeStepSuccessful}), \\
&\quad (\text{wcet}(\texttt{InvokeStepFailed}) + \text{wcet}(\texttt{InvokeSystemFailureLogger}))\}
\end{aligned}
$$
(9.3)

The TiCS Modeler needs several information from the automation engineer to calculate the average and worst-case execution time using Equation (9.2) and Equation (9.3). First of all, the send (snd) and receive (rcv) functions for average and worst-case execution time have to be defined. Figure 9.11 shows the use of a linear function $f(x) = mx + b$ to describe the send and receive performance of the BPEL4WS engine. Using another BPEL4WS engine will supposably result in different functions, but with the TiCS Modeler arbitrary formulas can be used. The rest of the configuration is omitted because it is irrelevant for the example.

Figure 9.11: Part of the engine configuration: configuring snd and rcv functions.

The next step is the specification of the real-time constraints applying to the process, as shown in Figure 9.12. The worst-case execution time is defined as 6 sec, whereas the average execution time is defined as 5 sec. Such constraints may also be applied to all structured activities, i.e. the Pick:Processing-Result, OnSuccessMessage, OnErrorMessage, and OnAlarm activities. Since the ProcessingStepN activity is the root-level activity of the process, the time constraints for this activity and for the entire process are identical.

The last and most important step is the specification of relevant parameters for each activity in the process. Figure 9.13 shows the parameters of the InvokeSystemFailureLogger activity that have to be defined by the automation engineer, namely the expected data volume and the expected web service

9.4 TiCS Modeler

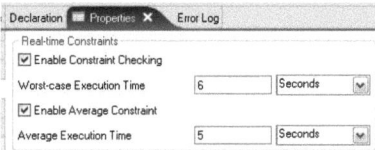

Figure 9.12: Setting the real-time constraints for the process.

execution time. In this example, the outgoing message (600 byte) contains the logging information and therefore is longer than the incoming reply message (350 byte). The execution time of the web service is considered to be constant (average: 200 msec, worst-case: 300 msec). Of course, the automation engineer may choose an arbitrary function (e.g. linear or quadratic) to describe the web service execution time, similar to the engine configuration shown in Figure 9.11.

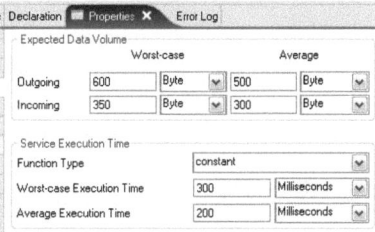

Figure 9.13: The data volume and the execution time for InvokeStepFailed.

The parameters for all other activities are given in Table 9.2. For the InvokeStepSuccessful and InvokeStepFailed activities, outgoing and incoming messages are considered having approximately the same length, since there are no large parameters involved. The same message size is considered for the asynchronous InvokeProcessing activity. The former two activities are also considered to have a constant execution time, because they only change a state in the parent process. The duration for the Pick:ProcessingResult activity depends on the actual processing of each step and is also modeled with a priori knowledge of the automation engineer.

Table 9.2: Relevant parameters for the remaining activities.

	worst-case	average
`Receive`		
input data size	350 byte	300 byte
`InvokeProcessing`		
output data size	350 byte	300 byte
`Pick:ProcessingResult`		
duration	5 sec	4 sec
`InvokeStepSuccessful` and `InvokeStepFailed`		
output data size	350 byte	300 byte
execution time (const.)	150 msec	100 msec
input data size	350 byte	300 byte

The `OnAlarm` activity is not relevant for the computation of average and worst-case execution time, since these times are only relevant if the process succeeded. However, the TiCS Modeler permits the definition of a real-time constraint directly on the `OnAlarm` activity. This allows to check the execution time of the error handling procedure, if required.

With the given parameters and derived equations, the execution time of the process can now be calculated, starting with the basic activities. For simplicity, only the calculation of the worst-case execution time is shown here.

$$\text{wcet}(\texttt{Receive}) = \text{rcv}_{\text{wcet}}(350\,\text{byte}) = $$
$$\left(0.00008\,\frac{\text{sec}}{\text{byte}} \cdot 350\,\text{byte} + 0.0375\,\text{sec}\right) = \quad (9.4)$$
$$0.0655\,\text{sec}$$

9.4 TiCS Modeler

$$\begin{aligned}
\text{wcet}\,(\texttt{InvokeProcessing}) &= \text{snd}_{\text{wcet}}\,(350\,\text{byte}) = \\
&\left(0.00008\frac{\text{sec}}{\text{byte}} \cdot 350\,\text{byte} + 0.0075\,\text{sec}\right) = \\
&0.0355\,\text{sec}
\end{aligned} \quad (9.5)$$

$$\begin{aligned}
\text{wcet}\,(&\texttt{InvokeStepSuccessful}) = \\
&\text{snd}_{\text{wcet}}\,(350\,\text{byte}) + 0.15\,\text{sec} + \text{rcv}_{\text{wcet}}\,(350\,\text{byte}) = \\
&\left(0.00008\frac{\text{sec}}{\text{byte}} \cdot 350\,\text{byte} + 0.0075\,\text{sec}\right) + \\
&0.15\,\text{sec} + \\
&\left(0.00008\frac{\text{sec}}{\text{byte}} \cdot 350\,\text{byte} + 0.0375\,\text{sec}\right) = \\
&0.251\,\text{sec}
\end{aligned} \quad (9.6)$$

$$\begin{aligned}
\text{wcet}\,(&\texttt{InvokeStepFailed}) = \\
&\text{snd}_{\text{wcet}}\,(350\,\text{byte}) + 0.15\,\text{sec} + \text{rcv}_{\text{wcet}}\,(350\,\text{byte}) = \\
&\left(0.00008\frac{\text{sec}}{\text{byte}} \cdot 350\,\text{byte} + 0.0075\,\text{sec}\right) + \\
&0.15\,\text{sec} + \\
&\left(0.00008\frac{\text{sec}}{\text{byte}} \cdot 350\,\text{byte} + 0.0375\,\text{sec}\right) = \\
&0.251\,\text{sec}
\end{aligned} \quad (9.7)$$

$$\begin{aligned}
\text{wcet}\,(&\texttt{InvokeSystemFailureLogger}) = \\
&\text{snd}_{\text{wcet}}\,(600\,\text{byte}) + 0.3\,\text{sec} + \text{rcv}_{\text{wcet}}\,(350\,\text{byte}) = \\
&\left(0.00008\frac{\text{sec}}{\text{byte}} \cdot 600\,\text{byte} + 0.0075\,\text{sec}\right) + \\
&0.3\,\text{sec} + \\
&\left(0.00008\frac{\text{sec}}{\text{byte}} \cdot 350\,\text{byte} + 0.0375\,\text{sec}\right) = \\
&0.421\,\text{sec}
\end{aligned} \quad (9.8)$$

$$\begin{aligned}
&\text{wcet}\,(\texttt{OnErrorMessage}) = \\
&\quad \text{wcet}\,(\texttt{InvokeSystemFailureLogger}) + \text{wcet}(\texttt{InvokeStepFailed}) = \\
&\quad 0.421\,\text{sec} + 0.251\,\text{sec} = \\
&\quad 0.672\,\text{sec}
\end{aligned} \qquad (9.9)$$

$$\begin{aligned}
&\text{wcet}\,(\texttt{Pick:ProcessingResult}) = \\
&\quad \max\{\text{wcet}\,(\texttt{OnSuccessMessage}),\text{wcet}\,(\texttt{OnErrorMessage})\} = \\
&\quad \max\{0.251\,\text{sec}, 0.672\,\text{sec}\} = \\
&\quad 0.672\,\text{sec}
\end{aligned} \qquad (9.10)$$

$$\begin{aligned}
&\text{wcet}\,(\texttt{ProcessingStepN}) = \\
&\quad \text{wcet}\,(\texttt{Receive}) + \text{wcet}\,(\texttt{InvokeProcessing}) + \text{wcet}\,(\texttt{Pick:ProcessingResult}) = \\
&\quad 0.0655\,\text{sec} + 0.0355\,\text{sec} + 5\,\text{sec} + 0.672\,\text{sec} = \\
&\quad 5.773\,\text{sec}
\end{aligned}$$

$$(9.11)$$

The results of the TiCS Modeler for the execution time calculation with the given parameters are shown in Figure 9.14. The example process does *not* violate the applied time constraints.

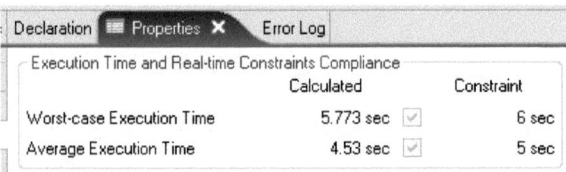

Figure 9.14: The results of the execution time calculation.

9.5 Summary

This chapter has evaluated the performance and usability of the SOAP4PLC engine, the SOAP4IPC engine, and the TiCS Modeler. The SOAP4PLC engine was evaluated by means of an experimental setup that consists of a PLC-controlled carriage. The carriage can be moved from left to right and vice versa using web services. The SOAP4IPC engine was evaluated on two different real-time operating systems (Ubuntu Studio and QNX Neutrino) by means of three example web services. The evaluation has shown that Ubuntu Studio does not work correctly in combination with JamaicaVM. The TiCS Modeler was exemplified and its internal time constraint calculation was shown by means of one step in a manufacturing process.

10
Related Work

10.1 Introduction

This chapter discusses ongoing research in related areas. More precisely, competitive research projects investigating the use of service-oriented architectures in general and web services in particular in industrial automation are discussed. Additionally, technologies related to key components of the TiCS framework are evaluated in detail:

- processing SOAP messages in real-time
- enhancing IPCs and PLCs with a web service interface
- composing time-constrained workflows
- describing time constraints using policies
- transmitting data efficiently within web service environments

Finally, a short view on real-time interconnection networks, data stream processing, and Grid computing is given.

10.2 Service-oriented Architectures in Industrial Automation

There are three major research projects related to the TiCS framework: Service Infrastructure for Real-time Embedded Networked Applications (SIRENA) [38, 103, 135, 136], Industrial Machinery Normalization Process (IMNP) [122, 123, 124, 175], and Service-Oriented Cross-Layer Infrastructure for Distributed Smart Embedded Devices (SOCRADES) [39, 134, 138, 139, 140, 159]. Besides these three, several minor related projects exist. The characteristics of these projects are discussed below.

10.2.1 SIRENA

The *Service Infrastructure for Real-time Embedded Networked Applications (SIRENA)* project [38, 103, 135, 136]—a part of the Information Technology for European Advancement (ITEA) research program—aims at the development of a framework for the integration of heterogeneous, resource-constrained embedded devices from the industrial and home automation, automotive, and telecommunication domains. SIRENA's integration efforts are based on two key assumptions: (1) integration is based on service-orientation, more precisely web services and (2) embedded devices offer enough computing power to process web services.

The SIRENA framework consists of the SIRENA Basic Framework, the SIRENA Framework Enhancements, and the SIRENA Framework Extension Interface. The SIRENA Basic Framework uses the Devices Profile for Web Services (DPWS) [82, 134] to integrate embedded devices (see also Section 10.3.1). The SIRENA Framework Enhancements are a set of tools to ease the development, deployment, integration, and maintenance of devices within a SIRENA-based network. The SIRENA Framework Extension Interface describes the requirements for not SIRENA-enabled devices to be integrated in the SIRENA framework.

SIRENA distinguishes *controlling devices* and *controlled devices* and six interaction patterns between these devices:

10.2 Service-oriented Architectures in Industrial Automation

- **addressing:**
  Each controlling and controlled device is assigned a unique address to enable communication (IPv4 or IPv6 addresses are used).

- **discovery:**
  A controlled device that enters a SIRENA network advertises its services, whereas a controlling device searches for services if it enters a SIRENA network.

- **description:**
  A controlling device requires detailed information about the properties of a controlled device, e.g. offered services, manufacturer, version, or serial number. This metadata is queried by the controlling device, the controlled device answers with a description containing its metadata.

- **control:**
  The controlling device sends a control message to the controlled device to trigger a service. The controlled device may answer with a response message.

- **eventing:**
  Eventing permits asynchronous communication between controlling devices and controlled devices. A controlled device offers events which correspond to its internal state. A controlling device subscribes a specific event. Once a new event is published by a controlled device, each controlling device which has subscribed to this event, receives a notification.

- **presentation:**
  Controlled devices offer a presentation interface, e.g. for maintenance purposes, which permits a status request by controlling devices.

The SIRENA project has run out in September, 2005. As a follow-up project, the *Service-Oriented Device and Delivery Architecture (SODA)* [40, 110] will continue research and development in the device integration area.

The SODA project is currently in the startup phase, no results are published until now.

At first glance, SIRENA shows several similarities to the TiCS framework: embedded devices that can also be PLCs within industrial automation, are interconnected using web services; the SIRENA Framework Enhancements offer tools to integrate devices in SIRENA-based networks, that is comparable with the TiCS tool support layer; web services are processed on the embedded devices (e.g. PLCs) directly, which is also enabled by the SOAP4PLC engine. However, the concrete realization of both frameworks differs. SIRENA only uses a restricted set of web service protocols (the so-called Devices Profile for Web Services (DPWS), see Section 10.3.1), whereas the TiCS framework permits to use the entire web service protocol stack. Even though SIRENA targets the industrial automation domain, it neither offers functionality to handle time constraints (especially real-time constraints) nor functionality to compose several web services to a workflow. Finally, SIRENA only outlines a conceptual blueprint for integration of embedded devices. No prototypical implementation other than the DPWS stack exists.

10.2.2 IMNP

Gilart-Iglesias et al. introduce the *Industrial Machinery Normalization Process (IMNP)* [122, 123, 124, 175]. It defines a service model for industrial machinery with the primary objective to raise abstraction. This normalization process is divided into three steps:

- **physical normalization:**
  The physical normalization step equips an industrial device with communication and computation functionalities via the use of specialized embedded devices.

- **middleware normalization:**
  Within the middleware normalization step, a minimal service container is implemented. It can be used to deploy and invoke services at the industrial machinery. For this purpose, the embedded device implements

10.2 Service-oriented Architectures in Industrial Automation 175

a complete web service protocol stack to enable the deployment and invocation of web services.

- **services normalization:**
  The services normalization step defines all services necessary to expose the industrial machinery's functionality. Gilart-Iglesias et al. distinguish between production, management, and utility services. A production service exposes the core functionality of the industrial device, a management service permits monitoring of the device, whereas the utility services are internally used to access actuators and sensors.

After successful realization of IMNP, an arbitrary industrial device can be accessed directly by the business layer using services. Consequently, IPCs and PLCs are not longer required by using IMNP.

Despite the fact that IMNP and TiCS are fueled by the same vision—arbitrary industrial devices are seamlessly integrated using web services—the focus of both projects differs. TiCS uses an evolutionary approach that integrates manufacturing devices by extending IPCs and PLCs with a web service interface. Consequently, TiCS promises increased protection of investment and acceptance by automation engineers compared to IMNP. Unfortunately, IMNP completely ignores the time constraints of production processes. Although Gilart-Iglesias et al. stipulate provision for real-time constraints during the normalization process, they present no solution to meet this requirement.

10.2.3 SOCRADES

The European Union funded *Service-Oriented Cross-Layer Infrastructure for Distributed Smart Embedded Devices (SOCRADES)* project [39, 134, 138, 139, 140, 159] is based on the principle of collaborative automation and targets three main objectives:

- definition of an architecture for a web service based communication infrastructure within industrial enterprises

- description of web services with agent-interpretable semantic markup to ease their composition

- investigation of existing and development of new wireless communication protocols for the interconnection of embedded devices

SOCRADES divides the industrial enterprise in a device layer, composition layer, middleware layer, and an application layer. The device layer contains web service enabled embedded devices. Since SOCRADES exploits the results of SIRENA, these devices use DPWS (see also Section 10.3.1) to expose web services to the higher layers. The composition layer combines several embedded devices to offer value-added functionality. This functionality is also offered as web services using DPWS. The middleware layer realizes the integration of the device and composition layer with the application layer. The application layer corresponds to the business layer in a traditional industrial enterprise.

The layers of SOCRADES show similarities to the TiCS layers: the SOCRADES device layer resembles the TiCS manufacturing layer whereas the composition and middleware layer of SOCRADES offer similar functionality as the TiCS real-time infrastructural and real-time service layer. An analogon to the SOCRADES application layer does not exist within TiCS. Unfortunately, SOCRADES completely disregards a key requirement of industrial automation: real-time processing. Up to now, SOCRADES completely lacks a prototypical implementation, proof of concept, and evaluation.

10.2.4 Miscellaneous

The European Union funded *End-to-End Quality-of-Service Support Over Heterogeneous Networks (EuQoS)* project [19, 113] is aimed at the design and development of an end-to-end quality-of-service (QoS) assurance system within SOAs. The project focuses on Universal Plug and Play (UPnP) [48] and extends the UPnP QoS architecture to enable layer-3 QoS assurances. Since this project is based on a completely different SOA realization and only best-effort assurances are given, an adoption in the area of web services based industrial automation seems to be difficult.

Kalogeras et al. [137] present a web service based system architecture for the vertical integration within industrial enterprises. This architecture completely lacks the specific real-time requirements within the manufacturing layer and tool support for automation engineers. The TiCS framework presented in this thesis can be used as a technical foundation for this architecture.

Delamer et al. [112] examine the use of event- and service-oriented architectures at the device level. Furthermore, semantic web services are investigated that enable automatic service selection. Timing requirements are completely ignored and therefore it is not applicable within industrial automation.

The European *High Integrity Java Application (HIJA)* project [25, 169] aims at the development of a Java based real-time middleware for embedded systems subject to soft and hard real-time constraints. This middleware contains features that replace the standard Java serialization/deserialization process to support deterministic network communication over appropriate interconnection networks by means of serialization/deserialization templates. HIJA is based on standard Java mechanisms for network communication like Remote Method Invocation (RMI). Since TiCS is based on web services for network communication, a use of HIJA's technologies is not possible.

10.3 Web Services on IPCs and PLCs

The SOAP4PLC and SOAP4IPC engines—two key components of the TiCS framework—permit the processing of web services on PLCs and IPCs, respectively. SOAP4IPC is based on profiling-and-monitoring whereas SOAP4PLC is based on the so-called sequence-controlled web services approach. To the best of the author's knowledge, no comparable engines for industrial automation purposes have been published so far. However, there are several research initiatives to use web services on embedded and resource-constrained devices. The most important initiatives—Devices Profile for Web Services (DPWS) and Web Services for Devices (WS4D)—are discussed in this section.

10.3.1 DPWS and WS4D

The *Devices Profile for Web Services (DPWS)* [82, 179] is a subset of the web service protocol stack—a so-called *web service profile*—tailored to the requirements of resource-constrained devices. The core protocols of DPWS are WS-Discovery, WS-Eventing, WS-MetadataExchange, WS-Transfer, WS-Security, WS-Policy, and WS-Addressing.

WS-Discovery [81] is used to discover web services by means of several multicast messages. The "Probe" message is used by a web service consumer to proactively discover a web service. An appropriate target web service answers with a "Probe Matches" message. A web service provider announces its availability by means of the "Hello" and "Bye" messages. For address resolving purposes, WS-Discovery offers a "Resolve" respectively "Resolve Matches" message. WS-Policy [96] is used to describe the characteristics of a web service in a generic way. WS-Policy defines an "ExactlyOne" element to describe several alternative properties and an "All" element to define several mandatory properties (see also Section 6.3). WS-Eventing [69] permits a publish/subscribe interaction among web services. A web service may subscribe to specific events that are published by event sources. Thereby, a loosely-coupled interaction among web services becomes possible. WS-MetadataExchange [83] and WS-Transfer [90] are used in combination to transfer the metadata of a web service. WS-MetadataExchange defines three request/response message pairs to retrieve the WS-Policy, the WSDL description, and the XML Schema of a specific web service. Therefore, a "GetPolicy", "GetWSDL", and "GetSchema" element are defined by WS-MetadataExchange. WS-Transfer can be used to retrieve all metadata of a web service, i.e. WS-Policy, WSDL description, and XML Schema, in one step. WS-Transfer offers HTTP-like messages for receiving ("Get") and sending ("Put") metadata. WS-Security [84] permits to sign and encrypt parts of or the complete SOAP message. WS-Addressing [87, 88, 95] defines so-called endpoint references and message information headers to identify web service providers and messages exchanged within a web service interaction. WS-Addressing offers a transport-neutral addressing schema, i.e. the addressing of providers and messages does not depend on the underlying transport protocol.

Since DPWS is only a web service profile, the use of DPWS on resource-constrained devices requires an appropriate implementation. Web Services for Devices (WS4D) [51] is a collaborative open-source implementation of the DPWS specification from the University of Rostock and the University of Dort-

10.3 Web Services on IPCs and PLCs

mund. WS4D is offered for three different target platforms respectively programming languages. WS4D-gSOAP permits the implementation of DPWS applications in C and C++ and is based on the gSOAP [24, 174] web service engine. The Java Multi Edition DPWS Stack (JMEDS) permits the implementation of DPWS applications in an arbitrary platform edition of the Java programming language. The Axis 2 edition of WS4D is intended for DPWS implementations on rich clients like regular desktop PCs.

The main focus of DPWS and WS4D is to offer a web service interface for resource-constrained devices. Consequently, DPWS contains only a small subset of all available web service specifications, and implementations of DPWS focus on a small memory footprint. Within industrial automation, a small memory footprint is desirable since PLCs have only less main memory. However, a far important requirement is the processing of web services within predefined deadlines. DPWS does not offer any functionality to describe or keep the deadlines of web services.

The use of WS4D limits the available web service protocols to those defined within DPWS. This a main drawback compared to the TiCS framework. TiCS permits the use of all web services protocols as long as they have been integrated in the SOAP4PLC and SOAP4IPC engines. Consequently, using TiCS, an arbitrary web service application—not only those which use protocols from DPWS—can be processed in real-time.

The use of DPWS requires in-depth knowledge about web service technologies. Additionally, WS4D or comparable implementations also require familiarization by automation engineers. Since DPWS has up to now not been integrated into a typical IEC 61131-3 [65] development environment—in contrast to SOAP4PLC—its use is problematical from an automation engineer's point of view.

10.3.2 Miscellaneous

Helander et al. [132] present a method for programming and controlling distributed tasks based on so-called *behavior patterns*. A behavior pattern is defined by an application and represents its temporal characteristics. It is used to automatically predict and reserve the application's resource requirements. The use of behavior patterns enables to distinguish what is executed and when it is executed, i.e. a separation of application logic and temporal logic is supported. Even though Helander et al. state that their prototypical implementation is based on a real-time SOAP engine, neither a blueprint of the engine nor implementation details are given. A detailed performance evaluation of the SOAP engine is lacking as well.

The *Open Real-Time Linux* project [32] investigates and benchmarks real-time Linux distributions from different vendors. Since the SOAP4IPC engine requires a real-time operating system, the results of this project may be used to select an appropriate real-time Linux distribution.

There are several programming languages for the formal description of the behavior of safety- and time-critical applications, e.g. Timber [102] and Hume [126]. *Hume* consists of three layers: expression layer, coordination layer, and declaration layer. The expression layer is a functional programming language for describing processes and offers bounded time and space behavior. The coordination layer is a finite state programming language that describes the interaction of processes. The declaration layer is used to define functions, values, exceptions, etc. All three layers permit to infer the time behavior of the underlying application. *Timber* is an imperative object-oriented, concurrent, and purely functional programming language and permits the analysis of the timing behavior of an application. Timber offers monadic constructs to define hard real-time properties. Even though both languages offer interesting approaches to automatically infer time behavior, they are not widely-used for the implementation of service-oriented architectures, especially web services.

10.4 Composition of Time-Constrained Workflows

There exists one major competing research project that investigates the composition of several web services to a time-constrained workflow called Grid-Enabled Remote Instrumentation with Distributed Control and Computation

10.4 Composition of Time-Constrained Workflows 181

(GRIDCC). This section illustrates the differences between GRIDCC and the TiCS Modeler and outlines several minor competing research initiatives.

10.4.1 GRIDCC

The European Union funded *Grid-Enabled Remote Instrumentation with Distributed Control and Computation (GRIDCC)* project aims at the integration of arbitrary scientific instruments (e.g. telescopes, particle accelerators, or power stations) into the Grid for conducting experiments [23, 109, 125, 154, 155]. Since scientific experiments normally consist of several steps that have to be realized with respect to several QoS parameters/constraints (e.g. execution time), GRIDCC offers a real-time workflow system for the Grid.

The GRIDCC Workflow Management Service consists of the GRIDCC Workflow Editor, the GRIDCC Workflow Planner, and the GRIDCC Workflow Observer. The GRIDCC Workflow Editor—implemented in ActionScript and Macromedia Flex XML [3]—is a portal-based, visual workflow editor that produces BPEL4WS v1.1 compliant workflow descriptions. The QoS parameters for a workflow are defined in a separate document using XPath [61] expressions. A workflow constraint may be labeled as strict (the constraint is mandatory) or loose (the constraint is optional). The GRIDCC Workflow Planner selects appropriated resources from all currently available Grid resources to execute a workflow. The resources are selected depending on the predefined QoS parameters. The GRIDCC Workflow Observer monitors workflow execution during runtime by means of status calls to the workflow engine. If necessary, the workflow is modified to satisfy its QoS parameters.

There are two fundamental differences between the GRIDCC Workflow Management Service and the TiCS Modeler. The QoS parameter validation in GRIDCC is deferred until runtime, i.e. a scientist designs and subsequently submits the workflow for execution to the Workflow Management Service. The Workflow Management Service validates the QoS parameters and, if necessary, rejects the workflow from execution. The runtime QoS parameter validation may result in numerous design-submission-validation iterations. The TiCS Modeler permits validation of time constraints during design time, which avoids these superfluous iterations. The second fundamental difference between GRIDCC and the TiCS Modeler concerns the selection of resources where web services are executed. In GRIDCC, resources are dynamically selected depending on its utilization and configuration, whereas TiCS selects resources statically. The statical resource selection approach results from the industrial automation domain where services are a priori bound to specific resources. Therefore, dynamic resource selection is not required using TiCS.

10.4.2 Miscellaneous

A formal verification of the timing behavior of orchestrated factory automation web services using the Ontology Web Language for Web Services (OWL-S) [71] is presented by Popescu et al. [158]. The verification is based on timed net condition/event systems. A simple web service is treated as a black box in this verification with a minimum and maximum execution time assigned to it. Since the TiCS Modeler is based on BPEL4WS, the results of this work can only be partially transfered.

Delamer et al. discuss the use of semantic web services for self-orchestration and choreography within manufacturing systems [111]. They also use OWL-S to describe the semantics of a web service and through this permit automatic discovery, invocation, composition, and monitoring of these. The use of semantically annotated web services should avoid the need for manual re-orchestration and should allow for automatic self-orchestration. Self-orchestration in the context of production process control is problematically, since only the automation engineer has in-depth knowledge about the structure of the production process. Consequently, it is almost impossible to re-orchestrate a production process only on the basis of ontologies.

Cambronero et al. [105, 106] use RT-UML [78] to model web services with time constraints. Interaction between web services and relevant time constraints are graphically modeled using RT-UML sequence diagrams and subsequently translated into Web Services Choreography Description Language (WS-CDL) [80] documents. Since the approach of Cambronero et al. has a generic nature, it is also adaptable for the automation domain. Unfortunately,

10.4 Composition of Time-Constrained Workflows

no adequate tool support exists at the moment.

Martinez et al. [145] present a visual web service composition tool based on BPEL4WS called ZenFlow. ZenFlow focuses on the visualization of a workflow by five different views: flow chart view (a graphical representation of the control flow of a business process), form view (a textual representation of the properties of a BPEL4WS activity), text tree view (an tree-like excerpt of the most-relevant BPEL4WS activities), error view (a list of warnings and syntactic errors), free text view (a plain text editor that permits the manual modification of the BPEL4WS code), and execution view (a graphical representation of the workflow execution). The design and implementation of ZenFlow and TiCS Modeler differ significantly: whereas ZenFlow focuses on the visualization of a workflow by different views, the TiCS Modeler permits the assisted orchestration of workflows with time constraints.

Foster et al. [117] present a model-based approach for the formal description of web service interactions. The Labeled Transition System Analyzer (LTSA) permits the specification of web service interactions using message sequence charts, verification of these specifications using labeled transition systems, and generation of orchestration and choreography descriptions using BPEL4WS and WS-CDL. Consequently, a workflow designer never composes a workflow directly using BPEL4WS, but starts with definition and verification of the interaction. An abstraction of the web service composition process permits the formal verification of the web service interaction which is undoubtedly useful in some cases. However, another level of abstraction complicates the composition process for non web service experts additionally. This conflicts with a general requirement of the TiCS framework: usability.

Wassermann et al. [176] describe their implementation of a Business Process Execution Language (BPEL) based environment for visual scientific workflow modeling called Sedna. It consists of a workflow engine based on ActiveBPEL [2] and a visual editor based on the Eclipse [16] platform. To ease the modeling of scientific workflows, the authors introduce several visual abstractions from the BPEL syntax. The visual abstractions are mapped to standard BPEL code so that no modifications to BPEL are necessary. The feasibility of their approach is demonstrated by a real-world example with completely automated workflows from computational chemistry. The authors state that Sedna as an Eclipse plug-in is extensible. However, they do not provide any further interfaces to extend the data model for adaptation to specific application domains. Consequently, an adaptation of Sedna to industrial domain needs is difficult.

In [133], Held et al. present a collaborative BPEL environment based on Web 2.0 technologies. It offers browser-based collaborative workflow modeling using Hobbes, a BPEL design tool running on a central server. The modeling tool features graphical editing of standard BPEL processes with sophisticated locking mechanisms. For this purpose, it holds a process's object model (BPEL object model) in an object tree on the server. Unfortunately, the authors do not provide any information whether the model is extensible or not. The implementation is based on the proprietary Adobe Flex framework that requires the Adobe Flash plug-in to be installed on client machines.

Tsai et al. [173] discuss workflow composition in a pay-per-use service domain. Each service is offered with several execution times and costs, where a lower execution time results in higher costs and vice versa. Workflow composition is determined by the total costs and the overall execution time. Consider a workflow that uses the services $S_1, \ldots, S_n$. Each service is offered at k different quality of service levels, i.e. combinations of execution time and costs. The workflow should be processed taking at most t_{max} execution time and c_{max} costs. Given these constraints, the selection of a QoS level for each service can be optimized with regard to two target parameters: minimization of total costs, minimization of overall execution time. Tsai et al. present a heuristic algorithm to solve this optimization problem. The derived algorithm is not suitable for the industrial automation domain scoped in this thesis, due to two reasons: (1) the presented algorithm is not generally applicable to BPEL4WS as workflow composition language and (2) industrial automation is not a pay-per-use domain since web service provider and web service consumer are located within the same enterprise.

10.5 Description of Time Constraints

This section discusses work and technologies related to the description of time constraints.

Garcia et al. [121] present an approach to ease the selection of a web service based on non-functional properties, especially QoS properties. Their approach is based on WS-Policy [96] and the Ontology Web Language (OWL) [72] to enable a semantics-enriched description of QoS properties, i.e. the intersection of the requirements and capabilities of a web service is eased. The approach of Garcia et al. is not suitable to describe QoS properties that vary over time, such as the response time in contrast to WS-TemporalPolicy.

Sahai et al. [161] introduce the term of an adaptive enterprise that consists of several layers, e.g. infrastructure virtualization layer, web services layer, business process layer, and the business layer. At these layers, policies can be specified using a multitude of languages, e.g. WS-Policy [96], and/or Extensible Access Control Markup Language (XACML) [76]. The authors argue that translation functionality between the different layers (i.e. the different policy languages) is needed. Furthermore, they state that policies usually deal with security, reliable messaging, QoS, privacy, or capabilities and constraints specific to a particular service domain. In contrast to this approach, WS-TemporalPolicy can be used to distinguish layers by means of their static and dynamic nature.

Tian et al. [170] introduce a standardized way to describe QoS parameters for web services that enables the efficient, dynamic, and QoS-aware selection and monitoring of web services. They define a QoS XML Schema which describes QoS offerings and requirements. WS-TemporalPolicy can be applied in a much broader area than only QoS, namely in every area where the management of dynamic properties is important.

Liang et al. [142] introduce a policy framework for managing a customization policy. The service provider declares its customization capabilities. The service consumer proposes a customization request within the scope defined in the policy, receives an updated service description and then invokes the updated service instance. Unlike WS-TemporalPolicy, the customization policy does not provide the management of dynamic properties.

Tosic et al. [172] extend WS-Policy by introducing *WS-Policy4MASC*. They define new types of policy assertions: goal, action, utility, and meta policy assertions. Goal policy assertions specify requirements or guarantees to be met (e.g. response time of an activity). Action policy assertions define actions to be taken as soon as certain conditions are met (e.g. if guarantees were not kept). Examples of these actions are removal, addition, replacement, skipping, and re-running of a sub-process or process termination. Utility policy assertions specify how to bill the execution of an action. Meta-policy assertions are used to specify which action policy assertions are alternatives and which conflict resolution strategy should be used. The policy assertion types do not address the idea of describing dynamic properties. The defined actions are executed in the middleware, so they highly differ from the event/action mechanism for policy management presented in this thesis. WS-TemporalPolicy may be used to add a temporal dimension to each of the different policy assertion types.

The WS-Agreement [85] specification defines the negotiation structure between a service consumer and a service provider to achieve an agreement on how a service is used with respect to service quality, for example. The provider may offer capabilities, the consumer may suggest requirements that the provider can evaluate and then accept or reject. Although WS-Agreement identifies the problem that not all properties of a service can be described statically, it only offers an expiration time for an agreement. No managing capabilities for dynamic properties are provided.

10.6 Efficient Data Transmission in Web Service Environments

This section discusses work related to the efficient transmission of data within web service environments.

Data-Oriented Transfer (DOT) [171] is an approach to transfer bulk data over the Internet, separating content negotiation from data transfer. DOT defines a transfer service that interfaces the application and network layer

10.6 Efficient Data Transmission in Web Service Environments 187

and allows developers to re-use transfer mechanisms in different applications. DOT has a main disadvantage: it completely lacks service-orientation and consequently is not applicably in modern service-oriented environments.

Fox et al. [119] present *NaradaBrokering*, an event brokering system to run a large network of cooperating brokers. The brokers can be organized in clusters, which can be organized in super clusters and so on. Interactions are encapsulated in events; clients can create and publish events and specify their interest in certain types of events. Therefore, NaradaBrokering provides a scalable publish/subscribe system. Furthermore, it can communicate with peer-to-peer (P2P) and Java Message Service (JMS) [44] networks. Intentionally, NaradaBrokering was not designed to work in a service-oriented architecture in contrast to Flex-SwA. Furthermore, NaradaBrokering does not provide different communication patterns for different application areas.

Allcock et al. [99] introduce *GridFTP* (Grid File Transfer Protocol) as a high performance data transfer protocol. GridFTP opens several network connections to efficiently transfer data from one node to another. Since GridFTP is a component of the Globus Toolkit [22], it is not suitable for general use in service-oriented environments. Additionally, it is completely decoupled from the service and thus violates a key characteristic of service-orientation. GridFTP is not very flexible, since data cannot be dynamically transferred after service invocation. However, with *RFT* [36] (Reliable File Transfer) a front-end Grid service that executes GridFTP in background exists. RFT is service-oriented but lacks the flexibility of dynamically transferring data during data production or service execution.

One reason for the bad performance of SOAP is the serialization- and deserialization processes, respectively. Abu-Ghazaleh et al. present an approach named differential serialization [98] that reuses a serialized SOAP message as a template for further messages. Furthermore, an approach to improve deserialization called differential deserialization [97] is proposed by Abu-Ghazaleh et al. This approach is interesting for future versions of the SOAP4PLC and SOAP4IPC engines to further improve their performance.

10.7 Real-time Interconnection Networks

A key requirement for a real-time enabled web service infrastructure is the use of a deterministic interconnection network, deterministic communication protocols, and a deterministic protocol stack implementation.

For example, ethernet and TCP/IP (Transmission Control Protocol/Internet Protocol) predominately used at the business layer offer no deterministic timing behavior. A standard ethernet uses CSMA/CD (Carrier Sense Multiple Access/Collision Detection) as medium access mechanism which may result in arbitrary delays due to collisions. TCP (Transmission Control Protocol), UDP (User Datagram Protocol), and IP (Internet Protocol) do not offer a deterministic timing behavior a priori, but there exist two widespread mechanisms to support at least quality-of-service within IP networks (see Section 10.8): Integrated Services (IntServ) and Differentiated Services (DiffServ). *IntServ* [53] is based on reservation of resources using the Resource Reservation Protocol (RSVP) [59], whereas *DiffServ* [60] classifies IP packets using the type-of-service field within the IP header.

For the use within industrial automation, several deterministic interconnection networks and protocols have been developed, e.g. Profinet. Profinet [33] is an open standard for industrial ethernet that is based on ethernet as the interconnection network and TCP, UDP, and IP as the communication protocols. Profinet offers two modes of operation: Profinet CBA for component-based automation and Profinet IO for fieldbus communication over ethernet. Profinet CBA is an object-oriented approach used for the configuration and operation of large systems that consist of several subsystems of similar type. Profinet IO is used to interconnect IPCs, PLCs, and sensors/actuators. Three different communication modes are distinguished by Profinet—non real-time, real-time, and isochronous real-time—that differ in the network delay guaranteed. Non real-time offers best-effort data transmission based on TCP/IP or UDP/IP (User Datagram Protocol/Internet Protocol), real-time guarantees network delays of 1 msec − 10 msec, and isochronous real-time guarantees network delays less than 1 msec. Additionally, Profinet supports security mechanisms like authentication, data encryption, or logging of security-relevant system events by segmenting the interconnection network in so-called secure automation cells. The network traffic between two cells is checked by specialized security network components.

The timing behavior of interconnection networks and communication protocols is out of scope in this thesis. It is assumed, that the technologies developed within this thesis are used on a completely deterministic network infrastructure.

10.8 Quality-of-Service

The terms real-time and quality-of-service (QoS) are often used synonymously, which is definitely *incorrect*. QoS defines several quality levels at which a service may be offered at different fees. The quality levels and corresponding fees are documented within a service level agreement (SLA). Breaking a SLA will result in financial penalties. QoS with regard to web services includes several aspects of a service, for example performance, reliability, scalability, robustness and exception handling, accuracy, availability, and security [67].

The *performance* of a web service describes how fast a web service invocation can be processed and may be measured in throughput or execution time. The *reliability* of a web service describes the ability to perform its functionality correctly. It can be measured, for example, in failures per hour, day, or week. *Scalability* addresses the adaptability of web services to new operating conditions like increased number of user requests or changes of the hardware infrastructure. A robust web service stays functional even though a part of its input parameters is incorrect or the input parameters are incomplete. An exception within a web service may occur due to several reasons, like erroneous input parameters, programming errors, or problems within the infrastructure used. Potentially occurring exceptions should be handled by the web service. This results in *robustness*. The *accuracy* of a web service describes its error rate, i.e. the produced errors per time unit. A web service should offer a high level of *availability*, i.e. the web service should be ready to use and accessible by potential clients. *Security* spans several aspects: authentication (identification of users), authorization (determining user rights), confidentiality (only authenticated and authorized user may access confidential data), accountability (a web service provider is accountable for the offered web services), traceability and auditability (use of web services is logged), data encryption (all data relevant to a web service is encrypted), non-repudiation (requesting a web service cannot be denied after the fact).

Research in the area of web services and QoS often focus on two aspects: describing QoS properties for web services and selecting the most suitable web service based on its QoS properties [170, 178]. Real-time requires that a web service is processed within a predefined deadline with a focus on enabling technologies, i.e. infrastructural technologies that permit the processing of a web service with time constraints. The technologies developed within this thesis to enhance PLCs and IPCs with time-constrained web service functionality may be also used in the QoS domain to achieve performance, but aspects like reliability, scalability, accuracy, and security are out of scope of this thesis.

10.9 Data Stream Processing Using PIPES

A completely different but promising approach for the integration of the business layer and the manufacturing layer is the use of a *data stream management system* (DSMS) that permits the continuous analysis of and reaction to sensor data collected at the shop floor.

The *Public Infrastructure for Processing and Exploring Streams* (PIPES) [37, 107, 108, 127, 141] provides the essential building blocks for realizing such DSMS by means of a library approach. Internally, PIPES is based on a push-based, time-interval operator algebra that distinguishes sources, sinks, and operators (pipes). An (initial) *source* produces input data that is consumed by a (terminal) *sink*. The interconnection of sources and sinks is realized by *operators*.

The main focus of PIPES is the efficient processing of stream data. Due to its library approach, PIPES can be easily adapted to several application domains, amongst others factory automation. Since the focus of the TiCS framework and the focus of PIPES differ significantly—offering a web service based infrastructure for industrial automation in contrast to efficiently processing stream data collected at the shop floor—both technologies may complement each other. For example, the SOAP4PLC engine or SOAP4IPC engine can be used as (initial) sources providing input data to PIPES.

10.10 Grid Computing

The research problems investigated in this thesis are not only interesting for the industrial automation domain but also for other application domains, e.g. service-oriented Grid computing. Grid computing environments are heterogeneous collections of networked hard- and software components located at different sites and hosted by different organizations. Foster et al. [118] have defined the Grid problem as flexible, secure, coordinated resource sharing among dynamic collections of individuals and institutions. To enable users to access these resources in a convenient manner using standardized interfaces, service-oriented Grid middleware (e.g. Globus Toolkit 4.x [22], gLite [18], or Unicore/GS [50]) provides a stack that implements the Web Services Resource Framework (WSRF) [31] specifications. Typically, service-oriented Grid middleware provides functionality for runtime components, execution and information management, data handling, and security. WSRF defines a Grid service, which—in short—is a normal web service plus state information. Consequently, the invocation of a Grid service is not idempotent but depends on the previous invocations.

Since service-oriented Grid computing is based on the same core functionalities as web services, i.e. WSDL [64, 89] for the description and SOAP [92, 93, 94] for the invocation of services, technologies developed within this thesis can be used within service-oriented Grid computing. For example, the SOAP4IPC engine can be used as a development basis for a Grid service engine that supports time constraints, whereas WS-TemporalPolicy may be used to describe the timing behavior of Grid services.

10.11 Summary

The comparison of TiCS with related research projects like SIRENA, IMNP, or SOCRADES shows several similarities but also fundamental differences. TiCS' main focus is to describe and keep deadlines of web services within the production process. For this purpose, TiCS takes an evolutionary approach that extends IPCs and PLCs with a web service interface, offers technologies to keep time constraints, and empowers automation engineers by several tools to describe and model time-constrained web services and workflows. Figure 10.1 outlines the relation between SIRENA, IMNP, SOCRADES, and TiCS. SIRENA is an early approach to use service-orientation for integration purposes within industrial automation. Consequently, SIRENA lacks a technical realization. The follow-up project SOCRADES offers first prototypical implementations with focus on integration. IMNP and SIRENA also have a visionary character, but no technical realization is provided. TiCS is based on the same vision as SIRENA, IMNP, and SOCRADES but offers a higher level of maturity.

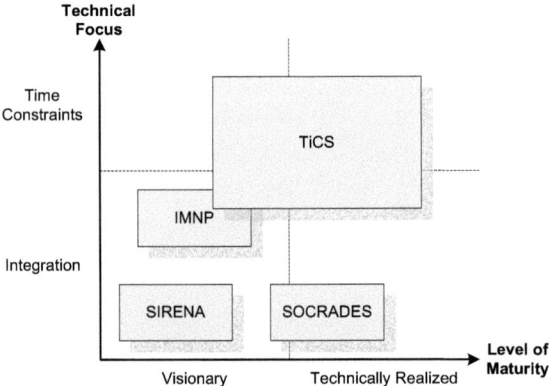

Figure 10.1: TiCS compared with related projects.

SOAP4PLC and SOAP4IPC permit the processing of web services in real-time on PLCs and IPCs, respectively. Only DPWS and its implementation

10.11 Summary

WS4D target the execution of web services on resource-constrained devices like PLCs. However, WS4D offers no functionality to keep use case dependent deadlines. Consequently, SOAP4PLC and SOAP4IPC offer the necessary basic technologies for the TiCS framework as well as related research projects.

In the areas of composition of time-constrained workflows, description of time constraints, and efficient data transmission within web service environments, several related research activities exist. Unfortunately, these activities have a general-purpose character, i.e. are not tailored to the demands of industrial automation, or are based on best-effort approaches which is unacceptable for the industrial automation domain.

In summary, the TiCS framework is the first development and execution framework for **time-constrained web services** focusing on industrial automation published so far.

11
Conclusions and Future Work

11.1 Conclusions

In this thesis, the Time-Constrained Services (TiCS) framework—a framework for the development, deployment, composition, publication, and execution of time-constrained web services and BPEL4WS workflows—was presented. The TiCS framework permits the seamless use of web services as a homogeneous communication backbone in industrial enterprises and leads to a reorganization of the layered architecture of these enterprises. At present, industrial enterprises are organized in three vertical layers—manufacturing, intermediate, and business layer—due to the heterogeneous communication paradigms on these layers. Future industrial enterprises are likely to have only the business layer and the manufacturing layer that are connected via a standardized web service communication backbone. The business processes and the production processes will be defined using web services and workflows and will be seamlessly integrated in the web service communication backbone. This will lead to a vertical integration of the industrial enterprises. At the same time the horizontal integration with suppliers and customers will be improved, since web services are based on standardized protocols. An additional benefit of using web services for inter-enterprise communication is increased flexibility with regard to process reengineering. Multi-step processes are represented using BPEL4WS workflows that contain several web services. Such workflows can be easily adapted to new market conditions. All these benefits of using web services as communication backbone in industrial enterprises come along with one key requirement: real-time processing, i.e. a task is processed prior to a predefined deadline.

The main challenges to use web services as a seamless communication backbone within industrial enterprises have been identified in this thesis:

- The manufacturing layer, more precisely the IPCs and PLCs used at the manufacturing layer for automation purpose, have to be enhanced with a web service interface.

- Since web services will be used to describe production processes, it is necessary that the TiCS framework offers functionality to process a web service invocation in real-time.

- The acceptance of the TiCS framework depends on the availability of tools that ease the implementation, deployment, publication, and invocation of web services.

- Since real-world business and manufacturing processes consist of several steps, the TiCS framework needs a tool that permits the composition of time-constrained web services to time-constrained workflows.

- A suitable mechanism to describe the time constraints of web services and workflows is required.

- The execution of a web service presumes that all relevant input parameters are available. Consequently, an efficient transmission of web service parameters is crucial for real-time processing.

The TiCS framework meets these challenges by several functional components that were designed and implemented during the course of this thesis.

The SOAP4PLC engine enhances PLCs with a web service interface. This permits to call a PLC function by means of a web service invocation.

11.1 Conclusions

SOAP4PLC uses a novel approach to interconnect the cyclic input-processing-output and on-demand processing of PLC functions and web services called sequence-controlled web services. Additionally, SOAP4PLC offers an intuitive user interface that permits the export of a PLC function as a web service.

The processing of web services in real-time on an IPC is realized by the SOAP4IPC engine. SOAP4IPC uses a profiling-and-monitoring approach to guarantee the concurrent processing of several web services in real-time. The core of SOAP4IPC offers a generic design that permits the execution of arbitrary protocols in real-time. The SOAP4IPC engine is implemented in plain Java extended by functionality from the Real-time Specification for Java [47]. For the prototypical implementation, aicas JamaicaVM [4] as real-time JVM and QNX Neutrino [34] as the real-time operating system were used.

The TiCS framework offers several Usability Wizards that assist an automation engineer during the development process. More precisely, TiCS offers a wizard for web service creation, a wizard for web service deployment, and a wizard for web service publishing. These wizards are realized as Eclipse [16] plug-ins.

The TiCS Modeler is a graphical BPEL4WS [100] workflow editor that is tailored to the needs of real-time processing. During the composition of a workflow, the average/worst-case execution time is calculated automatically. The execution time calculation is based on formal derivation of the time constraints of BPEL4WS activities.

For the description of time constraints, a policy language called WS-TemporalPolicy has been developed within this thesis. WS-TemporalPolicy permits to describe the validity period of a WS-Policy [96] or another WS-TemporalPolicy by means of a duration, start and end date, or expiration date. This mechanism can be used to describe time constraints during peak time and during off-peak time. Due to the generic character of WS-TemporalPolicy, it may also be used for the description of arbitrary dynamic web service properties.

The TiCS framework contains Flex-SwA for an efficient transmission of parameters in web service environments. Flex-SwA offers several communication patterns to improve efficiency, e.g. an eager, i.e. immediate, or lazy, i.e.

on-demand, transmission of parameters.

To summarize, the TiCS framework takes the first step towards a completely web service based automation infrastructure and offers the technical foundation to process web services in real-time.

11.2 Future Work

There are several areas for future work to improve the TiCS framework. First of all, some of the components presented in this thesis are only prototypically implemented for proof-of-concept purposes, e.g. the TiCS Usability Wizards. These components have to be extended in later releases of the TiCS framework. Additionally, there are several areas to enhance the functionality of the entire TiCS framework or the functionality of specific components as discussed subsequently.

Security

The TiCS framework is the technical foundation to use web services as the communication backbone within the entire industrial enterprise. IPCs and PLCs are enhanced with a web service interface that permits to access the manufacturing process using plain SOAP messages sent via HTTP. Since the manufacturing process is mission critical for industrial enterprises, i.e. production downtimes are not acceptable, it has to be protected against malicious damage and operating errors. Examples for malicious damage are virus and worm infections of the IT infrastructure or hacker attacks. Operating errors are, for example, a wrongly composed workflow or the invocation of a web service with incorrect input parameters. Consequently, future releases of the TiCS framework must support security with respect to the infrastructure and the user. Infrastructural security may be realized using a specific network topology, e.g. separated business and manufacturing networks coupled via a security gateway, and specific network protocols, e.g. HTTPS instead of HTTP as the transfer protocol. To avoid operating errors, a formal description of the correct system behavior is important. This permits the automatic check and

11.2 Future Work 199

possibly correction of misconfigured web services and workflows.

Real-time BPEL4WS Engine

The execution of a workflow in real-time requires:

1. the execution of each step of the workflow, i.e. each web service, in real-time

2. knowledge about the worst-case execution time of each activity

3. the processing of the workflow description in real-time

The TiCS framework covers the first and second requirement: the SOAP4IPC engine permits the execution of a web service in real-time; the TiCS Modeler calculates the worst-case execution time of a workflow based on a formal derivation of the timing behavior of each BPEL4WS activity. The third requirement is important for future releases of the TiCS framework. The BPEL4WS workflow description generated by the TiCS Modeler must be interpreted in real-time. Consequently, a *real-time BPEL4WS engine* is required. Since the SOAP4IPC engine is built on a general-purpose core that permits the interpretation of an arbitrary protocol in real-time, a real-time BPEL4WS engine can be based on these technologies.

Integration of Flex-SwA and WS-TemporalPolicy in SOAP4PLC

The SOAP4PLC engine offers a web service interface to PLCs. The sequence-controlled web services approach permits to embed a web service in the input-processing-output cycle of a PLC function. In future versions, SOAP4PLC may be extended by the Flex-SwA data transmission component and the WS-TemporalPolicy language.

Improvements to SOAP4IPC

The SOAP4IPC engine uses a profiling-and-monitoring approach to guarantee real-time processing of web services. The profiling step is currently realized manually by the automation engineer, i.e. after deployment of a new web service, the profiling step is triggered by the automation engineer. Future versions of the SOAP4IPC engine should support *auto-profiling* of newly deployed web services, i.e. an automation engineer only has to deploy the web service and the profiling is automatically done.

The SOAP4IPC engine handles deadline violations in a rudimentary way. If a task violates its deadline, an error message is printed to the console. A sophisticated deadline violation handling will be useful, e.g. a task that violates its deadline is aborted prematurely. This will result in more available resources for the remaining tasks.

The use of a Java-enabled microprocessor will additionally improve the performance of the SOAP4IPC engine. Future releases of the TiCS framework may include another SOAP engine for Java-enabled microprocessors in addition to the SOAP4IPC engine. Since most of the available Java-enabled microprocessors like aJ-100 from aJile Systems [5] support the Real-time Specification for Java, porting seems to be technically feasible with minimal effort.

One reason for the poor performance of SOAP for data transfer in general are the serialzation and deserialization of in-memory objects to the SOAP message format. An interesting approach to minimize the serialization/deserialization overhead is presented by Abu-Ghazaleh et al. [97, 98]: differential serialization/deserialization uses a template to speed up the serialization/deserialiazion process. This approach seems to be useful for future versions of the SOAP4IPC engine to additionally improve performance.

Improvements to the TiCS Modeler

The TiCS Modeler requires several parameters to calculate the average and worst-case execution time of a workflow, e.g. a function that describes the performance to send input parameters to a web service and a function that describes the performance to receive return parameters from a web service, respectively. These parameters either depend on the infrastructure (e.g. used BPEL4WS engine) or are provided by the automation engineer due to his/her expert knowledge about the manufacturing process. To further ease the work

11.2 Future Work

of an automation engineer, the TiCS Modeler should support a *testing and production stage* comparable to the profiling and monitoring steps of the SOAP4IPC engine. In the testing stage, all necessary parameters are collected via automated tests, whereas during production stage the automation engineer may modify the offered parameters due to his/her expert knowledge and the current system status.

To permit a more formal analysis of a time-constrained workflow, a transformation of the BPEL4WS workflow into a time Petri net [104, 166] seems to be useful. For this, the internal data model that represents a BPEL4WS workflow has to be extended by another data model that represents a time Petri net. This data model can be used as input for model checkers aware of time Petri nets.

Future versions of the TiCS Modeler will summarize all BPEL4WS engine dependent parameters, e.g. the average and worst-case execution time of the `terminate` activity, in an engine-specific profile. This enables an easy replacement of all these parameters in one step.

Improvements to Flex-SwA

The communication patterns, i.e. execution patterns, data transmission patterns, concurrency patterns, and blocking mode patterns, offered by Flex-SwA focus on a flexible and—compared to SOAP or SOAP Messages with Attachments [62]—efficient transmission of web service parameters. At present, there exists no mechanism to define the average or worst-case transmission time of parameters. Future versions of the Flex-SwA data transmission component should support a real-time communication pattern that supports the description of the transmission time.

List of Abbrevations

aet	Average Execution Time
BPEL	Business Process Execution Language
BPEL4WS	Business Process Execution Language for Web Services
CSMA/CD	Carrier Sense Multiple Access/Collision Detection
CVS	Concurrent Versions System
DAVO	Domain-Adaptable Visual Orchestrator
DiffServ	Differentiated Services
DOT	Data-Oriented Transfer
DPWS	Devices Profile for Web Services
DSMS	Data Stream Management System
ERP	Enterprise Resource Planning
FBD	Function Block Diagram
GC	Garbage Collector
GridFTP	Grid File Transfer Protocol
HTTP	Hypertext Transfer Protocol
IEC	International Electrotechnical Commission
IL	Instruction List
IntServ	Integrated Services
IP	Internet Protocol

IPC	Industrial PC	
IPO	Input-Processing-Output	
IPsec	IP Security	
IT	Information Technology	
J2SE	Java 2 Standard Edition	
JMS	Java Message Service	
JVM	Java Virtual Machine	
LD	Ladder Diagram	
MES	Manufacturing Execution System	
MIME	Multipurpose Internet Mail Extensions	
OWL	Ontology Web Language	
OWL-S	Ontology Web Language for Web Services	
PLC	Programmable Logic Controller	
POU	Program Organization Units	
QoS	Quality-of-Service	
RFT	Reliable File Transfer	
RMI	Remote Method Invocation	
RPC	Remote Procedure Call	
RSVP	Resource Reservation Protocol	
RT	Real-time	
RTOS	Real-time Operating System	
RTSJ	Real-time Specification for Java	
SFC	Sequential Function Chart	
SLA	Service Level Agreement	
SOAP	Simple Object Access Protocol (outdated)	

LIST OF ABBREVATIONS

SSH	Secure Shell
SSL	Secure Sockets Layer
ST	Structured Text
SVN	Subversion
SwA	SOAP Messages with Attachments
SWT	Standard Widget Toolkit
TCP	Transmission Control Protocol
TCP/IP	Transmission Control Protocol/Internet Protocol
TiCS	Time-Constrained Services
TLS	Transport Layer Security
UDDI	Universal Description, Discovery, and Integration
UDP	User Datagram Protocol
UDP/IP	User Datagram Protocol/Internet Protocol
UML	Unified Modeling Language
UPnP	Universal Plug and Play
URL	Uniform Resource Locator
wcet	Worst-Case Execution Time
WS	Web Service
WS-CDL	Web Services Choreography Description Language
WS4D	Web Services for Devices
WSDL	Web Service Description Language
WSFL	Web Services Flow Language
WSRF	Web Services Resource Framework
XACML	Extensible Access Control Markup Language
XML	Extensible Markup Language

LIST OF ABBREVATIONS

List of Figures

1.1	Real-time utility function.	3
1.2	Structure of a hierarchical production process.	4
1.3	Organizational layers of today's industrial enterprises.	7
1.4	Third industrial automation generation.	9
2.1	Architectural blueprint of the TiCS framework.	21
2.2	Smart devices at the manufacturing layer.	22
2.3	Using a SOAP engine for PLCs.	23
2.4	Using a SOAP engine for IPCs.	24
2.5	Bottom-up approach to define time constraints.	27
3.1	Logical structure of PLC applications.	35
3.2	Separation of concerns by using a web service interface.	37
3.3	Architectural blueprint of the SOAP4PLC engine.	39
3.4	Execution of a web service by means of a SOA function block.	44
3.5	Execution of handler code and SOA function block.	45
4.1	Architectural components of the SOAP4IPC engine.	55
4.2	Execution time of a web service.	56
5.1	Conceptual overview of DAVO's core components.	73
6.1	Dependency tree for several WS-TemporalPolicies and WS-Policies.	81
7.1	An example for a SOAP RPC interaction.	93
7.2	The Flex-SwA protocol stack.	96
7.3	Overview of Flex-SwA communication patterns.	99
7.4	Example of data movement reduction.	101
7.5	Example of simple load balancing using Flex-SwA.	102
8.1	Non real-time garbage collector.	107
8.2	Source code organization of the TiCS framework.	109

8.3	Implementation of SOAP4PLC using an IPC@CHIP PLC.	110
8.4	A simplified `Element` class hierarchy.	125
8.5	The property model of DAVO.	127
8.6	The `Element` extension mechanism.	127
8.7	The `EditPart` type hierarchy.	128
8.8	The `Property` adapter model.	129
8.9	A BPEL4WS translation process using the shadow model.	130
8.10	An example for policy weaving.	137
8.11	Implementation overview of Flex-SwA.	139
9.1	Carriage movement using a PLC.	147
9.2	A PLC control program for carriage movement.	147
9.3	Overview of the experimental setup.	148
9.4	Web service enabled carriage control application.	149
9.5	Test run of the `EchoService` on the SOAP4PLC engine.	153
9.6	Level of concurrency and resulting latency.	157
9.7	Execution time for each service operation.	158
9.8	Execution times during test run.	159
9.9	Examples for wcet violations.	161
9.10	A generic workflow for a step within a production process.	162
9.11	Part of the engine configuration: configuring snd and rcv functions.	164
9.12	Setting the real-time constraints for the process.	165
9.13	The data volume and the execution time for `InvokeStepFailed`.	165
9.14	The results of the execution time calculation.	168
10.1	TiCS compared with related projects.	192

List of Tables

5.1	Basic and structured BPEL4WS activities.	63
6.1	Overview of events concerning WS-TemporalPolicy.	82
6.2	Overview of actions concerning WS-TemporalPolicy.	82
8.1	Excerpt of the engine configuration parameters.	123
9.1	Evaluation of execution time for each operation.	158
9.2	Relevant parameters for the remaining activities.	166

List of Listings

2.1 Annotation for a web service operation with time constraints. . 26
6.1 Example of a WS-Policy using `ExactlyOne`. 78
6.2 Example of a WS-Policy using `All`. 78
6.3 XML Schema for the WS-TemporalPolicy language. 79
6.4 Example of using the `expires` element. 83
6.5 Example of using the `startTime` and `endTime` elements. 83
6.6 A WS-TemporalPolicy that affects other WS-TemporalPolicies. . 84
6.7 Using a WS-Policy to define QoS parameters for peak time. . . 86
6.8 Using a WS-Policy to define QoS parameters for off-peak time. . 87
6.9 A WS-TemporalPolicy for peak time. 87
6.10 A WS-TemporalPolicy for off-peak time. 88
6.11 Using a WS-Policy to define costs for a best-effort deadline. . . 89
6.12 Using a WS-Policy to define costs for a strict deadline. 89

7.1 Example of a MIME multipart/related message. 94
7.2 Example of a Flex-SwA reference. 96

8.1 Dynamic generation of WSDL descriptions. 113
8.2 Calling a PLC function. 116
8.3 Processing logic of the `EntryPoint`. 118
8.4 Example of dependencies.cfg. 119
8.5 Example output of the `SimpleProfiler`. 120
8.6 The `handleAsyncEvent` method of `ShutdownHandler`. 120
8.7 Adding a `OneShotTimer` to a `Task` object. 122
8.8 The implementation of the `IModelExtender` interface. 131
8.9 The `ElementExtender` for plain `Elements`. 132
8.10 The wcet property, that is applied to all `Elements`. 132
8.11 The wcet property, that is applied to all `ConnectedElements`. . 133
8.12 The wcet property, that is applied to all `ContainerElements`. . 134
8.13 The calculator for `flow` activities. 135
8.14 Using the `documentation` element for Flex-SwA. 142

8.15	An extension to WSDL to describe Flex-SwA parameters.	. . . 142
9.1	Thread scheduling and priorities within Ubuntu Studio.	 155
9.2	Thread scheduling and priorities within QNX Neutrino.	 155
9.3	Statistical information of the test run.	 159
9.4	Example output for deadline violations.	 160

Bibliography

[1] 3S – Smart Software Solutions.
http://www.3s-software.com/.

[2] Active Endpoints: ActiveBPEL.
http://www.activevos.com/community-open-source.php.

[3] Adobe Flex 3, Product Homepage.
http://www.adobe.com/products/flex/?promoid=BPDEQ.

[4] aicas: JamaicaVM.
http://www.aicas.com/.

[5] aJile Systems.
http://www.ajile.com/.

[6] Apache Ant, Project Homepage.
http://ant.apache.org/.

[7] Apache Axis 2, Project Homepage.
http://ws.apache.org/axis2/.

[8] Apache Axis, Project Homepage.
http://ws.apache.org/axis/.

[9] Apache Maven, Project Homepage.
http://maven.apache.org/.

[10] Apache Tomcat, Project Homepage.
http://tomcat.apache.org/.

[11] Beck IPC GmbH.
http://www.beck-ipc.com/.

[12] CVS, Project Homepage.
http://www.nongnu.org/cvs/.

BIBLIOGRAPHY

[13] D-Grid: FinGrid.
http://www.d-grid.de/index.php?id=405&L=0.

[14] Eclipse Draw2D, Project Homepage.
http://www.eclipse.org/gef/overview.html.

[15] Eclipse Graphical Editing Framework (GEF), Project Homepage.
http://www.eclipse.org/gef/.

[16] Eclipse, Project Homepage.
http://www.eclipse.org/.

[17] Eclipse Standard Widget Toolkit (SWT), Project Homepage.
http://www.eclipse.org/swt/.

[18] EGEE – Enabling Grids for E-Science, Project Homepage.
http://glite.web.cern.ch/glite/.

[19] End-to-End Quality of Service Support over Heterogeneous Networks (EuQoS), Project Homepage.
http://www.euqos.eu/index.php.

[20] EtherCAT Technology Group: EtherCAT – Ethernet for Control Automation Technology.
http://www.ethercat.org/.

[21] Festo AG & Co. KG.
http://www.festo.com/.

[22] Globus Toolkit, Project Homepage.
http://www.globus.org/toolkit/.

[23] Grid-Enabled Remote Instrumentation with Distributed Control and Computation (GRIDCC), Project Homepage.
http://www.gridcc.org/.

[24] gSOAP: C/C++ Web Services and Clients, Project Homepage.
http://www.cs.fsu.edu/~engelen/soap.html.

[25] High-Integrity Java Application (HIJA), Project Homepage.
http://www.hija.info/.

[26] IBM developerWorks: Which style of WSDL should I use?
http://www.ibm.com/developerworks/webservices/library/ws-whichwsdl/.

BIBLIOGRAPHY

[27] IBM WebSphere Application Server, Product Homepage.
http://www-01.ibm.com/software/webservers/appserv/was/.

[28] jetty, Project Homepage.
http://jetty.mortbay.com/jetty-6/.

[29] lookbusy – A Synthetic Load Generator, Project Homepage.
http://devin.com/lookbusy/.

[30] NetBeans, Project Homepage.
http://www.netbeans.org/.

[31] OASIS: Web Services Resource Framework 1.2 (WSRF).
http://www.oasis-open.org/committees/tc_home.php?wg_abbrev=wsrf.

[32] Open Real-Time Linux, Project Homepage.
http://www.open-realtime-linux.de/.

[33] PROFIBUS & PROFINET International.
http://www.profibus.com/pi/.

[34] QNX Neutrino, Product Homepage.
http://www.qnx.com/products/neutrino_rtos/.

[35] Real-Time Linux Wiki.
http://rt.wiki.kernel.org/.

[36] Reliable File Transfer, Project Homepage.
http://dev.globus.org/wiki/Reliable_File_Transfer.

[37] RTM – Realtime Monitoring GmbH.
http://www.realtime-monitoring.de/.

[38] Service Infrastructure for Real-time Embedded Networked Applications (SIRENA), Project Homepage.
http://www.sirena-itea.org/.

[39] Service-Oriented Cross-Layer Infrastructure for Distributed Smart Embedded Devices (SOCRADES), Project Homepage.
http://www.socrades.eu/.

[40] Service-Oriented Device and Delivery Architecture, Project Homepage.
http://www.soda-itea.org/.

[41] stress – A Simple Workload Generator for POSIX Systems, Project Homepage.
http://weather.ou.edu/~apw/projects/stress/.

[42] Subversion, Project Homepage.
http://subversion.tigris.org/.

[43] Subversive – SVN Team Provider.
http://www.eclipse.org/subversive/.

[44] Sun Microsystem: Java Message Service (JMS).
http://java.sun.com/products/jms/.

[45] Sun Microsystems: Java SE.
http://java.sun.com/javase/.

[46] The German Grid Initiative (D-Grid), Project Homepage.
http://www.d-grid.de/.

[47] The Real-Time Specification for Java (RTSJ), Project Homepage.
http://www.rtsj.org/.

[48] The UPnP Forum.
http://www.upnp.org/.

[49] Ubuntu Studio, Project Homepage.
http://ubuntustudio.org/.

[50] UNICORE, Project Homepage.
http://www.unicore.eu/.

[51] Web Services for Devices (WS4D), Project Homepage.
http://ws4d.e-technik.uni-rostock.de/.

[52] XLANG: Web Services for Business Process Design.
http://www.xml.com/pub/r/1153.

[53] IETF: Integrated Services in the Internet Architecture: An Overview, June 1994.
http://tools.ietf.org/rfc/rfc1633.txt.

[54] IETF: MIME (Multipurpose Internet Mail Extensions) Part Three: Message Header Extensions for Non-ASCII Text, November 1996.
http://tools.ietf.org/rfc/rfc2047.txt.

BIBLIOGRAPHY 217

[55] IETF: Multipurpose Internet Mail Extensions (MIME) Part Five: Conformance Criteria and Examples, November 1996.
http://tools.ietf.org/rfc/rfc2049.txt.

[56] IETF: Multipurpose Internet Mail Extensions (MIME) Part Four: Registration Procedures, November 1996.
http://tools.ietf.org/rfc/rfc2048.txt.

[57] IETF: Multipurpose Internet Mail Extensions (MIME) Part One: Format of Internet Message Bodies, November 1996.
http://tools.ietf.org/rfc/rfc2045.txt.

[58] IETF: Multipurpose Internet Mail Extensions (MIME) Part Two:Media Types, November 1996.
http://tools.ietf.org/rfc/rfc2046.txt.

[59] IETF: Resource ReSerVation Protocol (RSVP) – Version 1 Functional Specification, September 1997.
http://tools.ietf.org/rfc/rfc2205.txt.

[60] IETF: An Architecture for Differentiated Services, December 1998.
http://www.ietf.org/rfc/rfc2475.txt.

[61] W3C: XML Path Language (XPath) Version 1.0, November 1999.
http://www.w3.org/TR/xpath.

[62] W3C: SOAP Messages with Attachments, December 2000.
http://www.w3.org/TR/SOAP-attachments.

[63] IBM: Web Services Flow Language (WSFL) v1.0, May 2001.
http://www.ibm.com/software/solutions/soa/.

[64] W3C: Web Services Description Language (WSDL) 1.1, March 2001.
http://www.w3.org/TR/wsdl.

[65] IEC: Programmable controllers – Part 3: Programming languages (IEC 61131-3), January 2003.
http://www.iec.ch/.

[66] IETF: The Base16, Base32, and Base64 Data Encodings, July 2003.
http://www.ietf.org/rfc/rfc3548.txt.

[67] W3C: QoS for Web Services: Requirements and Possible Approaches, 2003.
http://www.w3c.or.kr/kr-office/TR/2003/ws-qos/.

[68] W3C: SOAP Version 1.2, 2003.
http://www.w3.org/TR/soap/.

[69] IBM: Web Services Eventing (WS-Eventing), August 2004.
http://download.boulder.ibm.com/ibmdl/pub/software/dw/specs/ws-eventing/WS-Eventing.pdf.

[70] OASIS: UDDI Version 3.0.2, 2004.
http://www.oasis-open.org/committees/tc_home.php?wg_abbrev=uddi-spec.

[71] OWL-S: Semantic Markup for Web Services, November 2004.
http://www.w3.org/Submission/OWL-S/.

[72] W3C: Ontology Web Language (OWL), February 2004.
http://www.w3.org/TR/owl-ref/.

[73] W3C: XML Schema Part 0: Primer Second Edition, October 2004.
http://www.w3.org/TR/xmlschema-0/.

[74] W3C: XML Schema Part 1: Structures Second Edition, October 2004.
http://www.w3.org/TR/xmlschema-1/.

[75] W3C: XML Schema Part 2: Datatypes Second Edition, October 2004.
http://www.w3.org/TR/xmlschema-2/.

[76] OASIS: eXtensible Access Control Markup Language (XACML), February 2005.
http://docs.oasis-open.org/xacml/2.0/access_control-xacml-2.0-core-spec-os.pdf.

[77] OASIS: WS-SecurityPolicy 1.2, July 2005.
http://docs.oasis-open.org/ws-sx/ws-securitypolicy/v1.2/ws-securitypolicy.html.

[78] OMG: UML Profile for Schedulability, Performance, and Time, January 2005.
http://www.omg.org/docs/formal/05-01-02.pdf.

[79] W3C: Web Service Modeling Ontology (WSMO), June 2005.
http://www.w3.org/Submission/WSMO/.

[80] W3C: Web Services Choreography Description Language, Version 1.0, November 2005.
http://www.w3.org/TR/ws-cdl-10/.

BIBLIOGRAPHY 219

[81] Web Services Dynamic Discovery (WS-Discovery), April 2005.
http://specs.xmlsoap.org/ws/2005/04/discovery/ws-discovery.pdf.

[82] Devices Profile for Web Service Specification, February 2006.
http://specs.xmlsoap.org/ws/2006/02/devprof/devicesprofile.pdf.

[83] IBM: Web Services Metadata Exchange (WS-MetadataExchange), Version 1.1, August 2006.
http://download.boulder.ibm.com/ibmdl/pub/software/dw/specs/ws-mex/metadataexchange.pdf.

[84] OASIS: Web Services Security: SOAP Message Security 1.1 (WS-Security), Februar 2006.
http://www.oasis-open.org/committees/download.php/16790/wss-v1.1-spec-os-SOAPMessageSecurity.pdf.

[85] OGF: Web Services Agreement Specification (WS-Agreement), October 2006.
http://www.ogf.org/documents/GFD.107.pdf.

[86] W3C: Extensible Markup Language (XML) 1.1 (Second Edition), August 2006.
http://www.w3.org/TR/2006/REC-xml11-20060816/.

[87] W3C: Web Services Addressing 1.0 – Core, May 2006.
http://www.w3.org/TR/ws-addr-core/.

[88] W3C: Web Services Addressing 1.0 – SOAP Binding, May 2006.
http://www.w3.org/TR/ws-addr-soap/.

[89] W3C: Web Services Description Language (WSDL) 2.0, June 2006.
http://www.w3.org/TR/wsdl20/.

[90] W3C: Web Services Transfer (WS-Transfer), September 2006.
http://www.w3.org/Submission/WS-Transfer/.

[91] MES Explained: A High Level Vision for Executives, August 2007.
http://www.mesa.org/.

[92] W3C: SOAP Version 1.2 Part 0: Primer (Second Edition), April 2007.
http://www.w3.org/TR/soap12-part0/.

BIBLIOGRAPHY

[93] W3C: SOAP Version 1.2 Part 1: Messaging Framework (Second Edition), April 2007.
http://www.w3.org/TR/soap12-part1/.

[94] W3C: SOAP Version 1.2 Part 2: Adjuncts (Second Edition), April 2007.
http://www.w3.org/TR/soap12-part2/.

[95] W3C: Web Services Addressing 1.0 – Metadata, September 2007.
http://www.w3.org/TR/ws-addr-metadata/.

[96] W3C: Web Services Policy Framework 1.5, September 2007.
http://www.w3.org/TR/ws-policy/.

[97] N. Abu-Ghazaleh and M. J. Lewis. Differential Deserialization for Optimized SOAP Performance. In *Proceedings of the ACM/IEEE Conference on Supercomputing (SC)*, pages 21–31, 2005.

[98] N. Abu-Ghazaleh, M. J. Lewis, and M. Govindaraju. Differential Serialization for Optimized SOAP Performance. In *Proceedings of the 13th IEEE International Symposium on High Performance Distributed Computing (HPDC)*, pages 55–64, 2004.

[99] B. Allcock, J. Bester, J. Bresnahan, A.L. Chervenak, I. Foster, C. Kesselman, S. Meder, V. Nefedova, D. Quesnel, and S. Tuecke. Data Management and Transfer in High-performance Computational Grid Environments. *Parallel Computing*, 28(5):749–771, 2002.

[100] T. Andrews, F. Curbera, H. Dholakia, Y. Goland, J. Klein, F. Leymann, K. Liu, D. Roller, D. Smith, S. Thatte, I. Trickovic, and S. Weerawarana. Business Process Execution Language for Web Services – Version 1.1, 2003.
http://www.ibm.com/developerworks/library/specification/ws-bpel/.

[101] G. Bernat, A. Burns, and A. Wellings. Portable Worst-Case Execution Time Analysis using Java Byte Code. In *Proceedings of the 12th Euromicro Conference on Real-Time Systems (ECRTS)*, pages 81–88, 2000.

[102] A.P. Black, M. Carlsson, M.P. Jones, R. Kieburtz, and J. Nordlander. Timber: A Programming Language for Real-Time Embedded Systems. Technical report, Oregon Health & Science University, 2002.

[103] H. Bohn, A. Bobek, and F. Golatowski. SIRENA - Service Infrastructure for Real-time Embedded Networked Devices: A service oriented framework for different domains. In *Proceedings of the International Conference on Networking, International Conference on Systems, and International Conference on Mobile Communications and Learning Technologies (ICN/ICONS/MCL)*, pages 43–47, 2006.

[104] G. Bucci, L. Sassoli, and E. Vicario. Correctness Verification and Performance Analysis of Real-time Systems using Stochastic Preemptive Time Petri Nets. *IEEE Transactions on Software Engineering*, 31(11):913–927, November 2005.

[105] M.E. Cambronero, G. Diaz, J.J. Pardo, V. Valero, and F.L. Pelayo. RT-UML for Modeling Real-Time Web Services. In *Proceedings of the IEEE Services Computing Workshops (SCW)*, pages 131–139, 2006.

[106] M.E. Cambronero, J.J. Pardo, G. Diaz, and V. Valero. Using RT-UML for Modelling Web Services. In *Proceedings of the ACM Symposium on Applied Computing (SAC)*, pages 643–648, 2007.

[107] M. Cammert, C. Heinz, J. Krämer, A. Markowetz, and B. Seeger. PIPES: A Multi-Threaded Publish-Subscribe Architecture for Continuous Queries over Streaming Data Sources. Technical Report 32, Department of Mathematics and Computer Science, University of Marburg, 2003.

[108] M. Cammert, C. Heinz, J. Krämer, T. Riemenschneider, M. Schwarzkopf, B. Seeger, and A. Zeiss. Stream Processing in Production-to-Business Software. In *Proceedings of the 22nd IEEE International Conference on Data Engineering (ICDE)*, pages 168–169. IEEE Computer Society Press, 2006.

[109] D.J. Colling, L.W. Dickens, T. Ferrari, Y. Hassoun, C.A. Kotsokalis, M. Krznaric, J. Martyniak, A.S. McGough, and E. Ronchieri. Adding Instruments and Workflow Support to Existing Grid Architectures. *Lecture Notes in Computer Science*, 3993:956–963, 2006.

[110] S. de Deugd, R. Carroll, K.E. Kelly, B. Millett, and J. Ricker. SODA: Service-Oriented Device Architecture. *Pervasive Computing*, 5:94–96, 2006.

[111] I.M. Delamer and J.L.M. Lastra. Self-Orchestration and Choreography: Towards Architecture-Agnostic Manufacturing Systems. In *Proceedings*

of 20th *International Conference on Advanced Information Networking and Applications (AINA)*, pages 5–9, 2006.

[112] I.M. Delamer and J.L.M. Lastra. Loosely-Coupled Automation Systems Using Device-Level SOA. In *Proceedings of the IEEE International Conference on Industrial Informatics (INDIN)*, pages 743–748, 2007.

[113] M. Ditze and I. Jahnich. Towards End-to-End QoS in Service-Oriented Architectures. In *Proceedings of the 3rd IEEE International Conference on Industrial Informatics (INDIN)*, pages 92–97, 2005.

[114] T. Dörnemann, T. Friese, S. Herdt, E. Juhnke, and B. Freisleben. Grid Workflow Modelling Using Grid-Specific BPEL Extensions. In *Proceedings of German e-Science Conference (GES)*, 2007.

[115] T. Dörnemann, M. Mathes, R. Schwarzkopf, E. Juhnke, and B. Freisleben. DAVO: A Domain-Adaptable, Visual BPEL4WS Orchestrator. In *Proceedings of the IEEE 23rd International Conference on Advanced Information Networking and Applications (AINA)*, pages 121–128. IEEE Computer Society Press, 2009.

[116] J. Engblom, A. Ermedahl, and F. Stappert. Validating a Worst-Case Execution Time Analysis Method for an Embedded Processor. Technical Report 2001-030, Department of Computer Sytems, Uppsala University, Sweden and Mälardalen Real-time Research Center, Sweden, 2001.

[117] H. Foster, S. Uchitel, J. Magee, and J. Kramer. Leveraging Eclipse for Integrated Model-Based Engineering of Web Service Compositions. In *Proceedings of the International Conference on Object-Oriented Programming, Systems, Languages, and Applications (OOPSLA), Workshop on Eclipse Technology eXchange (ETX)*, pages 95–99, 2005.

[118] I. Foster, C. Kesselman, and S. Tuecke. The Anatomy of the Grid: Enabling Scalable Virtual Organizations. In *International Journal of High Performance Computing Applications*, volume 15, pages 200–222, 2001.

[119] G. Fox, S. Pallickara, and S. Parastatidis. Toward Flexible Messaging for SOAP-Based Services. In *Proceedings of the ACM/IEEE Conference on Supercomputing (SC)*, pages 8–18, 2004.

[120] E. Gamma, R. Helm, and R.E. Johnson. *Design Patterns. Elements of Reusable Object-Oriented Software*. Addison-Wesley, 1995.

[121] D.Z.G. Garcia and M.B.F. de Toledo. Semantics-enriched QoS Policies for Web Service Interactions. In *Proceedings of the 12th Brazilian Symposium on Multimedia and the Web (WebMedia)*, pages 35–44, 2006.

[122] V. Gilart-Iglesias, F. Macia-Perez, A. Capella-D'alton, and J.A. Gil-Martinez-Abarca. Industrial Machines as a Service: A Model Based on Embedded Devices and Web Services. In *Proceedings of the IEEE International Conference on Industrial Informatics (INDIN)*, pages 630–635, 2006.

[123] V. Gilart-Iglesias, F. Macia-Perez, D. Marcos-Jorquera, and F.J. Mora-Gimeno. Industrial Machines as a Service: Modelling industrial machinery processes. In *Proceedings of the 5th IEEE International Conference on Industrial Informatics (INDIN)*, pages 737–742, 2007.

[124] V. Gilart-Iglesias, F. Macia-Perez, F.J. Mora-Gimeno, and J.V. Berna-Martinez. Normalization of Industrial Machinery with Embedded Devices and SOA. In *Proceedings of the IEEE Conference on Emerging Technologies and Factory Automation (ETFA)*, pages 173–180, 2006.

[125] L. Guo, A.S. McGough, A. Akram, D. Colling, J. Martyniak, and M. Krznaric. Enabling QoS for Service-Oriented Workflow on GRID. In *Proceedings of the 7th IEEE International Conference on Computer and Information Technology (CIT)*, pages 1077–1082, 2007.

[126] K. Hammond. Hume: A Bounded Time Concurrent Language. In *Proceedings of the 7th IEEE International Conference on Electronics, Circuits and Systems (ICECS)*, pages 407–411, 2000.

[127] C. Heinz, J. Krämer, T. Riemenschneider, and B. Seeger. Auf dem Weg zur allwissenden Fabrik – Vertikale Integration auf Basis kontinuierlicher Datenverarbeitung. *Lecture Notes in Informatics*, 110:339–344, 2007.

[128] S. Heinzl and M. Mathes. *Middleware in Java*. Vieweg+Teubner, 2005. ISBN-10: 3528059125, ISBN-13: 978-3528059125.

[129] S. Heinzl, M. Mathes, and B. Freisleben. A Web Service Communication Policy for Describing Non-Standard Application Requirements. In *Proceedings of the IEEE/IPSJ Symposium on Applications and the Internet (SAINT)*, pages 40–47, 2008.

[130] S. Heinzl, M. Mathes, T. Friese, M. Smith, and B. Freisleben. FlexSwA: Flexible Exchange of Binary Data Based on SOAP Messages with

Attachments. In *Proceedings of the IEEE International Conference on Web Services (ICWS)*, pages 3–10, 2006.

[131] S. Heinzl, M. Mathes, T. Stadelmann, D. Seiler, M. Diegelmann, H. Dohmann, and B. Freisleben. The Web Service Browser: Automatic Client Generation and Efficient Data Transfer for Web Services. In *Proceedings of the 7th IEEE International Conference on Web Services (ICWS)*, pages 743–750. IEEE Computer Society Press, 2009.

[132] J. Helander and S. Sigurdsson. Self-Tuning Planned Actions – Time to Make Real-Time SOAP Real. In *Proceedings of the 8th IEEE International Symposium on Object-Oriented Real-Time Distributed Computing (ISORC)*, pages 80–89, 2005.

[133] M. Held and W. Blochinger. Collaborative BPEL Design with a Rich Internet Application. In *Proceedings of the 8th IEEE International Symposium on Cluster Computing and the Grid (CCGrid)*, pages 202–209, 2008.

[134] F. Jammes, A. Mensch, and H. Smit. Service-Oriented Device Communications Using the Devices Profile for Web services. In *Proceedings of the 21st International Conference on Advanced Information Networking and Applications (AINA)*, pages 947–955, 2007.

[135] F. Jammes and H. Smit. Service-Oriented Architectures for Devices – the SIRENA View. In *Proceedings of the 3rd International Conference on Industrial Automation (INDIN)*, pages 140–147, 2005.

[136] F. Jammes and H. Smit. Service-Oriented Paradigms in Industrial Automation. *IEEE Transactions on Industrial Informatics*, 1(1):62–69, February 2005.

[137] A.P. Kalogeras, J. Gialelis, C. Alexakos, M. Georgoudakis, and S. Koubias. Vertical Integration of Enterprise Industrial Systems Utilizing Web Services. In *Proceedings of the IEEE International Workshop on Factory Communication Systems (WFCS)*, pages 187–192, 2004.

[138] S. Karnouskos, O. Baecker, L.M.S. de Souza, and P. Spiess. Integration of SOA-Ready Networked Embedded Devices in Enterprise Systems via a Cross-Layered Web Service Infrastructure. In *Proceedings of the IEEE Conference on Emerging Technologies and Factory Automation (ETFA)*, pages 293–300, 2007.

BIBLIOGRAPHY 225

[139] S. Karnouskos, A. Colombo, F. Jammes, and M. Strand. Towards Service-oriented Smart Items in Industrial Environments. *Microsystems Technology (MST)*, 2:11–12, 2007.

[140] S. Karnouskos and M.M.J. Tariq. An Agent-Based Simulation of SOA-Ready Devices. In *Proceedings of the 10th International Conference on Computer Modeling and Simulation (UKSIM)*, pages 330–335, 2008.

[141] J. Krämer and B. Seeger. PIPES – A Public Infrastructure for Processing and Exploring Streams. In *Proceedings of the ACM SIGMOD International Conference on Management of Data*, pages 925–926. ACM Press, 2004.

[142] H. Liang, W. Sun, X. Zhang, and Z. Jiang. A Policy Framework for Collaborative Web Service Customization. In *Proceedings of the 2nd IEEE International Symposium on Service-Oriented System Engineering (SOSE)*, pages 197–204, 2006.

[143] M. Lindgren, H. Hansson, and H. Thane. Using Measurements to Derive the Worst-Case Execution Time. In *Proceedings of the 7th International Conference on Real-Time Systems and Applications (RTCSA)*, pages 15–22, 2000.

[144] C.L. Liu and J.W. Layland. Scheduling Algorithms for Multiprogramming in a Hard-Real-Time Environment. *Journal of the ACM*, 20:46–61, 1973.

[145] A. Martinez, M. Patino-Martinez, R. Jimenez-Peris, and F. Perez-Sorrosal. ZenFlow: A Visual Web Service Composition Tool for BPEL4WS. In *Proceedings of the IEEE Symposium on Visual Languages and Human-Centric Computing (VL/HCC)*, pages 181–188, 2005.

[146] M. Mathes, J. Gärtner, H. Dohmann, and B. Freisleben. SOAP4IPC: A Real-Time SOAP Engine for Time-Constrained Web Services in Industrial Automation. In *Proceedings of the 17th Euromicro International Conference on Parallel, Distributed, and Network-Based Processing (Euromicro PDP)*, pages 220–226, 2009.

[147] M. Mathes, S. Heinzl, and B. Freisleben. Towards a Time-Constrained Web Service Infrastructure for Industrial Automation. In *Proceedings of the 13th IEEE International Conference on Emerging Technologies and Factory Automation (ETFA)*, pages 846–853, 2008.

[148] M. Mathes, S. Heinzl, and B. Freisleben. WS-TemporalPolicy: A WS-Policy Extension for Describing Service Properties with Time Constraints. In *Proceedings of the 1st IEEE International Workshop On Real-Time Service-Oriented Architecture and Applications (RTSOAA) of the 32nd Annual IEEE International Computer Software and Applications Conference (COMPSAC)*, pages 1180–1186, 2008.

[149] M. Mathes, S. Heinzl, T. Friese, and B. Freisleben. Enabling Post-Invocation Parameter Transmission in Service-Oriented Environments. In *Proceedings of the International Conference on Networking and Services (ICNS)*, pages 55–60, 2006.

[150] M. Mathes, R. Schwarzkopf, T. Dörnemann, S. Heinzl, and B. Freisleben. Orchestration of Time-Constrained BPEL4WS Workflows. In *Proceedings of the 13th IEEE International Conference on Emerging Technologies and Factory Automation (ETFA)*, pages 1–4, 2008.

[151] M. Mathes, R. Schwarzkopf, T. Dörnemann, S. Heinzl, and B. Freisleben. Composition of Time-Constrained BPEL4WS-Workflows using the TiCS Modeler. In *Proceedings of the 13th IFAC Symposium on Information Control Problems in Manufacturing (INCOM)*, pages 892–897. Elsevier, 2009.

[152] M. Mathes, C. Stoidner, and B. Freisleben. SOAP4PLC: Web Services for Programmable Logic Controllers. In *Proceedings of the 17th Euromicro International Conference on Parallel, Distributed, and Network-Based Processing (Euromicro PDP)*, pages 210–219, 2009.

[153] H. McGhan and M. O'Connor. PicoJava: A Direct Execution Engine for Java Bytecode. *IEEE Computer*, 31(10):22–30, October 1998.

[154] A.S. McGough, A. Akram, L. Guo, M. Krznaric, L. Dickens, D. Colling, J. Martyniak, R. Powell, P. Kyberd, and C. Kotsokalis. GRIDCC: Realtime Workflow System. In *Proceedings of the 2nd Workshop on Workflows in Support of large-scale Science (WORKS)*, pages 3–12, 2007.

[155] A.S. McGough and D.J. Colling. The GRIDCC Project. In *Proceedings of the 1st International Conference on Communication System Software and Middleware (COMSWARE)*, pages 1–4, 2006.

[156] R. Murugesan. Evolution of Industrial Automation. *International Journal of Computer Applications in Technology*, 25:169–174, 2006.

[157] S.M. Petters and G. Färber. Making Worst-Case Execution Time Analysis for Hard Real-Time Tasks on State of the Art Processors Feasible. In *Proceedings of the he 6th IEEE International Conference on Real-Time Computing Systems and Applications (RTCSA)*, pages 442–449, 1999.

[158] C. Popescu and J.L.M. Lastra. Verification of the Consistency of Timing Constraints of the Orchestration of Factory Automation Web Services. In *IEEE International Conference on Industrial Informatics (INDIN)*, pages 785–790, 2007.

[159] L.M. Sa de Souza, P. Spiess, D. Guinard, M. Köhler, S. Karnouskos, and D. Savio. SOCRADES: A Web Service based Shop Floor Integration Infrastructure. In *Proceedings of the 1st International Conference Internet of Things (IoT)*, pages 50–67, 2008.

[160] G. Saez, A.L. Sliva, and M.B. Blake. Web Services based Data Management: Evaluating the Performance of UDDI Registries. In *Proceedings of the IEEE International Conference on Web Services (ICWS)*, pages 830–831. IEEE Computer Society Press, 2004.

[161] A. Sahai, C. Thompson, and W. Vambenepe. Specifying and Constraining Web Services Behaviour through Policies. W3C Workshop on Constraints and Capabilities for Web Services, 2004.
http://www.w3.org/2004/09/ws-cc-program.html.

[162] R. Salz. Transporting Binary Data in SOAP, August 2002.
http://webservices.xml.com/pub/a/ws/2002/08/28/endpoints.html.

[163] W. Shen and D.H. Norrie. Dynamic manufacturing scheduling using both functional and resource related agents. *Integrated Computer-Aided Engineering*, 8:17–30, 2001.

[164] F. Siebert. The Impact of Realtime Garbage Collection on Realtime Java Programming. In *Proceedings of the IEEE International Symposium on Object-Oriented Real-Time Distributed Computing (ISORC)*, pages 33–40, 2004.

[165] S. Siewert. *Real-time Embedded Systems and Components*. Charles River Media, 2006.

[166] V.S. Srinivasan and M.A. Jafari. Monitoring and Fault Detection in Shop Floor using Time Petri Nets. In *IEEE International Conference on Systems, Man, and Cybernetics (SMC)*, pages 355–360, 1991.

[167] J.A. Stankovic. Misconceptions about real-time computing: a serious problem for next-generation systems. *Computer*, 21:10–19, 1988.

[168] C. Stoidner, M. Mathes, and B. Freisleben. Sequence-Controlled Web Services for Programmable Logic Controllers. In *Proceedings of the 13th IFAC Symposium on Information Control Problems in Manufacturing (INCOM)*, pages 2186–2191. Elsevier, 2009.

[169] D. Tejera, A. Alonso, and M.A. de Miguel. Predictable Serialization in Java. In *Proceedings of the 10th IEEE International Symposium on Object and Component-Oriented Real-Time Distributed Computing (ISORC)*, pages 102–109, 2007.

[170] M. Tian, A. Gramm, H. Ritter, and J. Schiller. Efficient Selection and Monitoring of QoS-aware Web Services with the WS-QoS Framework. In *Proceedings of the IEEE/WIC/ACM International Conference on Web Intelligence (WI)*, pages 152–158, 2004.

[171] N. Tolia, M. Kaminsky, D.G. Andersen, and S. Patil. An Architecture for Internet Data Transfer. In *Proceedings of the 3rd Symposium on Networked Systems Design & Implementation (NSDI)*, pages 19–33, 2006.

[172] V. Tosic, A. Erradi, and P. Maheshwari. WS-Policy4MASC – A WS-Policy Extension Used in the MASC Middleware. In *IEEE International Conference on Services Computing (SCC)*, pages 458–465, 2007.

[173] W.T. Tsai, Y.-H. Lee, Z. Cao, and Y. Chen. RTSOA: Real-Time Service-Oriented Architecture. In *Proceedings of the 2nd IEEE International Symposium on Service-Oriented System Engineering (SOSE)*, pages 49–56, 2006.

[174] R.A. van Engelen and K.A. Gallivan. The gSOAP Toolkit for Web Services and Peer-to-Peer Computing Networks. In *Proceedings of the 2nd IEEE/ACM International Symposium on Cluster Computing and the Grid (CCGrid)*, pages 128–135, 2002.

[175] J. Vicente Berna-Martinez, F. Macia-Perez, H. Ramos-Morillo, and V. Gilart-Iglesias. Distributed Robotic Architecture based on Smart Services. In *Proceedings of the 4th IEEE International Conference on Industrial Informatics (INDIN)*, pages 480–485, 2006.

[176] B. Wassermann, W. Emmerich, B. Butchart, N. Cameron, L. Chen, and J. Patel. *Workflows for e-Science*, chapter Sedna: A BPEL-Based

Environment for Visual Scientific Workflow Modeling, pages 428–449. Springer, 2007.

[177] B.S. Yang, S.-M. Moon, S. Park, J. Lee, S. Lee, J. Park, Y.C. Chung, S. Kim, K. Ebcioglu, and E. Altman. LaTTe: A Java VM Just-in-Time Compiler with Fast and Effcient Register Allocation. In *Proceedings of the International Conference on Parallel Architectures and Compilation Techniques (PACT)*, pages 128–138, 1999.

[178] T. Yu, Y. Zhang, and K.-J. Lin. Efficient Algorithms for Web Services Selection with End-to-End QoS Constraints. *ACM Transactions on the Web*, 1(1):6–31, 2007.

[179] E. Zeeb, A. Bobek, H. Bohn, and F. Golatowski. Service-Oriented Architectures for Embedded Systems Using Devices Profile for Web Services. In *Proceedings of the 21st International Conference on Advanced Information Networking and Applications Workshops (AINAW)*, pages 956–963, 2007.

Die VDM Verlagsservicegesellschaft sucht für wissenschaftliche Verlage abgeschlossene und herausragende

Dissertationen, Habilitationen, Diplomarbeiten, Master Theses, Magisterarbeiten usw.

für die kostenlose Publikation als Fachbuch.

Sie verfügen über eine Arbeit, die hohen inhaltlichen und formalen Ansprüchen genügt, und haben Interesse an einer honorarvergüteten Publikation?

Dann senden Sie bitte erste Informationen über sich und Ihre Arbeit per Email an *info@vdm-vsg.de*.

Sie erhalten kurzfristig unser Feedback!

VDM Verlagsservicegesellschaft mbH
Dudweiler Landstr. 99   Telefon +49 681 3720 174
D - 66123 Saarbrücken   Fax   +49 681 3720 1749

www.vdm-vsg.de

Die VDM Verlagsservicegesellschaft mbH vertritt

Printed by Books on Demand GmbH, Norderstedt / Germany